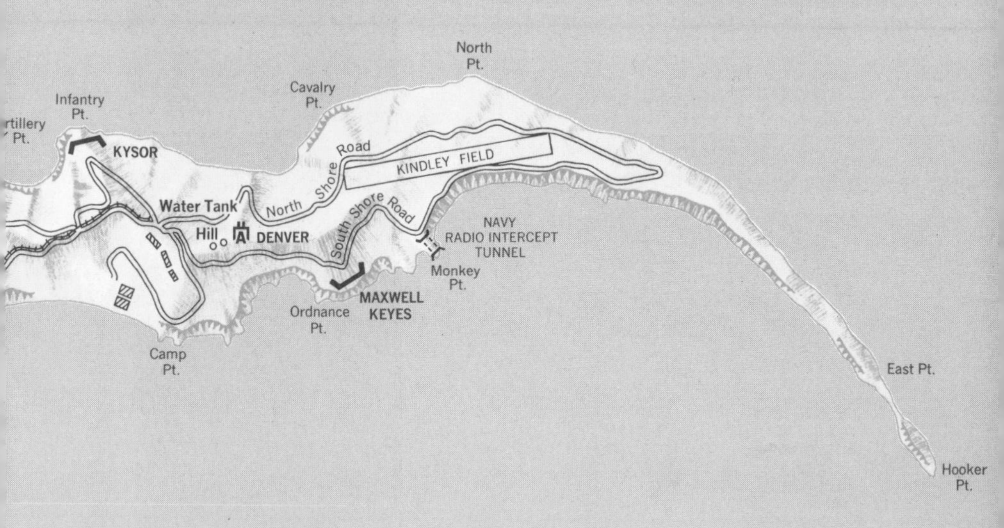

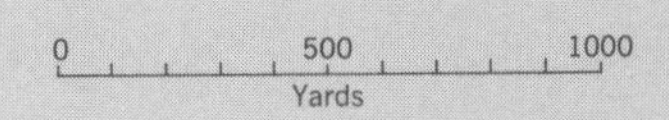

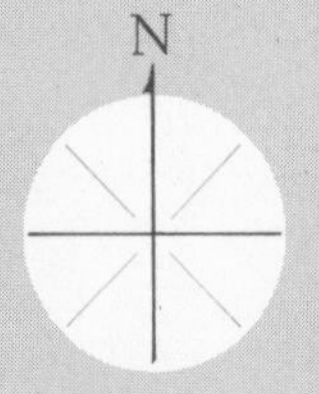

Map by Harry Scott

CORREGIDOR

CORREGIDOR

THE SAGA OF

by James H. *and* William M. Belote

Foreword by Robert Leckie

A FORTRESS

Harper & Row, Publishers • New York, Evanston, and London

To all who served on the Rock in war and peace this book is dedicated.

LIBRARY OF CONGRESS CATALOG CARD NUMBER: 66-21723

E-R

☆ Contents

MAPS

☆ Foreword

One of the outstanding lessons to be learned from World War II is that there is no such thing as an "impregnable" fortress. From the turning of the Maginot Line through the taking of Singapore from the rear to the leapfrogging of Japan's chain of island forts, the war repeatedly demonstrated that the side which relied on the defensive, especially the static defensive, was foredoomed to defeat.

In *Corregidor: The Saga of a Fortress,* the brothers Belote have written a compelling statement of this thesis. This, of course, is not their chief purpose. Rather, they have sought to tell in human as well as military terms the story of what happened to the Americans and Filipinos who tried to hold Corregidor against the Japanese in those hopeless yet gallant days of 1942, and of the other Americans whom General MacArthur led back to "the Rock" 32 months later to reclaim the island fortress. In this, they have succeeded admirably. They have the rare gift of making military history exciting and interesting as well as meaningful and informative. Because the Belotes combine a grasp of top-level strategy with a compassionate concern for the front line, low-level foot slogger who carries the strategy out, they have made their book a moving, gripping adventure story as well as accurate and authentic history. And just because their book is so complete—a wealth of detail diligently amassed and expertly organized into a neatly-woven narrative—it bears testimony to the futility of the fortress in modern war.

Indeed, to rely upon the strength of a fortress in any era generally has been a mistake. Military history suggests that the fort usually falls.

Troy was deceived and undone by the ruse of the wooden horse, Jericho was betrayed to Joshua by the harlot Rahab, Jerusalem crumbled under the catapults of Titus, Constantinople was stormed by Crusader and Saracen alike, Quebec was surprised by Wolfe and Vicksburg succumbed to siege guns and starvation. Century after century bears doleful testimony to the crossing of impassable waters, the scaling of inaccessible cliffs, the march through impenetrable swamps or the bursting by force of arms or the opening by guile or deception of unbreakable walls. Yet men continue to put their faith in forts, probably because of mankind's immemorial bad habit of mistaking the part for the whole.

A fort is only part of the defensive. It is not meant to defeat the enemy but to delay or deter him. Of course, if a fort harbors the enemy's true objective, some person or some treasure, then to hold it successfully is to defeat the besieger. Commonly, however, the true objective is the opposing army, and a fort in the enemy's path is meant to bar his passage until reinforcements can arrive. "Hold the fort, I'm coming," Sherman signaled one of his commanders in Georgia, and when he did arrive the joint forces went over to the attack. Thus, the fort is the shield which parries the enemy's blow until the sword of the nation, her armed forces, is drawn from its sheath.

Unfortunately, popular democracies have a bad habit of forgetting that the shield without the sword is only half an armament, and, at that, the lesser half. They tend to put all their faith in the shield while allowing the sword to rust. One reason for this is that fortresses already in being are much more inexpensive to maintain than sizeable military establishments supporting ample forces-in-readiness. They are not only cheaper, they are less obtrusive, way out there on the edge of nowhere. A third reason is what may be called the habit of fortress thinking, the classic example of which is the Maginot Line of France. In the twenties, that nation, bled white and weary of war, built a formidable line of fortifications which was to prevent the Germans from invading her soil again. It was not completed west to the sea because it was not intended to be anything more than the shield which was to deflect the German armies in that direction, where the French sword, the reserve, was to cut them down. But so much was said about the strength of the Maginot Line that the French, and most of the rest of the world, came to think of it as invincible. Eager to believe, the French did believe, and as they put their trust in the Maginot Line they allowed their army to deteriorate. Thus, when the Germans penetrated the "impenetrable" Ardennes forest on the Maginot's open left flank, the French were utterly demoralized. Their will to fight had been weakened, among other reasons, by a belief that they would not need to fight.

A similar habit of thought was current in America before World War II. Pacifists and those who were disillusioned by World War I—the war fought to end all wars—got the naive notion that it takes two to make a war. If you tell a man you will not fight, not resort to violence, he will not hit you. Unhappily, as Hitler proved, it only takes one to make a war. The pacifists, however, did not understand that the only way to avoid a war is to accept an occupation. Nor did their isolationist allies realize that the age of American isolation was over. Ignoring the development of the airplane, they still thought that our two oceans served as impassable moats; or else, this time ignoring America's dependence on world trade, they proposed that we arm only to defend our own shores.

Between pacifism and isolationism then, Americans before the war also thought that they would not need to fight. They not only hung up the sword, they forgot that they even had a buckler. Places such as the island of Corregidor in Manila Bay among the far-off Philippines received so little attention that, as this remarkably well-detailed book shows, a hospital there was not allowed to replace its antiquated coal-fired heating plant with an efficient oil system because the oil would cost $185 more annually! Yet Corregidor had to be held. American plans called for it. Manila Bay must be held as a Philippines "keep" until the United States Navy fought its way across the Pacific. Few of the planners, of course, believed that this was possible. Most of them realized that the nation had not the military means to effect such a rescue in less than two years. Still, for political and psychological reasons, the plan was put into effect. And thus, after the lesson of the futility of the fort, we come to the second lesson learned from World War II: woe to the guardians of the outposts of democracy. Hold the fort, they are entreated, until we come. But no one comes, the fort falls and its gallant defenders pass into captivity.

This is what happened at Corregidor, and the glory and the tragedy of it all is the theme of this splendid book.

ROBERT LECKIE

Mountain Lakes, New Jersey

September, 1966

☆ Preface

The subject of Corregidor has fascinated the authors since the days of the siege of 1942. Then, as young R.O.T.C. students at the University of Washington, they studied avidly the meager information provided by the daily communiqués, American and Japanese. The fall of the Rock on May 6 seemed to them a personal loss. Their own war experience afterward, however, took them to the opposite side of the earth, to North Africa and Italy, and their deep interest in Corregidor had to remain dormant.

After the war and some years of graduate study, government service, and teaching, they decided to take up the study of the history of Corregidor again, determined to make their research about the fall in 1942 and the recapture in 1945 as complete as possible. This volume represents the fruition of approximately seven years of effort. The authors hope that the reader will find in the story of the Rock the same fascination that has so long held them.

Although they bear full responsibility for the conclusions drawn in this volume, the debt of the authors to others has been considerable. At the World War II Records Division, National Archives, Mr. Wilbur Nigh and his staff have been most co-operative. At the Army Administration Center, St. Louis, the staff of Colonel M. J. Halper, U.S.A., has met every request. The authors are especially grateful to Messrs. Lester J. Spall, Robert E. Wyrsch, and Joseph A. Pentz. At the office of the Chief of Military History, U.S. Army, Mr. Stetson Conn, Chief Historian, Mr. Israel Wice, and Miss Hannah Zeidlick have been especially helpful, as were Messrs. Michael O'Quinlivan and John H. Marley at the Historical Section, U.S. Marine Corps Headquarters. At the U.S. Navy's Division of Naval History, Rear Admiral E. M. Eller and his Executive Officer, Captain F. Kent Loomis, are to be thanked, and especially Mr. Dean Allard.

For their complete photographic collection on Corregidor, the authors are indebted to Mrs. Norma Sherris at the Office of the Chief of Military History, to Mrs. Donna Traxler at the Still Pictures Branch, Signal Corps, Pentagon, U.S. Army, and to Colonel Riley E. McGarraugh, U.S.A. (Ret.), of Lewes, Delaware.

Messrs. Norbert Slepyan and Marion S. Wyeth, Jr., of Harper & Row, have been most understanding and patient editors. The authors have had sage counsel from Dr. E. Ray Lewis of Oregon State University and Mr. Robert L. Underbrink of MacMurry College.

Finally, the authors owe much to their respective wives, Edith W. Belote and Marilyn P. Belote, and to their mother, Mrs. Adelaide Belote, of Bellevue, Washington, for constant encouragement and for performing many tasks connected with preparing the manuscript.

September, 1966

JAMES H. BELOTE
Elsah, Illinois
WILLIAM M. BELOTE
Annapolis, Maryland

CORREGIDOR

1 ☆ America's Rock of Gibraltar

IN THE NEVER-NIGHT of the U.S. Navy's Radio Intercept Tunnel at Monkey Point on Corregidor a young Navy bluejacket, muffed in huge padded earphones, was sitting at the console of his complex electronic gear. Beside him others also probed the air waves, carefully adjusting dials, listening intently for those faint enciphered dits and dahs that might pinpoint the location of a Japanese convoy of transports. Suddenly, the young man stiffened, seized his pad, and wrote hurriedly. When the message ended he rushed it to the desk of his duty officer, Lieutenant Rudolf J. Fabian, who glanced at it and reached for his telephone. The message on the pad, which had come in the clear from the U.S. naval radio station at Honolulu, read: "Air raids on Pearl Harbor. This is not drill," and "Hostilities commenced with air raids on Pearl."

Thus on December 7, 1941—December 8, Corregidor time—war, long-anticipated and feared, had broken out between the United States and the Empire of Japan.

When his phone rang seconds later in his quarters on Topside, Corregidor's commander, Major General George F. Moore, a soft-spoken, self-possessed veteran Coast Artilleryman, was not surprised by the news. He had had this island, long known as the Rock, on the alert, ready to fire on unidentified ships or planes, since November 29, the day after Lieutenant General Douglas MacArthur had told him that negotiations with Japan were breaking down and that he should ready his men for war. Hastily dressing, Moore drove to his

Harbor Defense Command Post, H Station, ordered his Seaward, Antiaircraft, and Beach Defense Commands to double their surveillance, and radioed a warning to Colonel Napoleon Boudreau commanding Fort Wint at Subic Bay. Forty-two years before, a careless Spanish commander had allowed Commodore George Dewey to slip past Corregidor into Manila Bay, there to destroy Spain's Far Eastern Squadron and force the surrender of Cavite and Corregidor itself. Moore did not think the Japanese would challenge with their fleet his powerful armament, but he dared not take chances. His primary mission, which was clearly spelled out, was to keep Japanese warships out of the bay and away from Manila. With daybreak his post quartermaster would begin the laborious task of transferring supplies to and moving ammunition from bombproof Malinta Tunnel to make room for the post hospital, headquarters, and support units.

To most of Corregidor's garrison Pearl Harbor day had an aura of unreality about it despite the bustle of activity. In a vague sort of way the men had been expecting war, but now that it had come they were sobered and a bit surprised that Japan had had the temerity to take on the might of the United States. Yet the day was something of an anticlimax. The expected heavy air attack on the Rock's antiquated defenses did not develop. The only action came at 1:15 P.M., when three medium bombers flew at a high altitude between Corregidor and a nearby island, Fort Hughes. The green and excited antiaircraft crews of Batteries Idaho and Denver fired enthusiastically, but with no more result than a dubious claim of one plane damaged. Earlier, the Navy had rounded up thirty of the seemingly omnipresent Japanese fishermen who for years had been objects of suspicion as they plied their trade in the waters about Corregidor. Otherwise, Pearl Harbor day was quiet for the Rock, since 1908 America's Gibraltar in the Far East. The enemy was elsewhere.

Some four thousand miles eastward this day had closed on a scene of disaster unparalleled in the history of American arms. Five battleships, the core of American naval might, lay pathetically sunk in

Pearl Harbor's mud. Struck by torpedoes and an armor-piercing shell converted into a heavy bomb, the *Arizona* had blown apart at her moorings. Likewise caught by torpedo planes, the *California* and *West Virigina* had foundered at anchor, surrounded by pools of blazing oil. Holed by three torpedoes, the *Oklahoma* had capsized. Struck near the bow, the *Nevada* had sortied, only to be battered by dive bombers as she went, so that she had to beach herself at the harbor's mouth to avoid sinking and blocking the channel. Damaged by bombs, the remaining three battleships had escaped the torpedo planes, but none could be used immediately, nor could two cruisers, the victims of torpedoes. All these ships except the *Arizona* and *Oklahoma* were salvageable, but all needed many months of repair and refitting before they could be combat-ready. While naval aviators could rejoice that none of the Pacific Fleet's three aircraft carriers had been hit, since none had been present, they and their Army comrades could but shake their heads sadly at the terrible blasting the Japanese had dealt Hawaiian air power. The two attacking waves of 358 "Zekes," "Vals" and "Kates" had destroyed or crippled 244 Army and Navy aircraft.

Nor was this blow at Oahu all. At tiny, strategically located Wake Island, high-level bombers followed by strafers had wiped out seven Marine Corps fighters in five minutes, in an obvious pre-landing raid. At remote Guam, essential steppingstone for any expedition that might be mounted to relieve the Philippines, several bombing attacks from close-by Japanese islands served plain notice that an American tenure dating from 1898 soon would end. Guam's handful of marines, sailors, and Insular Guards could offer only a token resistance.

From the standpoint of Hawaii's harried defenders, and for America's defenses as a whole, Pearl Harbor day could have been very much worse. Had Admiral Chuichi Nagumo's six large carriers lingered near Oahu, repeating their attacks, they might easily have ended American chances for even a minor riposte for a year or longer. Simply by wrecking naval base installations and burning the

Navy's fuel oil supply—then stored above ground in vulnerable tanks—the enemy aviators could have insured this result. Still, as it affected the defense of the Philippines—including Corregidor—the outcome of December 7 was total and irretrievable. All lingering hopes in the Navy and War Departments that somehow relief convoys might sail to bolster MacArthur's forces had sunk with the battle line. It was well that the Rock's defenders knew little of the details of this day that would "live in infamy." Had they known, only the optimistic or unreflective could have failed to realize that the Pearl Harbor blow had sealed their destiny. A new Alamo was in the making.

Like Guam and the rest of the Philippine Islands, Corregidor had been a prize of the war with Spain. Even in 1898 it had already acquired an aura of mystery and foreboding. Expecting Commodore George Dewey's arrival when war broke with the United States, the Spanish authorities in Manila had placed small batteries on the Rock and on two of its five satellite bay islands, augmenting these with unfounded rumors, planted at Dewey's Hong Kong base, of mighty fortress cannon, controlled mine fields, and nests of torpedo boats. Discounting these myths, Dewey had brushed past the Rock on the night of April 31, 1898, in a surprise night approach, to penetrate the bay and to score during the morning his overwhelming victory over Admiral Don Patricio Montojo's decrepit squadron anchored at Cavite. At Dewey's demand Corregidor and its sister islets had promptly surrendered. The Rock passed into American hands as a lighthouse station, a summer home site for a handful of Manila residents, and a convalescent hospital for American soldiers injured or sickened during the dreary warfare which ensued for years against the Filipino guerrilla followers of Emilio Aguinaldo and other champions of Philippine national sovereignty. Except in Filipino mythology the Rock seemed destined to fade into renewed neglect and obscurity.

In olden times, so local Filipino legend has it, the mouth of Manila

Bay was but a salt marsh; no sea lay between the Bataan and Cavite headlands. At the bottom of the high mountain on the Bataan side stood a monastery and nearby a convent. One day, in the years before the Renaissance, a young friar fell in love with one of the nuns, the lovely Mariveles, who reciprocated his ardor. Deciding to flee, the couple procured a horse from the nearby village and started across the marsh. Almost at once they were missed, the hue and cry resounded, and the pursuit began. The lovers' horse became bogged in the mire, forcing them to transfer their flight to that faithful but slowest of Filipino draft animals, the carabao. On their swift steeds the pursuers gained, and the lovers took to foot. They were caught by the horsemen and remanded to the local magistrate, the haughty Corregidor, who decreed that they must be punished for their crime and sin and separated from each other, with one on either side of the marsh.

However, the merciful deity who watches over lovers took pity, and was displeased by the haughtiness of the judge. "I will show this proud Corregidor," he said, "that he may not decree eternal punishment for anyone, much less for a pair of faithful lovers." Nevertheless, they had broken the solemn vows of their orders, taken before God, and so the deity determined to make them a permanent example of his justice as well as a monument to fidelity.

He therefore decreed that Mariveles should lie in eternal rest atop the mountain on Bataan that now bears her name. The outline of her figure may be seen from the marsh which is now the channel between the two headlands. The friar he placed on the other side of the channel where he could look always on his beloved. His scowl is preserved in stone—the island, El Fraile. The proud magistrate also was transformed into stone and placed between the two lovers—the island of Corregidor. Nor did he forget the horse and carabao, as the islands of Caballo and Carabao testify.

Of the five islands at the Manila Bay entrance, Corregidor is by far the largest, with an area of 1,735 acres. It lies two miles from Bataan and seven from Cavite Province, naturally dividing the bay's mouth into two channels, called by the Spaniards the Boca Chica and Boca Grande (Small Channel and Large Channel) and by the Americans the North Channel and South Channel. Corregidor's nearest sister, Caballo Island—seventy-five acres—which was destined to become Fort Hughes, lies a thousand yards to the south and east. El Fraile—less than an acre—which was transformed into Fort Drum, the "concrete battleship," lies five-and-a-half miles to the south-southeast. Carabao—forty-five acres—juts abruptly from the sea only a few hundred yards from the Cavite shore, and out of its hard rock the American engineers blasted Fort Frank. Only La Monja, the nun, a tiny islet about the size of El Fraile, lying halfway between Corregidor and the Bataan shore, has remained in its pristine state.

Corregidor resembles a tadpole. When viewed from above, its high bulbous head thrusts bellicosely west into the South China Sea, and its spiny body and tail curl east and south back into Manila Bay. At one time in its geologic history Corregidor undoubtedly was part of a huge volcano that blew out on one side and gradually eroded to disappear partially beneath the sea. To the observer flying into Manila from the west, the tail and Caballo Island appear to comprise part of a volcanic crater that forms almost a circle. Corregidor also lies in the center of a fault and is subject to frequent earthquakes, a phenomenon known to the Spaniards and taken into account by the American engineers who designed the batteries. The crumbly volcanic rock also posed construction difficulties in places, although there is much hard rock present.

Nature has separated Corregidor, later named Fort Mills, into five parts. The major and most spectacular portion, the high, round head of the island, rises 628 feet at its highest point, and is the site of the lighthouse built originally by the Spaniards in the 1830s. Appropriately called "Topside" by the Americans, it forms an uneven area about a mile in diameter on which the engineers and quartermasters placed all of the heavy batteries, the post headquarters, a nine-hole golf course, the huge Topside Barracks for the enlisted men, a parade ground, and the majority of the living quarters. Three ravines, James,

Cheney, and Ramsay, permit access from the water's edge. Elsewhere, although narrow, rocky beaches permitted sight-seers to walk all around the head of the island at low tide, cliffs varying from a hundred to five hundred feet in height bar access except for a few steep trails. Militarily, Topside was vulnerable only from the ravines or the slopes to the rear and east leading to the remainder of the island.

Topside tapers an average of a hundred feet downward and rearward to a plateau the American garrison called Middleside. This extensive area contained the station hospital, the post stockade, numerous service buildings and warehouses, and more barracks and quarters. A ravine on the south, or Cavite, side became known as Government ravine, because a reservation there was earmarked for the bullion, important documents, and selected officialdom of the Philippine Commonwealth, if it became necessary—as it did—for the island to serve as a refuge for them. A ravine called Power Plant Ravine dropping from the north, or Bataan, side, contained the fort's vital electric generating plant, the indispensable heart of the defenses. A climb from sea level to Middleside and Topside up the "golden staircase" was short but breath-robbing; a trip by streetcar or road was hundreds of yards longer around numerous twists, turns, and bends.

From Middleside the terrain slopes steeply downward another three hundred feet or so to the third portion of the island, "Bottomside." As its name implies, this smallish area, about three hundred yards from beach to beach, by two hundred yards wide, is the lowest part of the island. It sheltered warehouses and various post utilities as well as the small barrio (village) of San Jose, where dwelt in both Spanish and American times most of the island's workers. Two docks on the Bataan (north) shore and one on the Cavite (south) shore enabled small ships to unload supplies.

To the east of Bottomside a miniature mountain rises abruptly to 390 feet. Called "Malinta" by the Spanish and Americans, it severs Bottomside from the tail of the island. Two narrow, dangerous roads carved from its precipitous slopes, the North and South Shore roads, girdled the hill and ran on down the curving tadpole tail. To facilitate passage and to create a bombproof headquarters, hospital, and storage area, the Americans drove a shaft from a rock quarry at Bottomside directly through the hill, creating the famous Malinta Tunnel in which General Douglas MacArthur established his wartime headquarters in 1942. Thus the interior of the hill as well as its commanding summit was converted into a military asset.

Until the Malinta Tunnel was built, Bottomside served as the terminus of that remarkable installation, the Rock's electric trolley line. Authorized in 1907 and beginning service in 1910, its streetcars proved to be a handy and economical means of getting men and supplies about Fort Mills. The line ran to all the batteries and all important points on the Rock, and when the main shaft of the Malinta Tunnel was completed in 1934, straight through the hill to a terminus at Kindley Field. From a station near the post Ciné (theater) on Topside, its open-sided, heavy-duty trolleys wound around hairpin turns down a 4 percent grade. It had one bad day in 1925, when a car lost its braking power and ran wild down the hill, killing eight and causing Corregidor's worst peacetime disaster; but otherwise, in thirty-one years of peacetime operations, the trolley line served well and faithfully, hauling uncounted passengers and all classes of freight, from groceries to dangerous high-explosive powder charges.

The fifth and remaining portion of Corregidor is its long, twisting tail, which was given no particular name by the garrison. The western half of this narrow, two-and-a-half-mile area consists of a low ridge with several distinct hills which assumed crucial military importance both in the 1942 siege and in the 1945 recapture. The remaining half, being a fairly level plateau, was partially graded off to form a small airstrip, Kindley Field, some three thousand feet in length. Although taking off and landing from its uneven surface was something of an adventure, the strip saw use from the 1920s onward. A small Air Corps installation, including barracks and hangars, was built at the strip's western end just after the First World War. The extreme tail of the island proper is known as East Point; it contained only a small cemetery. Beyond it is a tiny prominence, Hooker Point, which is periodically separated from East Point by tides, and was a favorite exploring place of hikers and sight-seeing parties in the early years of American tenure. Corregidor's tail was the best place for an amphibious landing—it had thousands of yards of traversable beach below fifty-foot cliffs—but once ashore an enemy would have a long way to go to reach the more important parts of the fortress.

Although Corregidor is only some thirty miles from Manila, it enjoys several natural advantages over the Philippine capital. It has a more salubrious climate, for offshore breezes bring welcome relief from the heat, making the Rock in all seasons about seven degrees cooler than Manila. During the cooler months of the winter and spring, blankets are mandatory at night. Shrubs and flowering trees abound and include flame and fire trees, frangipani, bougainvillaea, hibiscus, and cadena di amour. Orchids bloom profusely amid the branches. A number of palms, planted later, enhanced the tropical appearance of the island.

American officers who served there in the pleasant peacetime years of the twenties and thirties remember the Rock with nostalgia and affection. Lieutenant General Charles E. Kilbourne, who as a captain served as the island's first defense commander, recalls how, sitting on the veranda of his quarters in the evening, he used to watch the automobile headlights on Dewey Boulevard in Manila. Others remember the loom of the Bataan Peninsula to the north and the cloud cap that perpetually seems attached to Mount Bataan. Still others recall the intense blue of the China Sea to the west, and how it changed to gold as the sun dipped low. After the sudden tropic night descended, a thousand stars twinkled among the clouds racing overhead, only to be obscured by the brilliance of a silver moon.

When viewed from the lighthouse on Topside, Caballo Island appears as a wedge of rock jutting from the sea. In Dewey's time, El Fraile resembled a sail, but now it looks like a squat ship with its bow projecting into the China Sea. Of the four so-called Fortified Islands, Carabao is perhaps the most unusual, with sheer cliffs rising a hundred feet from the beach, except for one spot on the eastern shore. To fortify it, the engineers had to emplace all of the armament on a narrow north-south ridge running along its top and on a promontory jutting from the west side.

In a military sense all four islands are dominated by much higher ground on the nearby mainland. From the south the Pico de Loro hills of Cavite Province tower to 2,230 feet above Carabao. From the north Mount Mariveles on the Bataan Peninsula overlooks Corregidor from 4,660 feet. Moreover, both mainland heights, north and south, contain many valleys and ravines defiladed—protected—from observation and shellfire from the islands. This factor, as much as any other, doomed the defenders in World War II.

The conversion of Corregidor and its satellites into fortresses began on a hot July day in 1904 when the Manila Army Engineers received orders from Washington to commence building emplacements for heavy rifle and mortar batteries. After hard work, much of it done with pick and shovel, the first gun was ready to fire on January 27, 1909. At the order of Captain Kilbourne, Coast Artillery Corps, a 12-inch rifle of Battery Wheeler flamed into the tropical sky, and a shell whished toward a target bobbing behind a small tug far out in the China Sea. Already the Spanish gesture at arming the Rock—three museum-piece 8-inch muzzle-loading rifles—seemed pitiful beside the weaponry the United States was to install seven thousand miles from its shores.

On Corregidor the big guns were arranged in semicircular fashion around the rim of the island from Geary Point to Rock Point (see map in front of book). Batteries Crockett, Wheeler, and Cheney each mounted a pair of 12-inch disappearing rifles. Battery Grubbs, further around toward the north side, contained a pair of 10-inchers. The disappearing carriages of these cannon raised the piece above a low concrete parapet. On firing the recoil sank the gun on its mount into position to be quickly reloaded manually under the protection of the parapet. Although disappearing guns were inconspicuous to observers on ships, their main purpose was to supply maximum crew protection and rate of fire at minimum cost. Vulnerable to plunging shells from siege howitzers, to ships mounting high-angle guns, or—later—to aerial bombs, Corregidor's open emplacements were admittedly less effective than the armored turrets favored in European fortresses. But because turrets cost five times as much and were hard to maintain, the uncovered disappearing weapons were selected. The limited 15-degree gun elevations permitted by the mounts deprived the rifles of 40 percent of their maximum possible range, but the 12-inchers could still fire 17,300 yards, equaling the ranges of the ship's guns of their era.

Corregidor's two mortar batteries, Geary and Way, held, respectively, eight and four squat, ugly, almost vertically elevating 12-inch mortars in sunken concrete pits. Way, sited to the northwest of Topside Barracks, contained old but accurate and reliable M-1890 weapons. Geary, situated behind and somewhat eastward of Battery Crockett, had one pit similar to Way, and another equipped with faster-firing M-1908 mortars. With remarkable accuracy these archaic-looking pieces—which resembled something from a Civil War lithograph—could loft a shell as much as 15,200 yards in any direction. They were ideally suited to penetrate the thin deck armor of ships, or to "search" for enemy siege batteries hidden in Bataan's ravines. Despite their antiquity, they remained the most effective weapons on the Rock during the siege of 1942.

The two long-range 12-inch rifles of Batteries Smith and Hearn, mounted high above Corregidor's westernmost tip, were the pride of the garrison. When elevated to 30 degrees, each barbette-mounted weapon could lob a seven-hundred-pound, deck-piercing shell to within *feet* of a target 29,500 yards distant, be it at sea or deep within Bataan's jungles. The trouble with both was that although their crews and ammunition had bombproof tunnels for shelter, the pieces themselves were completely in the open, on circular concrete pads a thousand feet apart which resembled from the air two huge bull's-eyes. Authorized in 1915, but not ready for service until 1921, these batteries were the last completed in the harbor defenses.

Fearing with some reason that a sudden turn of Philippine defense policy might halt appropriations, the constructing engineers had elected to ready Corregidor's basic armament first, leaving its lesser sister islands until later. In consequence the fortification of Carabao, Caballo, and El Fraile lagged several years behind. Delay furnished one blessing. Except for Batteries Smith and Hearn, Forts Frank, Hughes, and Drum received more modern arms than had Fort Mills on Corregidor.

Because they were anxious to blanket the wide South Channel with heavy weapons as soon as possible, the Manila engineers began the other defenses at Carabao Island, which they named Fort Frank. Topography dictated placing Battery Greer's 14-inch disappearing rifle at the northernmost end, and a similar weapon, Battery Crofton, on a promontory on the westward side. Between the 14-inchers the engineers found room to excavate two pits for the eight M-1908 mortars of Battery Koehler. But after they had stripped off the island's vegetation, the engineers realized that the garrison could quickly be decimated by shells fired at point-blank ranges from the close-by Cavite hills. Consequently they blasted a deep, bombproof trench between all battery locations, a feature destined to save many lives in wartime.

Caballo, named Fort Hughes, also received two 14-inch rifles, one on either end of the island. Battery Woodruff occupied the low rear and Battery Gillespie the steep face of the fort. From the rear a tunnel ran upward and forward to a shelf about halfway to the island's crest. Here the engineers sited what were potentially the most valuable weapons in the harbor defenses, the four mortars of Battery Craighill. These late-model M-1912 weapons, two in each pit, could sink ships 19,300 yards out to sea, could neutralize enemy batteries on Bataan or Cavite, or blast vessels deep within the confines of Manila Bay, should a foe emulate Commodore Dewey's feat of slipping past the harbor forts.

When armed and renamed Fort Drum, the last islet, El Fraile (The Friar), was unique in the American seacoast service. The engineers razed the tiny rock to the water line, erected a twenty- to thirty-foot-thick concrete casemate around it, and then decked it over to create an all-but-impregnable fortress. As completed shortly after the First World War, Fort Drum looked like a squat battleship, or more precisely a monitor, thrusting its bow into the China Sea. Four 6-inch rifles for mine-field defense bristled from armored casemates in its rear; two massive twin-gun 14-inch turrets, one above the other, dominated its broad foredeck. A cage mast topped by a searchlight and a caretaker's shack on the stern completed the ship-like effect. Currents passing the fort crested like the bow wave of a moving warship, and more than one afterward embarrassed Navy skipper so reported it, estimating its speed at three to four knots. The challenging engineering feat of building Fort Drum took from 1909 until 1919, but was worth the time and cost. The booming salvos of "the concrete battleship" provided more support for the defenders and more trouble for the Japanese attackers than any other installation in the harbor defenses.

Of course the big guns were only the most spectacular feature of the harbor defenses of Manila Bay. They were not necessarily the most important, given the sort of war the garrison would have to fight. Searchlight positions, a very large number of command, fire control, and observation posts, pillboxes, casemates for housing switchboards to trigger controlled mines, light fixed batteries to cover mine fields, and especially mobile artillery, heavy and light—these elements of the defenses occupied positions far too numerous to detail. All were as essential to the island's defense as the heavy batteries.

Several items deserve special mention. Two of Corregidor's light fixed batteries bore directly on Bataan. Designed to cover an electrically controlled mine field in the North Channel, the two 6-inch rifles of Battery Morrison and the four 3-inchers of Battery James were well placed to hit an enemy on Bataan. Unfortunately, both were clearly visible from the Peninsula's heights as was 10-inch Battery

Grubbs. Fortunately, a shipment of mobile field guns had been sent to the Rock shortly after World War I consisting of twenty-four 155 mm. guns of a French model, the famous *Grande Puissance Fillioux* (G.P.F.) of the Western front, and forty-eight 75 mm. rapid-firing pieces of a British model with high, wooden-spoked wheels. As scattered about the island on semifixed "Panama mounts," the 155's greatly added to the island's firepower, as each could range as far as a 12-inch disappearing rifle. Although odd-looking and less effective than the famous French *Soixante-Quinze,* the British-model 75's, copies of an old eighteen-pounder, were suitable as beach defense weapons. When backed by 37 mm. guns and dozens of light and heavy machine guns, they sufficed to lead many officers to believe—erroneously as it turned out—that no enemy could land successfully on Corregidor.

In summary, the armament of Corregidor and its lesser sisters could by 1941 be termed obsolescent but still formidable. By any standard Manila Bay was protected by an exceptionally powerful seacoast defense. If an enemy fleet ventured near, the rifles of Batteries Smith and Hearn could plunge shells through the thinly armored decks of the enemy flagship. If it had the temerity to close the range, then an array of sixteen other rifles of major caliber and twenty-four 12-inch mortars could pummel all its ships with rapid fire. With reason the coast artillerymen of Fort Mills were convinced that no admiral anywhere, Japanese or other, would dare risk his command, reputation and life by venturing within thirty thousand yards of the Rock. The Harbor Defenses could and did fulfill their "primary mission"—that of closing Manila Bay to an enemy fleet—without firing a shot in anger. In some ways Corregidor's sobriquet, "the Gibraltar of the Far East," was an understatement rather than an exaggeration.

2 ☆ "A Strategic Liability"

AT FIRST LIGHT on December 8, only minutes after receipt of the grim message from Pearl Harbor announcing the outbreak of war, Navy launches were speeding toward half a dozen Japanese owned fishing boats plying their trade about the entrance to Manila Bay. A few minutes later, the boats and their crews were in American captivity on Corregidor. Thus ended a Japanese threat which for years had gravely concerned every Harbor Defense commander, many of whom had expected Japan to begin hostilities by mounting a surprise attack using troops concealed in the seemingly omnipresent boats.

Japan's interest in Corregidor had coincided with the emergence of her rivalry for power with the United States. Suspicious of all foreigners, but recognizing after Commodore Perry's visit in 1854 that imitation of the West was essential to compete in a modernized world, Japan in a burst of energy had quickly transformed herself into a first-rank military and industrial power. Victories over China in 1895 and Russia in 1905 had proved that Japan could employ modern weapons with medieval ardor, and had whetted the appetites of her military leaders for further conquests.

With the defeat of Russia, the United States had become the only power capable of checking Japanese expansionist designs in China. Increasingly heated diplomatic exchanges with the United States charged an already tense atmosphere, until a seemingly minor incident in San Francisco brought on a crisis.

In October of 1906 the school board of that city had segregated children of Japanese ancestry, thereby implying that Orientals were unfit to associate with whites. As a wave of indignation swept Japan, the incensed government protested vehemently. Although at President Theodore Roosevelt's insistence the order was rescinded, the damage had been done; the crisis continued, and since it seemed likely that if war broke Japan would seize the Philippines—if only to acquire a bargaining chip for the peace table—Roosevelt ordered Philippine defense stepped up. Work was rushed on Corregidor's batteries, and the only major American combat unit, the Philippine Division on Luzon, was ordered to prepare a defense perimeter at Subic Bay, there to hang on, if possible, until reinforcements could come from the United States.

For its part the Japanese General Staff strove to complete its intelligence portfolios concerning American defenses. Mysterious Corregidor interested it greatly, as did prospects of exploiting a renewed Filipino insurrection against American rule. Although the immediate threat of war faded during 1907, Japanese intelligence activity continued unabated, as the commander of the Philippine Division, Major General William P. Duvall, discovered the following year.

In late August of 1908 one "Major K. Inouye" of the Japanese General Staff suddenly appeared at Duvall's headquarters, demanding blanket permission to inspect various American combat organizations, including Corregidor. Pointedly refusing an escort, he based his request on reciprocity, alleging that similar privileges had been granted to an American officer in Tokyo. He received a polite brush-off, and an amazed Duvall hastily inquired into Inouye's prior activity. What he discovered led him to cable Washington posthaste, warning that a Japanese attack on the Philippines might be imminent.

According to the Philippine Constabulary's agent "Number 11," Inouye was really Major General Inouye, Chief of the Intelligence Section of the Japanese General Staff, come to Luzon to spy out the land for himself and to check reports from his networks of agents. Prior to his request he had been busily seeing Japanese residents, spending money lavishly, and had been treated with great deference by the Japanese colony. He had shown special interest in a "commercial" steamer that had anchored first in Lamon Bay and then in Lingayen Gulf, already estimated to be the probable debarkation points for an enemy expeditionary force. Other agents reported that Japanese naval officers had directed crew members at sounding the anchorages. Inouye had also been seen pouring over maps of Luzon, especially those portions covering roads from prospective beachheads to Manila. Duvall feared that he might be plotting an invasion route for immediate use.

No one in Washington took Duvall's cables seriously. President William Howard Taft set the tone when he minuted, "I don't think there is anything to be done, and I don't attach any particular significance to it." That ended matters for the time being.

Yet, however thoroughly official Washington might erase Inouye from its collective mind, Duvall could not. Constabulary agents continued to report meetings of Japanese with the local underground, attempts to gather information, and even purported arms deliveries. And in March, 1910, Duvall's counter-intelligence discovered that two Japanese attached to the staff of the consul general in Manila were rather ineptly trying to bribe an American engineer private first class and a German-born photographer—promising them twenty-five thousand dollars—for photos of Corregidor. At the third meeting with the pair, officers burst into their Manila hotel room rendezvous and seized the Japanese. On orders from Washington the Japanese were released, but the consul general was declared *persona non grata* to the United States.

Throughout its career the Rock continued to attract attention from the Japanese (and probably other) intelligence services. Japanese fishing boats, equipped with such unconventional gear as spotting telescopes and direction-finding equipment, prowled about the three-mile limit, sometimes venturing within it. Their skippers, often believed to be naval reserve officers, were surly and uncooperative when caught. That at least some of its secrets remained unplumbed by the

Japanese now seems incredible in the face of the persistent snooping. The 1942 attackers had large and detailed maps of the island, but the combat troops seemed uninformed about key headquarters tunnels and even the locations of some batteries. Perhaps it was the old story of intelligence operations: the spies and fishing boats got the data, but the information somehow failed to reach the troops in the field.

While Duvall chased spies in the Philippines, Army and Navy leaders were reappraising the defense prospects of the island in the light of continuing unsettled relations with Japan. America had lightheartedly annexed the islands, but could she hold them against an expansionist Japan capable of mounting a powerful attack? Already the Congress had proved unwilling to furnish enough combat troops to defeat a landing on Luzon. Nor could the Navy risk uncovering the continental United States by transferring the entire fleet to the Far East. For want of a better strategy American planners had to find a "keep," a refuge where the Philippine garrison could hold out until forces mustered in the United States could be dispatched to relieve it.

Deciding on the location of the "keep" produced the worst clash of wills between Army and Navy chieftains since the Civil War. The Navy insisted on Subic Bay, but Army objections that infantry could not hold this splendid harbor prevailed. On August 24, 1908, Corregidor was chosen. The Philippine Division commander was ordered in event of war to defend Manila as long as possible, and then to withdraw to the Rock. He was immediately to arm, stock, and equip Corregidor for a prolonged siege. After six months, so the planners estimated, the island would be the sole territory still flying the American flag.

For its part the Navy had decided to limit Subic Bay to the status of a small naval station, to develop the former Spanish base at Cavite inside Manila Bay only as an installation for its Asiatic Squadron, and to build its main base at Pearl Harbor in the Hawaiian Islands. Thus relief for Corregidor's beleaguered troops would have to be staged at Pearl Harbor and convoyed the breadth of the Pacific.

The Army leaders soon came to realize that as a "keep" the Rock had a number of serious drawbacks. But because construction was already well advanced and no practicable alternative seemed feasible, few modifications were made to the island's armament to accord with its additional mission. Corregidor's primary task still was to deny Manila Bay to an enemy fleet. Now it would also have to fight off bombardment and follow-up amphibious landings from the Bataan and Cavite shorelands, holding an enemy off for at least six months, until the arrival of reinforcements. For this purpose its armament was ill-suited. Most of its heavy guns bore southward and westward and few bore on the Bataan Peninsula just two miles away. Moreover, most were rifles, with a relatively flat trajectory, and were incapable of lobbing a shell onto the reverse slope of a hill. Behind Bataan's many ridges an enemy could be expected to emplace siege howitzers which only the high-angle mortar batteries, Geary and Way, could touch. Also, all the batteries, the mortars included, were in open emplacements, vulnerable to plunging fire. To replace them with guns in turrets would be too costly; the House Appropriations Committee would never approve. To cover them with overhead concrete or armor protection would be almost as expensive and technically very difficult. In the end, all that the best efforts of many concerned officers could produce from 1909 onward was a series of remedial half measures.

In studying the problem of defeating enemy siege howitzers—for example, the deadly 11-inch Japanese weapons that had wrecked Russia's Port Arthur forts in 1904—boards of officers convened by the Philippine Division's commanders soon realized that no single measure would suffice. Besting enemy howitzers and preventing the Rock from being softened up for a landing was a threefold proposition. First, Corregidor had to be able to "take it"; vital structures had to be made as shellproof as possible. Second, the enemy howitzers had to be located. And third, they had to be counterbatteried and silenced.

Task one, that of shellproofing vital installations, began at once. As designed, the huge Topside Barracks received a second floor thickened by five-and-a-half feet of concrete, sufficient to resist a 7-inch shell. Ordnance warehouses, machine shops, and the telephone exchange likewise were bombproofed. The post power plant, indispensable in furnishing electricity to all installations, received a nine-foot-thick concrete roof, with earth over that. Originally merely splinterproofed, the magazines of the mortar batteries, Way and Geary, were given an eleven-foot concrete and earth cover. In vulnerable James ravine, a likely enemy landing point, an infantry bombproof was built, and atop Morrison and Malinta Hills, protected infantry command posts were installed. But no battery received so much as a concrete roof for its emplacement, and before World War I no one seems to have proposed tunneling under Corregidor's numerous hills.

After much debate concerning task two, locating the enemy's batteries, the Harbor Defense Command in 1914 sponsored a practical test. Captain Harrison Hall, then commanding Battery Way, was ordered to bombard the Rock with four old 7-inch howitzers from behind a hill near Mariveles Harbor on Bataan. Observers on Corregidor would try to locate him. Hall lobbed a number of shells at Battery James, whose 3-inch weapons had been removed for the test. Not only did he place several rounds within a few yards of the empty mounts while firing unfamiliar weapons and using only an improvised ranging system, but none of the observers had spotted the smoke or the flash of his old 7-inchers. Had a regiment of Japanese heavy artillery been firing, the results would have been disastrous.

Most of the officers believed that aerial observation promised the best solution, and so from 1915 to 1927 seaplanes were based on the Rock. But air spotting was hardly a definitive answer. If Japanese planes controlled the air, as in a prolonged siege they were bound to do, neither seaplanes nor land observation planes stationed at the Kindley Field base could survive. Under the circumstances only improved flash and sound ranging equipment offered much hope, plus a measure recommended in 1913, maintaining secret plotting stations high in the Bataan and Cavite mountains. Unfortunately, no improved ranging equipment became available, and no clandestine radio posts were established. In 1941 the Rock was still helpless to locate enemy batteries.

The third task, that of enhancing the Rock's counterbattery fire, was hardly approached before the end of the First World War. The only effective measure taken was the establishment on Fort Hughes of the modern four-gun mortar battery, Craighill. But like Geary and Way on Corregidor, and Koehler on Fort Frank, its pits were open to fire from enemy siege howitzers. To be sure, some of the seacoast rifles—such as the weapons of Fort Drum—could bear, but their relatively flat trajectory could not touch a howitzer snuggled behind a hill. Also, for both the 12-inch rifles and 12-inch mortars, land bombardment ammunition with instantaneous fuzes was in short supply. Thousands of rounds of armor- and deck-piercing heavy-case projectiles were available, but in 1941 only 900 of 1,300 thin-case rounds, originally sent in 1921 and later, remained. The 14-inch batteries had no land projectiles at all. Delay-fuzed shells were fine against enemy ships but were ill-suited for counterbattery use against enemy guns. Tests had shown that they would bury themselves so deeply into the earth before exploding that their blast effect would be limited.

After World War I, ideal counterbattery weapons, including heavy howitzers, became available from stocks returned from the Western front. In 1921 twelve modern, efficient 240 mm. howitzers, with a high trajectory capable of "searching" any of Bataan's ravines, were loaded aboard ship and dispatched. But these never arrived, for Washington had concluded that diplomatic measures were superior to heavy field howitzers for defending Corregidor and the Philippines.

During the First World War diplomacy had acquired added burdens. The naval arms race between the United States and Japan had coincided with Japanese occupation of the German-owned Marshall, Caroline, and Mariana islands lying between Hawaii and the Philippines. In an attempt to improve international relations and end the arms race, the Harding Administration in 1921 convened in Washington a conference at which Japan, the United States, and seven other countries agreed to respect one another's possessions in the Pacific. The nations also agreed to a fifteen-year treaty drastically paring naval strength. In order to persuade the reluctant Japanese to sign, an article was added, the "Nonfortification Clause," specifying that the United States could not strengthen its naval bases or seacoast defenses west of Midway Island. That meant that Guam could not be fortified and that nothing could be added to Corregidor's armament. Hence the decision to off-load at Hawaii the twelve 240 mm. howitzers. Soon literally dozens of projects, including provision of critically needed gasproofing equipment for all batteries, were likewise cancelled.

Close on this blow came another of equal severity. To economize, the Harding Administration slashed the military budget repeatedly, until the Army could muster barely enough men to insure domestic order. On Corregidor and its sisters first batteries and then entire forts had to be reduced to caretaker status. Only the expedient of creating two understrength regiments of Philippine Scout artillerymen, who cost half as much to maintain as Americans, left even a semblance of defense at Manila Bay. By 1925 even Fort Drum, whose turret machinery needed constant maintenance to remain serviceable, had been moth-balled. At Fort Mills penury denied converting a coal-fired heating plant in the hospital to more efficient oil because oil would cost $185 more annually than coal. The post prison officer had his charges collect scrap for sale on the Manila commercial market to raise funds for purchase of barbed wire for the Rock's beach defenses.

To Harbor Defense commanders it must have seemed as if America was attempting to keep the peace by unilateral disarmament. Far from living up to her obligations under the Washington Treaties, Japan had barred her mandated Pacific islands to outsiders, and, as intelligence reports correctly indicated, was violating the terms of the treaties, thereby tilting the military and naval balance in the western Pacific further in her favor.

Although improvement of Corregidor's defenses seemed an impossibility, three remarkable officers refused to adopt a do-nothing policy, and risked their careers to tackle anew the Rock's most vexing tactical problem, bombardment from Bataan. Shortly after World War I a Harbor Defense commander had proposed emplacing a secure headquarters and storage area under Malinta Hill. In 1931 Brigadier General Charles E. Kilbourne blandly announced in a routine dispatch his intention of constructing a "tunnel road" through the hill for the convenience of the Air Corps garrison at Kindley Field. Covered by Major General John Gulick, who permitted no discussion of the true nature of the project at Coast Artillery Headquarters, Kilbourne used his post maintenance allowance to begin construction, employing old mining equipment and prison labor. His friend and successor, Brigadier General Stanley D. Embick, continued the task, lining the main corridor and laterals with concrete and laying out the north and south supplemental storage areas. Work went on until the system was substantially completed in 1938.

Despite the boost given to its defenses by the Malinta Tunnel, the Rock remained an uncertain "keep." Even if its commanders had managed to meet the threat of land-based artillery, the danger to the island would have been almost as great. For unless a relieving United States fleet could cross the Pacific, safely passing the Japanese mandated islands, the defenders eventually would be starved into submission.

In the Pacific, the years of the 1920s had been tranquil. In 1931, however, a Japanese army, without the permission of its home government, began the conquest of Manchuria. By 1937, Japan had embarked on an all-out attempt to subdue China, inducing the Rock's Harbor Defense commanders to keep one antiaircraft battery constantly manned and a skeleton beach defense force on the alert—just in case. The assumption remained that if Japan attacked, and if Corregidor could hold out for approximately six months, the Navy would come to the rescue.

A Navy war plan of 1911 had sketched just such an operation; and in 1924, as a result of deliberations by the Joint Board of the Army and Navy, a formalized joint Army-Navy war plan embodied the same assumption. It was called War Plan Orange, the code term "Orange" identifying the prospective enemy, Japan. As finally worked out after several changes, its essential features were simple; the Army's "mobile" forces in Luzon would abandon Manila to retire into the natural jungle fortress of the Bataan peninsula, while the coast artillerymen protected their rear. The Navy would fight its way across the Pacific, seizing Japanese-held islands as it advanced. At some point, probably near Guam, a decisive Jutland-type naval battle would erupt between the battleships of the rival fleets and Japan would lose, giving America command of the seas and access to the beleaguered forces on Bataan and Corregidor.

Generally speaking, the Navy planners were more enthusiastic about Plan Orange than was the Army, which did not relish a defensive strategy of retreat. As one of the naval planners, Captain L. M. Overstreet, put it in 1922, the Philippines constituted a pawn to be sacrificed in the larger interest of winning the decisive naval battle. If the Corregidor-Bataan stand diverted Japanese naval strength, it would be worth it, whatever the outcome.

The Orange Plan was not even a good staff study. Not by the wildest stretch of the imagination could the Army have mustered the trained divisions to fulfill the plan (fifty thousand men were to be en route from the West Coast to Hawaii by D plus ten!), nor did the Navy have the logistical capacity to project its Pacific Fleet into the midst of Japan's advanced bases. And as if these problems were not enough, the transports and landing craft needed to boat the men and equipment did not exist. Only concerning Corregidor's capability were most knowledgeable officers optimistic. They not only expected the Rock's garrison to hold the specified six months, but were confident the defenders could withstand the siege for a time limited only by available stocks of food and ammunition—provided, of course, the Japanese used only "fair" methods of attack, and not poison gas. Yet, from what soon transpired in China no one could be sanguine about even that.

The military clique dominating the Japanese government was ruthless in its conquest of China, going so far as to sink the American gunboat *Panay* in the Yangtze River in 1938. Already it had become clear that the time was fast approaching when the United States would have to make a clear-cut decision: to move in enough forces to defend the Philippines effectively or to get out.

The decision was to get out—eventually. Congress in 1934 passed the Tydings-McDuffie Act guaranteeing the Philippines unconditional independence on the Fourth of July, 1946. At that time the United States would relinquish its sovereignty over the islands, and Corregidor and other Army installations would be transferred to Philippine control. Passage of the act virtually doomed plans to modernize Corregidor's elderly armament after the Arms Limitation Treaty's expiration, which was due in 1937. A trickle of funds began flowing to the armed forces as international affairs worsened, but most went to the Navy and Air Corps. Understandably, the less-favored Army was loath to pour money into an obsolescent fortress soon to leave its hands.

In the Philippines, colorful, already controversial Douglas MacArthur, leaving his post as Chief of Staff of the Army to accept a commission as Field Marshal from the Philippine Commonwealth Government, devised in 1935 and 1936 an imaginative "do it yourself" defense plan for the islands. With United States forces gone in 1946, he predicted, the Philippines could nevertheless protect themselves. By building up a force of 400,000 infantry reservists, by creating a small cadre of regulars, by establishing a small but efficient Air Corps and a Navy featuring motor torpedo boats for coastal operations, the new nation could become an "Asiatic Switzerland." Japan *could* overrun the islands, but MacArthur and the new President of the Philippine Commonwealth, Manuel Quezon, hoped to make the effort too costly to be worth it. For the next five years, against formidable odds, MacArthur strove to implement the scheme.

He was aided initially by a small staff which included Majors James B. Ord and Dwight D. Eisenhower. Despite meager accomplishments he remained optimistic that he could enlist, arm, and train combat-worthy forces.

Meanwhile, in the United States doubt grew steadily in ranking Army circles that Plan Orange, still in effect should war come before independence, would prove workable. Leading the skeptics among Coast Artillery officers were Generals Kilbourne and Embick. Both officers were inclined to regard Corregidor and Bataan as a mere trap for American forces if Japan attacked. In May of 1927 Kilbourne wrote in the *Coast Artillery Journal,* "We must accept [the Philippines] . . . as a strategic liability," and he suggested that rather than reinforcing the islands, the best course would be to strike directly at the vitals of the enemy. His friend Embick was even more specific and emphatic, writing officially during his tour as Harbor Defense commander: "To carry out the present Orange Plan with the provision for an early dispatch of our fleet to Philippine waters would be an act of madness." Later, as an influential chief of the Army's War Plans Division, Embick pointed out repeatedly that the Army lacked sufficient troops to fulfill its part of the joint relief operation; with existing forces an attempt would be suicidal.

Still clinging to hopes of drawing the Japanese fleet into a decisive naval battle, the Navy's leaders disagreed, as late as 1938 accepting only more realistic modifications, not an alteration, of Plan Orange. Events, however, forced their hand. When war broke out in Europe in 1939, a disaster followed closely by the near defeat of Great Britain in 1940, they finally agreed with Embick. Realizing that the United States would have to maintain substantial naval forces in the Atlantic as well as the Pacific, in 1940 and again in 1941 Admiral Harold R. Stark, the Chief of Naval Operations, reverted to a 1915 strategy decision, specifying that if war broke in the Pacific the Navy would not send its squadrons west of the 180th meridian. With this decision the Navy in effect wrote off the Philippines and Corregidor as its "keep," even though Orange remained officially unchanged.

In such a climate of policy Corregidor got short shrift. From 1938 to 1941 maintenance and construction annual allocations did not exceed thirty-nine thousand dollars and usually were less. To quote Major General George F. Moore, who became commandant of the Rock in the spring of 1941, this was ". . . inadequate for ordinary repair and maintenance work." Quartermaster and fortification allowances were equally slighted. The only new major appropriations for construction after 1938 came from naval funds, the most important being for a Navy radio intercept tunnel at Monkey Point to house special electronic machinery the Army and Navy had developed to break Japanese codes. This, it turned out, was a tremendous bargain, for the Corregidor installation picked up and passed on to American headquarters the Japanese messages making possible the American naval victories in the Coral Sea and at Midway. Since the Navy also expected to lose Cavite's base facilities when war came, it released funds in 1939 to the Army Engineers to drive four tunnels into the south side of Malinta Hill, to be connected by a shaft to the Army's South Tunnel complex. The largest, Tunnel Queen, was an elaborate affair designed to refuge the headquarters of the Sixteenth (Philippines) Naval District. The other tunnels held stores, foodstuffs, spare torpedoes for Asiatic Fleet submarines, and a naval radio station. Two, set in soft rock, were incomplete when war began.

By mid-1941 tension between the United States and Japan had become critical. The Japanese forced their way into Thailand, preparatory to further expansion into Malaya and the Netherlands East Indies. President Franklin D. Roosevelt responded by freezing Japanese assets, instituting an oil embargo, and, with the Dutch, British, and Australians, working toward the development of an Allied command aimed at discouraging Japanese expansion into their so-called "Greater East Asia Co-Prosperity Sphere." Abruptly Washington had shifted its policy from one of isolation and nonintervention to another, which was akin to containment.

As a front-line territory in this effort the Philippines assumed a position of first-rank importance in American strategy. Built up to the strength envisaged by General MacArthur in his plan for the Philippine Commonwealth armed forces, the islands would constitute, so Washington hoped, a formidable deterrent to a Japanese drive southward. As America's western Pacific strategy was reversed, no longer was the loss of the Philippines accepted as inevitable.

General MacArthur had been a long-time foe of the proposition that the Philippines were indefensible. Now the War Department recommissioned him as a Lieutenant General and appointed him to command all American Army forces in the Far East. It also accepted his proposal to mobilize 200,000 Filipino reservists into ten infantry divisions with supporting units, including two regiments of coast artillery. Both MacArthur and the War Department seem to have become convinced that if these men could achieve a reasonable stage of training and if enough B-17 and B-24 heavy bombers and P-40 fighters could reach the islands by April, 1942, a deterrent barrier to Japanese invasion would exist, and a Pacific war would be averted.

MacArthur, buoyed by the support he was receiving from Chief of Staff George C. Marshall and the War Department, now pushed ahead with optimistic plans of his own. Dropping the local Philippine section of the Orange War Plan, which had called for a retreat into Bataan and a last stand at Corregidor, he proposed a new strategy which assigned to his reservists the mission of defending Luzon's beaches and driving enemy landing forces into the sea. By November 4 he had secured War Department approval of his changes and was ready to formalize his command structure to conform to the new strategy.

Already the dispatch of matériel to the Philippines had reached, by previous standards, flood-tide proportions. New planes, two battalions of tanks, an antiaircraft regiment, field guns, millions of rounds of ammunition, and sundry other items already had arrived. More was coming on every ship: some new and some surplus from World War I stocks and depots in the United States. For the first time in its history the United States was endeavoring to provide its Philippines dependency with the equipment and men necessary for a successful defense.

Yet Corregidor shared little in this largesse. If the plan to build up powerful land and air forces could be completed in time, the Rock would lose one of its two missions; it no longer would be needed as a "keep," but only for what it originally had been designed—a fortress to prevent enemy naval forces from entering Manila Bay. Nevertheless, a number of long-deferred projects found approval. In early 1941 a local board recommended and Washington approved expending over half a million dollars to gasproof Malinta Tunnel. However, no material arrived before the outbreak of war, and it was well for the "tunnelites" of 1942 that Nippon elected not to use mustard gas or lewisite. A fortuitous acquisition of forty thousand dollars to purchase sandbags locally proved of much greater practical importance. So also did reviving old plans to build several bombproofs, including projected major tunnels near Battery Wheeler and at Middleside for Seaward Defense and Harbor Defense headquarters. Routine handling in Washington of these urgent requests delayed start of the work until just before war began, but enough equipment and labor had been gathered to continue it after Pearl Harbor day.

Acquiring more men proved easier than acquiring more equipment. Early in January, 1941, Chief of Staff Marshall approved sending 1,465 recruits to bring the 59th and 60th Coast Artillery Regiments, manning respectively the "concrete artillery"—the heavy coast defense guns—and the antiaircraft batteries, almost to wartime strength. These men arrived in April to give General Moore, the new Harbor Defense commander, a total of 4,810 troops, enough to man all the antiaircraft weapons and most—but not all—of the seacoast pieces.

By the beginning of November, 1941, the chances of deterring Japan and keeping the peace had become slight. The question was not "if" Japan would strike, but "when." The long era of peace on the Rock was drawing to a close.

3 ☆ A Month of Disaster

At 1:30 in the morning of December 8, 1941, a force of 5,300 Japanese troops sped in their landing barges for the beaches of Malaya. Their objective: to seize the important British airfield at Kota Bharu, a coastal town close to the narrow Malaya-Thailand frontier, and in so doing to begin the conquest of the entire British colony with its prize, the great island fortress and naval base of Singapore. Even as the boats neared the shore, on the other side of the international date line—it was 7:30, December 7, Honolulu time—the Pearl Harbor striking force was making its attack approach on Oahu.

Thus on that fateful morning Japan plunged into all-out war against the United States and the British Empire and its Commonwealth of Nations.

As they neared the Malayan shore line, the spray-drenched soldiers of the Takumi Detachment, many of whom were coal miners from northern Kyushu and hardened veterans of the China campaign, were in for a stiff fight. More than three hundred of them would perish and another five hundred would suffer wounds. Early morning air attacks would sink two of the three transports that had brought them to these shores. But by the afternoon of the following day Kota Bharu's airfield would be in their hands.

A full year and a half earlier, in late July of 1940, Japan's ruling military clique had decided to conquer, at the earliest favorable opportunity, Burma, Malaya, Borneo, the Philippines, and the

Netherlands East Indies (Indonesia), lands rich in oil, nickel, copper, aluminum, rubber, and rice; lands they euphemistically called the "Southern Resources Area." With this accomplished, the clique reasoned, China could be fully pacified in three to four years, and with Manchuria could be welded into a powerful union with the Japanese home islands. The Takumi Detachment at Kota Bharu was therefore beginning one of history's most daring and comprehensive schemes of conquest. If Japan could win the war, His Imperial Majesty, the deified Hirohito, would reign over more than half the people of the earth.

Japan's main thrust, so the planners had decreed, would be into Burma, Malaya, Sumatra, and Java, with a powerful secondary blow struck at the Philippines to eliminate the American threat from the flank and rear. Subsidiary operations would seize Hong Kong, Guam, Wake, and many other small islands. Expansion then would follow into the Admiralties, New Britain, and New Guinea to guard the Southern Resources Area from the southwest. In six months the entire region should be in Japanese hands—assuming the Pearl Harbor attack force had crippled America's Pacific Fleet. Luzon—and presumably Corregidor as well—would be fully "secured" in fifty days. Here prophecy stopped, but the planners apparently believed that the United States and its Allies could not retake the area and would ultimately settle for a treaty recognizing Japan's gains.

Although the clique and its planners undoubtedly believed their chances for victory depended mostly on Japan's own resources, and especially on the fanatical willingness of the ordinary Japanese soldier, aviator, and sailor to discard his life in combat—"spiritual strength," they called it—their prospects really hinged on a Nazi victory in Europe. Had Hitler's renewed attack in 1942 destroyed the Soviet Union, who could say that the Japanese gamble might not have paid off? At the least the road to victory for America and Britain would have been made excruciatingly slow and bloody.

As set down on paper Japan's chances looked good. Its Army boasted 2,400,000 combat troops, backed up by an additional

3,000,000 reserves, many of whom were combat-hardened in China. Against these forces the British, Dutch, and Americans could muster a mere 350,000 men in eastern Asia, of whom only a handful of British imperial units in Malaya could be considered combat ready. Moreover, although the Allies did not realize it prior to hostilities, the Japanese Army and Navy air forces enjoyed superiority both in numbers and quality in some types of combat aircraft. For example, no Allied fighter could boast half the combat radius of the Navy Mitsubishi A6M, better known as the Zero. Also, as the British would discover to their shock, this graceful aircraft could outmaneuver even the famous Spitfire, of Battle of Britain fame. Japan's weak link was its Navy, which nevertheless had more warships, including aircraft carriers, in Pacific waters than the combined Allied navies. Here, the Pearl Harbor attack was intended to be the decisive blow that would convert superiority into lopsided preponderance. With the American battle force lying wrecked at Pearl, the Japanese Navy easily could overpower whatever sea strength the Allies could muster in eastern Asia.

Hitler had practiced blitzkrieg (lightning war) on land; now Japan would do the same by land, sea, and air. Bad as it was, the disaster at Pearl Harbor was in some ways the least tragic of a dolorous series of reverses to Allied arms in the first six months of the Pacific War. Prewar United States intelligence had not credited the Japanese with the capacity to undertake more than one major amphibious operation at a time. But beginning with the Kota Bharu landing, there were literally dozens of landings in the next three months, involving the often simultaneous movement of tens of thousands of troops. Just one failed, the initial attempt to take Wake Island on December 11. And as we shall see, the last attempt in Japan's march of conquest only narrowly averted failure.

Against Malaya and Singapore the Japanese blitzkrieg reached its zenith. The troops landed at two other beachheads in addition to Kota Bharu, and two days later, on December 10, land-based planes of the 22nd Air Flotilla torpedoed and sank the great British warships *Repulse* and *Prince of Wales,* liquidating Allied hopes of offering effective naval opposition. Then, through Malaya's dense jungles, hard-fighting Japanese infantry of the 5th, 18th, and Imperial Guards Divisions drove back thousands of the British Empire's finest, including Gurkhas, Australians, Britons, Malays, and troops of many other nationalities. Japanese cleverness at the art of jungle warfare was one part of the story; British ineptitude at a command level was another; but the clincher was the Japanese ability to make amphibious "end runs" around the successive jungle defense lines the British managed to establish inland along the Malay coast. Repeatedly outflanked, the defenders could only withdraw.

In a little over two months the Japanese reached the narrow strait opposite the island of Singapore, and on February 15, 1942, the great fortress surrendered. Among other weaknesses it, like Corregidor, had big guns that pointed seaward, rather than landward across the narrow causeway to the Malay shore.

Even before Singapore's fall the Japanese began the conquest of the Netherlands Indies, landing in Borneo on December 17 and in the Celebes on January 11. Consolidating their hold against feeble opposition, they quickly brought in planes and gathered strength to assail Bali, Sumatra, and Java. Against these thrusts the Allies mustered what remained of their naval power, which after the loss of the two British capital ships consisted merely of cruisers and destroyers. But a series of battles and skirmishes, climaxed by the gallant last fight of the American cruiser *Houston* and the Australian *Perth* at midnight of February 28, cost them nearly all of their remaining ships. Withdrawing what men, planes, and warships they could, the Allies yielded the Netherlands Indies and grimly prepared to make their next stand in New Guinea and Australia. By March 9 the Japanese conquest of Java was virtually completed; the Philippines and Corregidor lay isolated hundreds of miles deep in enemy territory.

In their assault on Burma from Thailand the Japanese proved their skill in overland jungle warfare. British forces, supported by Chinese troops, could not stem the advance, and the fall of Lashio on April 30 closed the western terminus of China's last life line, the Burma Road. Now Burma's oil fields and other resources belonged to Japan, whose empire spanned the entire Far East. If Japan could consolidate her gains, complete the conquest of China and convert that gigantic country into a satellite, she would emerge, as her militarists had intended, the most powerful nation on earth. In speed, ruthlessness, and smoothness of execution, the Japanese lightning war had equaled and often was superior to the best campaigns Nazi Germany had waged. In fact, Hitler was a bit jealous.

That MacArthur had activated a number of divisions of Filipino reservists had not alarmed the Japanese planners, for they correctly estimated that none of these would be a serious combat threat. What did concern them was the American air build-up in the prewar months, especially of Major General Lewis H. Brereton's force of thirty-five B-17 heavy bombers. Capable of reaching targets a thousand miles distant, the fast, high-altitude Flying Fortresses constituted the only really potent offensive weapon the Allies had. Also, the United States Navy, although weak in surface ships, had a strong force of twenty-nine submarines which were counted on to take a heavy toll of Japanese transports and supply ships. Potentially, the B-17's and submarines presented a considerable danger to Japan's main supply artery running past Luzon.

As a consequence, Japan's first goal in attacking the Philippines was to neutralize with repeated air strikes all American air and naval power. They therefore massed on Formosan airfields five hundred aircraft of the Navy's 21st and 23rd Air Flotillas and the Army's Fifth Air Group. This was almost twice the number of planes General Brereton had. Except for the B-17's and 107 modern P-40 fighters, all of Brereton's other aircraft were obsolete and sitting ducks for the faster and more agile Zeros.

Because morning at Pearl Harbor was still the middle of the night in the Philippines, the Japanese, expecting the Americans to be alerted by daylight, did not expect to catch Brereton's air force on the ground. In addition, a heavy ground fog further delayed their own take-off from Formosa. But this delay became diabolically fortuitous. Expecting an early morning attack, Brereton had ordered his planes airborne, only to have them land for refueling shortly before the noon hour, when the Japanese did attack. For reasons still obscure, his improvised air warning network, based on visual observation and telephone, broke down completely, enabling the enemy to surprise his main base at Clark Field while many of the American pilots lunched in their mess hall. Damage from attacking high-level bombers was considerable, but far worse was strafing from the deadly Zeros, which had escorted the bombers the full five hundred miles from their Formosan bases. On their departure an hour later a dismayed Brereton found that eighteen of his B-17's and fifty-three of his P-40's had been destroyed. The Japanese had lost only seven Zeros.

With its strength nearly halved, Brereton's Far East Air Force had little chance in the short, merciless air war of attrition that followed. Lacking adequate dispersal fields, as well as an effective air control and warning system, his pilots could only stab against enemy shipping in hit-and-run attacks. The surviving Flying Fortresses were too few to mount counterattacks on Formosa's airfields. By mid-December, a week after the campaign started, Brereton was reduced to hoarding his few remaining P-35's and P-40's for reconnaissance. Already he had dispatched his ten surviving B-17's to Australia to prevent their being destroyed on the ground.

Likewise for the Navy's twenty-nine submarines disaster came early. In one devastating raid on December 10 fifty-four Japanese high-level bombers completely burned out the compact and crowded Cavite navy base. They damaged one submarine beyond repair, and what was perhaps worse, destroyed 230 torpedoes. From then on the submarines were forced to refuel and take on torpedoes from Corregidor, as the Orange Plan had foreseen. What nobody had foreseen, however, was how difficult submarine operations would be with the Japanese commanding the air over Manila Bay. And so by December 31, all of the submarines had left for Fremantle in Australia.

As offensive weapons the submarines had proved disappointing.

Instead of taking the anticipated heavy toll of Japanese shipping, they had been of little more than nuisance value. The boats were good, their skippers and crews were well-trained and aggressive, but their torpedoes were defective. Repeatedly, the torpedoes ran too deep and failed to explode, or "prematured" before reaching their targets, or harmlessly glanced from the sides of enemy ships as their detonators failed.

Not expecting a hard fight, the Japanese planners counted on securing Luzon Island, including Bataan and presumably Corregidor, in just fifty days. Apparently, they had no inkling of the pre-war Orange Plan and did not expect MacArthur to withdraw into the Bataan Peninsula. Bataan, "being a simple, outlying position, would fall quickly," they had assumed. They made no estimate of the time needed to reduce Corregidor, and in fact all but ignored the Rock.

For the amphibious landings Tokyo had assigned Lieutenant General Masaharu Homma's 14th Japanese Army, consisting of the 16th and 48th Divisions and the 65th Brigade plus supporting units—in all, about a hundred thousand men, exactly the number the Orange Plan had estimated Japan would use. The total was considerably fewer than MacArthur had, although the Japanese were much better trained, equipped, and led.

On paper General MacArthur had calculated that his troop strength was sufficient to defeat a Japanese landing. He therefore had scrapped the local adaptation of the Orange Plan, which had called for an anticipated thirty-five thousand defenders to retire slowly into Bataan's jungles, there to set up a short, easily defended line anchored on the water on each side. The war's outbreak had found him still confident that he could drive his foes into the sea with his superior numbers of Filipino reservists. Under Major General Jonathan M. Wainwright, a tall, spare ex-cavalryman, he had organized the North Luzon Force of four divisions to defeat the expected major enemy landing above Manila at Lingayen Gulf. Under Brigadier General George M. Parker, Jr., he had established the South Luzon Force of two divisions to defend airfields and the beaches of Lamon Bay, the other anticipated landing point. Wisely, he held in reserve his best troops, the U.S. Philippine Division, composed of the 31st American and 45th and 57th Philippine Scout infantry regiments and the 1st Division of Philippine Army regulars. He intended to use them to support either of his beach defense forces as needed.

If Luzon was to be kept from enemy hands, MacArthur's plan or something closely akin to it was the only alternative, but admittedly the scheme was a desperate gamble. MacArthur had assumed that the Japanese would leave him alone until April, 1942, by which time most of the Filipino reservists would have completed their basic training. But if the Japanese struck before then—as they did—then the plan might prove far worse than the Bataan withdrawal alternative, because his units might become cut off and trapped. However, MacArthur did not change his dispositions when Japan attacked, and he stubbornly adhered to his plan until almost too late.

Shortly after the initial Japanese landings at Aparri and Vigan in far northern Luzon on December 10, Wainwright realized that his reservists could not possibly drive the Japanese into the sea, or even form a defense line to check them. In his own words, "The rat was in the house"; he well knew that his yet untrained Filipinos had virtually no knowledge of basic infantry fire and movement tactics. Short of almost every type of support weapon, armed with Enfield rifles too big and too heavy for them, and further handicapped in many cases by an inability to understand the Tagalog speech of their officers, many of them did what Wainwright doubtless expected—they prudently fled at the first sign of the enemy's approach.

Precisely on schedule on December 22, 1941, the Japanese landed their main force at Lingayen Gulf, flicking aside the few reservists scattered thinly along the beaches. The situation now was critical. When two days later they landed again south of Manila, MacArthur's entire Luzon command was enveloped in a gigantic trap. Already, the optimistic general, who had had such faith in his Filipinos as fighters, and who perhaps had underestimated the Japanese as soldiers, knew he had no recourse but to adopt the old Orange Plan he had earlier scored as defeatist, and to hope that somehow he could successfully pull his men and their supplies into Bataan and organize a jungle defense line. On December 23, fifteen long days after the outbreak of war, days which already had seen his air force crushed, his naval base destroyed, and his Manila depot and command center pummeled at will from the air, he sent Wainwright and his other field commanders the order: "WPO-3 [Orange] is in effect."

That the Filipino and American forces scattered north and south of Manila managed to retire successfully into Bataan is attributable to MacArthur's sound over-all direction and to skillful field generalship. At MacArthur's order Wainwright's North Luzon Force established a series of defense lines south from Lingayen Gulf, each of which held just long enough to delay the Japanese and enable other units to retire in order into Bataan. In holding these lines a number of units fought hard and well: the 26th Cavalry Regiment, a Philippine Scout horse cavalry outfit; the Provisional Tank Group, a Minnesota National Guard unit; and—surprisingly—several of the Filipino reserve regiments and battalions.

A battle typical in its ferocity of several others took place at the Zaragoza bridge across the Dalagot River. There a platoon of tanks of Company A of the 192nd Tank Battalion and the 3rd Battalion of the Philippine reservist 11th Division were given the mission of delaying the enemy. Had the Japanese broken through at this point, they might have succeeded in turning the left anchor of Wainwright's entire defense line, cutting off his withdrawal. The fight began when an alert tanker spotted a Japanese infantry column of the Kanno Detachment advancing on bicycles toward the bridge and opened point-blank fire, killing or wounding about eighty. Then the bridge was blown, the tankers pulled out, and delay of the Japanese was left to the 3rd Battalion of reservists. Though under a heavy artillery barrage, the 3rd Battalion counterattacked the Japanese crossing the river, surprising and disconcerting the unit commander, and then withdrew to form still another defense line. Of the 550 men of the battalion only 156 remained at the end of the action, many of them with wounds, but they and the tankers had inflicted considerable losses on the Kanno Detachment, delaying it for a full twenty-four hours.

For their part the Japanese co-operated with Wainwright by not altering their strategy of driving straight for Manila. They realized that the Filipinos and Americans were escaping into the Bataan Peninsula, but made little effort to shift the direction of attack to stop them. Especially, their aviators left alone the vital Calumpit River bridge, which was essential to the retreat of the South Luzon Force. When that structure blew into pieces in a gigantic demolition blast on New Year's Day, 1942, the explosion signaled the success of half of MacArthur's new strategy, the withdrawal of the South Luzon Force into Bataan. Shortly thereafter, when a rear guard held the town of San Fernando nine miles north of Calumpit just long enough to complete the escape of the last elements of the North Luzon Force, MacArthur's goal was realized. The bulk of his units had escaped into Bataan.

On December 26 General MacArthur had declared Manila an open city to spare it further destruction. The once busy streets of the charming Philippine capital now were empty, the hotels and night clubs were more like funeral parlors than gay places of entertainment. As was their custom, however, the Japanese ignored the "open city" declaration and continued their bombing of the port area, unwittingly assisting the efforts of demolition teams, until the first troops entered on the late afternoon of January 2. The city's silent, glum citizenry could do no more than watch with apprehension. Fortunately, unlike in Nanking and other Chinese cities, the Japanese troops behaved themselves, and there was no mass looting or rape.

In the meantime the Bataan forces were busily readying their jungle defense line on the peninsula. This would secure their front door. Corregidor's big rifles and mortars would guard their back door open on Manila Bay. MacArthur's delay in revising his strategy had been costly; his quartermasters had lacked the time to furnish Bataan from Manila and forward depots with the vital foodstuffs and medicines his horde of over eighty thousand hungry and weary troops so badly needed. An inventory of food supplies on January 3 produced consternation at headquarters, now established on Corregidor. Instead of enough food for forty-three thousand men for six months, as the Orange Plan had specified, Bataan held only enough for eighty thousand men for thirty days. All troops, including the Corregidor garrison, went on half rations on January 5.

4 ☆ Clearing For Action

TO DECEMBER'S GRIM SPECTACLE of Allied defeat on land, sea, and air, Corregidor's garrison had been an ill-informed, vitally concerned spectator. For the Rock, war action during those crucial days had been limited to repeated air raid alarms—twenty-eight in all by December 28—and a few firings by the antiaircraft batteries against Japanese bombers passing over en route to other targets.

After the first action—on Pearl Harbor day—when Denver and Idaho Batteries had fired at three enemy bombers, two days passed before another Japanese plane was sighted, and then it was twenty-seven of them flying very high—at 30,000 feet—on their heading for the Cavite Navy Yard. They were far above the range of all of the batteries except Captain Arthur Huff's Boston, located on Topside near the parade ground. The eager crews of the other batteries fired anyway, many of the men hearing the sound of their 3-inch guns for the first time. Brief as the action was, it steadied them and made them veterans.

On December 13 the gunners scored first blood. A Japanese flight that had been bombing the Manila port area took a short cut home, this time at only 22,000 feet. All batteries fired; the bursts from several "looked very good," and one of the seventeen planes tumbled wing over wing into the North Channel. Denver, stationed on the tail of the island, ultimately received credit for the kill, but when Corporal Jerome B. Leek of Headquarters Battery congratulated First Sergeant Dewey G. Brady on his men's performance, that crusty old veteran growled, "Congratulations, hell. If we hadn't a whole raft of recruits on the guns we'd a got 'em all."

Denver's success provided only a momentary lift in an otherwise dismal month. When Technical Sergeant Bernard O. Hopkins, the intelligent and highly literate clerk of Battery Chicago, an antiaircraft outfit, learned of the fall of Manila, he predicted grimly, "They'll eventually get us, but they'll pay dearly for their efforts." But he was an exception, for most of the officers and men confidently expected that a convoy of reinforcements soon would arrive from the States to make good the terrible initial losses.

From the beginning of hostilities the garrison had been working around the clock to bolster defenses and restow supplies and ammunition. With the exception of Captain Godfrey R. (Rolly) Ames's Chicago, none of the antiaircraft batteries had constructed splinterproof positions before war came. Consequently, while the ack-ack gunners were belatedly filling sandbags, digging gun pits, and entrenching data feed lines and height finders, the quartermasters were directing details from other units at emptying Malinta Tunnel of its ammunition, at shifting fuel and foodstuffs from vulnerable wooden shelters to dispersed dumps, and at unloading additional stores and rations from Manila. Perhaps the biggest single job was the transfer of the Fort Mills station hospital from its quarters at Middleside to its wartime haven in the north complex of the tunnel.

Many men took too much with them. Colonel Louis J. Bowler, General Moore's imperturbable adjutant and personnel officer (G-1), found in one space in the jungle a complete "office" equipped with desks, swivel chairs, filing cabinets, and electric fans. A full-length mirror leaned against a banana tree, and nearby a porcelain toilet bowl with its bottom broken out covered a hole in the ground. Alongside a sign warned sternly, "NCO's only."

Running day and night, the electric trolley line was the key installation. Had the Japanese elected to bomb it out of business the Rock would have been in deep trouble. As it was, Colonel Chester H. Elmes, the Post Quartermaster, transferred some 25,800 tons of food to wartime storage in two weeks. On December 22 a quartermaster officer noted in relief, "Completed transferring 90 per cent of our equipment. The balance is to [sic] bulky, such as stove parts, etc."

But he rejoiced too soon. The next day General MacArthur put War Plan Orange into effect. This called for U.S. Far East Command Headquarters (USAFFE—pronounced "You-saf-fe") and Philippine President Manuel Quezon to come to the Rock, along with part of the staff of the United States High Commissioner, the Honorable Francis B. Sayre. It also called for more food stocks and supplies; instead of enough stores to sustain seven thousand men for six months, the Rock would have to stock enough for ten thousand. In short, the Fort Mills quartermaster was in for a lot more work. As the quartermaster officer, who remains unidentified, put it,

> Dec. 24—2:30 A.M. This was one hectic day. MacArthur and his whole dam Staff swarmed to Corregidor. Just completed making all transportation and unloading details. They pulled in about 11 P.M. Whata mess, thousand one questions about this and that, I never in my life have seen such disorder and excitement, officers and men swarming around like ants. . . . Barges and barges of supplies are being pushed over to Corregidor, yes, supplies and equipment we have been crying for for months and then could have handled in orderly fashion but now it's one hell of a job. Dogtired, good nite.

Nevertheless, the "job" was completed in just twenty-four hours while the Japanese aviators considerately stayed away. Even the critical Sergeant Hopkins was satisfied. "Oh," he confided to his notebook, "there were blaring cases of materiel which wasn't moved —of negligence and oversight—but these only emphasize the great good fortune of our being let alone for over three weeks. . . . The failure of the Japs to bomb Corregidor [has] enabled all the echelons to get completely moved."

One serious tragedy marred an otherwise successful performance by the Corregidor garrison in those December days. On the seventeenth, shortly after midnight, the steamer *Corregidor,* a fast passenger ship loaded with refugees outbound for the southern islands from Manila, struck an American mine in the North Channel and sank in a few minutes with heavy loss of life. Of at least eight hundred passengers and crew estimated to have been aboard, only 287 were saved, many oil-soaked and naked. Colonel Frank Griffin, a retired seventy-year-old officer, survived more than four hours in the water.

The 60th Coast Artillery Regiment was one echelon that did not have to move during the hectic scramble of December; it had only to dig. Five of its 3-inch batteries—Boston, Chicago, Denver, Flint, and Hartford—had shifted to their wartime stations on the Rock several weeks before; another, Battery Globe, had gone to Mariveles on Bataan at the outbreak of war. One machine-gun battery, Mobile, had temporarily gone to Manila, but later had pulled back to join three sisters in furnishing the Rock with a close-in defense. Four other antiaircraft batteries, not a part of the 60th, served on the lesser islands: Exeter of the 59th CA at Fort Drum; Idaho of the 59th at Fort Hughes; and Ermita and Cebu of the 91st CA (PS) at Forts Frank and Wint, respectively. Together, all these batteries comprised the Antiaircraft Defense Command of the Fortified Islands of Manila and Subic Bays, under Colonel Theodore M. Chase, who also commanded the 60th.

Because of its long service in the Philippines—it had come to the islands as a battalion in 1924—the 60th contained many professional soldiers of the old breed. Its commander, Colonel Chase, was an experienced, strict, conservative, no-nonsense type of officer. He had a competent staff headed by Lieutenant Colonel Arnold D. Amoroso, and good battalion commanders. These included Lieutenant Colonels Howard E. Breitung and Elvin L. Barr, both fated for execution by the Japanese for trying to escape from prison camp, and Major William Massello, Jr., who was to become one of Corregidor's great combat heroes. Many of the battery commanders, such as Captains Godfrey Ames of Battery Chicago, Arthur Huff of Battery Boston, Jack Gulick of Cebu and Aaron Abston of Globe, to name but a few, were young West Pointers of exceptional ability. Very few survived captivity.

As most soldiers know, a good first sergeant can make an outfit, and the 60th had some good ones. Doubtless the most colorful was crusty, gruff Dewey G. Brady, who was destined to perish the very day he was commissioned a second lieutenant for his long years of faithful service. The men of his Denver Battery hated this "brilliant, rough, tough soldier" in peacetime and loved him in war. Others included Bezalle O. Fooshee of Battery Hartford, with twenty-nine years of service, and William E. Beeman of Battery Chicago, with one week less than thirty years in the Army when war came.

Of Beeman a former member of Chicago, Gene W. Wooten, has written, "If the army has such a thing as a typical first sergeant, I would say our top kick . . . would be the first to qualify. Slender, with thinning hair, a firm jutting jaw, straight as a ramrod, [he was] fiercely proud of himself, his regiment, and battery." Beeman had served in the cavalry, field artillery, and infantry, coming to the Philippines with the 31st Infantry, following the regiment's sojourn in Vladivostok after World War I. Despite his strict sense of loyalty and duty, Beeman was called "Willie" or "Bill" (sometimes "Pop" behind his back), and during Chicago's long ordeal in 1942 his dry humor emerged when the going was roughest. When the battery surrendered, Wooten recalls, Beeman's eyes were filled with tears; he did not, he said, care what happened to himself, but was worried over the ordeal the younger men would have to face. Ironically he perished from the blast of a bomb dropped by an American B-29 as he worked as a stevedore in Japan. Colonel Paul R. Cornwall, then a captain and Chicago's executive officer, confesses that before hostilities began he thought that Beeman delegated too much of his authority, especially to the extremely able Technical Sergeant Bernard Hopkins, who nominally was the supply clerk. But when he saw Beeman everywhere under fire, encouraging and steadying the younger men, "I realized what a great soldier he was."

By no means were all of the 60th's men seasoned veterans. Like most regular units it had been far understrength in the interwar years and had built up to its authorized table of organization only after President Roosevelt had declared a national emergency in 1940. The transport *Republic* had brought the regiment 1,200 raw recruits on April 23, 1941. They had not stayed rookies long! Before their first twenty-four hours in the Philippines had ended they had found themselves with rifles in their hands, and for the next month they took a condensed version of the ninety-day Coast Artillery basic training course "on the double" under the merciless supervision of Colonel Barr. As Private Harold Shrode of Denver Battery later described it, "We lived a life of hell the first month. The heat was terrific and the training officers in our regiment took no pity on us." Boys became men very quickly—tough, hard, bronzed, and in much better physical shape than many of the infantrymen of the 31st American regulars stationed in Manila. It was claimed that one could always tell a soldier from the Rock by his healthy tan in contrast to the gin-mill pallor of those infantrymen who had been enjoying the "pleasures" available in the Oriental capital. By June 1, 1941, the 60th had integrated its new men and had mingled experienced gunners with recruits to form several new batteries, bringing it to full wartime strength.

A few men of the 60th were no good. One enlisted man was a thief. In the stockade when Corregidor fell, he passed into captivity with his buddies only to be caught and executed by the Japanese for going over the prison wire to loot in a nearby Filipino village. A few men, including some officers, for psychological or other reasons proved unable to take it during the long siege and had to be transferred or hospitalized. However, these were exceptions.

The equipment of the 60th was as good as in most contemporary U.S. antiaircraft regiments, although by the standards of the combatants in Europe much of it was rapidly approaching obsolescence. The six heavy gun batteries each had four 3-inch guns. Their all-important fire control directors—we would call them computers today—calculated electrically, but their height-finders were optical. Two radar sets provided adequate early warning of Japanese air attacks, but could not provide altitude resolution helpful to the gunners. Neither could several radar sets, some of which were operational, attached to the two searchlight batteries, Albany and Erie. Nevertheless, even without the aid of radar, the well-trained height-finder operators obtained astonishingly accurate data with their optical gear, and were instrumental in scoring a record which few radar-directed units would be able to equal later in the war.

The great weakness of the batteries was in the type of fuze used in the 3-inch shells. All batteries except Boston had the Scovil Mark III powder time train fuze, a type first used in the Philippines in 1926, which was cut by a fuze-setter on the gun mount to trigger an explosion at a predetermined altitude. Atmospheric pressure affected its rate of burning, and duds were numerous, but an even more serious defect was its altitude limitation. At approximately 8,300 yards altitude (24,900 feet) the fuze burned out and exploded the shell. In the Philippines this maximum fuze range was a little higher, for the warm climate heated the powder in the shells and gave the guns a slightly increased muzzle velocity, adding a bonus of 125 to 150 yards of range. This proved very important, for it enabled the 60th to engage planes at a maximum altitude of just over 8,400 yards (25,200 feet), a height at which the attacking "Sallys" often flew.

Captain Arthur Huff's Boston was more fortunate in having a new mechanical fuze which permitted firing to 10,600 yards (32,000 feet), the extreme vertical range of the 3-inch gun. This fuze was activated by the discharge of the gun. Only a number sufficient to equip one battery was on hand when war began. Later, in February, Chicago also received mechanical fuze ammunition brought directly from Hawaii by submarine.

For close-in defense against strafers and dive bombers Corregidor was protected by the forty-eight .50 caliber machine guns of Batteries Indiana, Kingston, Lansing, and Mobile. These weapons were mounted on towers rising above the trees, so as to give clear fields of fire. The 3-inch units also had one .50 and four .30 caliber weapons for use against strafers, but the .30's proved ineffective.

Although the .50's were good, reliable guns and remained standard throughout the war in Army service, they could not fire accurately above 3,000 feet. Since the 3-inch guns could not track a fast aircraft below about 5,000 feet, a gap existed between these altitudes for the enemy to exploit. To cover it a Navy 1.1-inch pom-pom gun with four barrels (sometimes referred to as a "Chicago organ"), originally intended for the USS *Houston* and salvaged from the wrecked Cavite naval base, was mounted atop Malinta Hill. Its water-cooling system gave some trouble, but Gunner Otto ("Wiley" to the others), the Navy chief supervising installation, improvised a pump operated by a Crosley automobile motor, and a Mobile Battery crew under Lieutenant Stanley O. Friedline manned it. It missed the first Japanese air blitz, but by February 11 it was ready for action. The gun had no fire control director, but Friedline's men could aim by following the track of their own tracers, and the piece effectively discouraged attacks between 3,000 and 5,000 feet until destroyed late in the siege.

As December, the first month of war, neared its end, Corregidor stood ready and even eager to meet the vanguard of the Far Eastern blitzkrieg—Japan's air power. The men of the 60th and the garrison they defended did not have long to wait.

5 ☆ The Big Raids

WHEN the air raid sirens screamed on Corregidor just before noon on December 29, 1941, most of the men paid scant attention. During the month of fighting on Luzon and the withdrawal of American-Filipino forces to Bataan, which was now almost completed, there had been only a few inconsequential air raid alerts. A few who saw the neat twenty-seven-plane vees split into groups of nine to begin their bombing runs lingered a few dangerous moments to watch, but the high-pitched screech of the falling bombs, mingling with the crack of the 3-inchers of the 60th Coast Artillery, sent them scrambling for the nearest cover.

The first bombers, two-motored Mitsubishi KI 21's (later code-named "Sallys" by the American forces), were flying relatively low, at only 18,000 feet. As the shells began bursting among them, they discovered that they had made a dangerous mistake. Three dropped smoking from the first nine-plane formation. Ten light bombers which peeled off into shallow dives over the island also had made a mistake. The .50's of Batteries Lansing and Mobile peppered them so liberally that four plunged into the sea. Successive formations continued bombing, but raised their altitudes to 22,000 feet and above. At about 1:30 P.M. the Japanese Navy's 22nd Air Flotilla took over, also releasing their bombs at high altitude from their graceful twin-engine, twin-tail "Nells."

The Japanese decision to launch this "big raid," as Corregidor's men later thought of it, had been made only the previous day when Lieutenant General Hideyoshi Obata had ordered his Army 5th Air

Group to join the naval bombers in striking Corregidor "with full strength." His plan called for his medium bombers to strike at high noon, followed closely by light bombers and dive bombers. Two fighter regiments would furnish high and low cover, ready to pounce should any surviving P-40's of the Far East Air Force rise from their field at Cabcaben on Bataan. By 1:00 P.M. all Army bombers were to clear the target area, giving the sixty Navy "Nells" a chance to make their runs.

Doubtless the Japanese expected their attack to devastate Corregidor as thoroughly as earlier full-strength raids had wrecked Clark Field and the Cavite Navy Yard. They had expected to wreck or burn out most of the crowded installations by blanketing the island with bombs of 110 to 550 pounds. Lieutenant General Masaharu Homma and his 14th Army staff, who had conceived the raid, were even more optimistic. A heavy air attack on the "center of the American Far Eastern Army Command," they had reasoned, not only would destroy Corregidor's installations, but also would demoralize the defenders of the island and of Bataan. They may have hoped that the attack would elicit a surrender offer from General MacArthur, but if so, they had misjudged their man.

In keeping with his nature Douglas MacArthur had scorned bombproof protection when the raid began. Emerging from his headquarters, which he had established in the 59th Coast Artillery's vacated Topside Barracks, he stood in the open counting off the planes in each formation and watching the technique of his enemies as the 60th's shells burst amongst them, while nearby men pressed themselves against the bottom of slit trenches. When the bombs began falling extremely close, his Filipino orderly, Sergeant Domingo Adversario, and his driver, Solomon Bayoneta, a former Philippine Scout, attempted to shield him with their bodies. While Adversario held his helmet over MacArthur's head, a fragment hit Adversario in the hand and a rock struck the General on the shoulder. The Japanese bombs—they must have been light ones in this instance or

MacArthur surely would have been killed—fell very close; some observers claim within a few feet.

Contemptuous as he was of enemy fire and anxious to inspire his men by an example of bravery, MacArthur nevertheless realized that to remain in the open would be suicidal. During a lull in the attack he ordered his headquarters staff out of Topside Barracks into the bombproof telephone exchange nearby. Then he drove down to Malinta Tunnel, and after the attack established USAFFE headquarters in Lateral Three. However distasteful this concession was to him, he had no other alternative, because even though its ground floor had five-and-a-half feet of protective concrete, Topside Barracks was no place for a headquarters.

On this day all over the island, a standard of heroism was set. On the tail, at Kindley Field, where a machine-gun section of Mobile was located, two 0-49 observation planes caught fire when a bomb struck an oil storage tank in a hangar. When the flames threatened to spread to the other three planes on the field, veteran First Sergeant William F. ("Bull") King and Private John Ballow of Mobile, aided by two Filipino KP's, fought the flames for two hours, pushing one plane to safety and beating out grass fires about the two others, and ignoring the falling bombs.

Newcomers to the Rock were the fifteen hundred marines of the 4th Marine Regiment. Members of an old-time unit that had been stationed in Shanghai until just before the outbreak of the war, they had moved first to Subic Bay, then to Mariveles, where they had absorbed other marine units in the Philippines, and from thence to Corregidor to serve as the island's beach defense force. The gyrenes —to use the old Army epithet for them—had just arrived; and for the time being, while their commander, Colonel Samuel L. Howard, was conferring with his officers and the Rock's command as to their deployment, they had been quartered in the 60th's barracks at Middleside.

Like Topside Barracks, those at Middleside also had a cover of thick concrete over the ground floor. When the "Sallys" arrived and bombs screamed down, the marines were grateful to be ordered to the ground floor. "There we were," Quartermaster Clerk F. W. Ferguson recalls, "the whole regiment flat on our bellies. . . ." Bombs fell all around, blowing out windows, ripping off doors, and filling the air with debris. Several bombs hit the barracks and one belied the bombproof reputation of the building by penetrating—so the marines claimed—right to the bottom floor. Only one man, Corporal Verl W. Murphy, was killed, but the marines were more than pleased to leave the structure for the beaches the next day. They much preferred taking their chances in foxholes to remaining in a conspicuous aiming point for Japanese bombardiers.

When the attack ended, Japanese reconnaissance pilots were gratified at the numerous fires and immense clouds of smoke billowing upward. They reported Corregidor finished as an American command center, with every battery silenced, a claim Japanese propaganda quickly repeated. However, the attackers had paid a heavy price; the 60th claimed nine medium and four light bombers shot down. In keeping with their custom of sweeping such incidentals under the rug (and saving the commander's face), Japanese records do not specify losses but do confess to the meeting of "fierce enemy antiaircraft fire." Assuming that the 60th shot down half as many planes as claimed—a rule of thumb used with fair success in assessing losses during World War II—this still would mean that the antiaircraft defense of Corregidor was second to none for that stage of the war. A loss of six or seven of about ninety-one attacking aircraft to optically directed antiaircraft fire was exceptionally heavy.

For their part the Japanese bombardiers proved skillful. Many of their 110-, 220-, and 550-pound bombs fell into the water, but enough hit the island to sprinkle it liberally with craters, especially in the interior. About eighty tons of bombs hit. Many barracks, quarters, and warehouses were destroyed or damaged. San Jose barrio at Bottomside was set ablaze and reduced to "one huge mass of jagged and bent sheet iron." Topside Ciné, where the men only a few days before had watched Gary Cooper in *Sergeant York,* was wrecked, as was the vacant station hospital, the post exchange, and the Officer's and Enlisted Men's Clubs. The electric railroad was torn up and cut in so many places that only a local service was restored about Bottomside later.

Even so, genuine military damage was slight. Battery Smith's long-range gun, for example, was struck squarely on the racer, but its crew emerged unharmed from their bombproof magazine to have it in working order in six hours. Although open, the antiaircraft positions by this time were so well splinterproofed that only three men were killed—Lieutenant Benjamin A. Kysor and two enlisted men—by a missile that landed on one of Boston's guns. Elsewhere personnel losses were heavy, with nineteen more men slain and about eighty wounded, mostly men who had not taken cover when the alarm sounded.

Some of the 60th's gunners had displayed reluctance to dig in before the big raid; their officers had no difficulty getting them to do so afterward. They had, rather, to be kept from pilfering sandbags, for all hands knew the Japanese would be back. Exposed units all over the island began digging tunnels for added safety. Before the campaign had ended, hundreds of the defenders owed their lives to those tunnels.

For three days after the attack of December 29 no bombs fell. Only one plane appeared, a low-flying fighter, which Mobile's .50's shot into the sea. New Year's Day came and went, moving Captain Rolly Ames to comment, "New year, new war, new lack of knowledge about the future."

On January 2 the bombers were back, fifty-four "Sallys" of the 5th Air Fleet. As before, they attacked at noon, the normal time of arrival after an early morning take-off from Formosa, bombing through cloud cover at 5,000 feet. This gave them an opportunity to duck through, drop, and then zoom hastily out of sight before the 60th could begin tracking. Again they bombed at random. Again losses to the Rock's garrison were high, with ten killed, including

Battery Lansing's commander, Captain Alva W. Hamilton. Thirty were wounded.

The bombers returned on January 3, 4, 5, and 6, dropping their bombs from very high altitudes—24,000 to 28,000 feet and losing planes on each raid. On one occasion Chicago's gunners watched a shell strike a "Sally" squarely in an engine nacelle, blowing off its wing. On another, Battery Flint's men had to take cover when a wing fell toward them, an attached engine still roaring. Toward the end of the period the Japanese pilots had become so respectful of the 60th that they switched their tactics, bombing in threes instead of nines, approaching from different directions, and changing course after releasing bombs. Although the 60th believed that only eight of the original attacking aircraft were left, the last raid, on the sixth, was a very heavy one, second only to the big raid of the twenty-ninth in tonnage dropped. Either the 60th's observers were mistaken, as seems likely, or reinforcements had arrived.

Chicago scored brilliantly on this last day. Firing on the lead plane of a vee of three, Ames's men put a shell neatly into its bomb bay, exploding the bombs reserved for a second run in a blast which also engulfed the planes on either side.

Chicago's men also were impressed by the continuing courage of their commander-in-chief. General MacArthur arrived on the sixth to inspect the battery just as an air alarm sounded. With Rolly Ames begging him to get down as the "Sallys" came in, MacArthur stayed up, watching through his binoculars, counting off the attacking planes, and remarking calmly that the bombs would fall close. A sweating Ames stayed up too, but when the bombs were about due, the rest of the men ducked.

To fire effectively at such extreme altitudes the 60th had to overcome many difficult problems. Sometimes only Boston, with its mechanical fuzes, could fire; at other times the remaining batteries could get away only four to six rounds per gun before the Japanese planes passed out of range of the powder train fuzes. Nevertheless, the 60th enjoyed some advantages. The Japanese pilots had to take a lead-in course toward the island and fly "straight and level" long enough for the bombardiers to align their sights—and for the 60th's height-finder operators to get good readings. That meant that for a given course and altitude the planes bombed from about the same "window" in the sky each time. Moreover, they flew at about 190 miles per hour—the "Sally" was not a fast plane—and their formations prevented rapid maneuvers immediately after release of bombs.

When the radar picked up the enemy, the gunners would crank their pieces to about 60 degrees, aiming into the "window" through which the Japanese would have to fly. When the dim specks showed, the height-finder operators would carefully track the targets in, focusing on the lead plane, slowly turning the dials of their stereoscopic instruments until the double images in their scopes merged. Ranges would then be read off and transmitted for director computation; the guns would begin tracking, and the loaders would wait, shells in hand, for the order from the battery commander to fire. The planes would release their bombs. As the bombs fell, the guns would keep going up and up, until, just before they hit their elevation stops at 80 degrees, the planes would finally enter fuze range and each weapon would spit four to six rounds in ten to fifteen seconds. Then everyone would drop to the bottom of the gun pits, for the bombs would be impacting seconds later. Sometimes, however, the gunners would stay up and begin tracking the next flight, ignoring the falling missiles.

The crews quickly discovered that it did little good to fire more than six rounds. Either the height-finder operator was on, or he wasn't, and usually a plane shot down was the lead bomber of the formation. The effective kill radius of the 3-inch shell was not great. Moreover, after six rounds the enemy would be banking away and a miss was virtually certain.

To stay at their posts, literally peering around falling bombs to keep their delicate instruments on target, demanded courage and devotion to duty of the highest order by the height-finder operators. It also took steady hands and nerves for the men on the gunwheels to keep their pointers precisely matched on the numbers flowing to the dials from the range section. The shell handlers and rammers became remarkably proficient. Chicago's, for example, operated so smoothly during their four- and six-round shoots that they attained the almost unbelievable rate of fire of thirty-four rounds per minute. The usual maximum rate for a good crew was reckoned at twenty-seven or twenty-eight rounds.

As in the big raid of December 29, the renewed attacks of the first week of January caused little serious military damage. On the fifth a bad fire on the Engineer Dock at Bottomside threatened to get out of control and engulf the unbombproofed new powerhouse, incensing MacArthur's chief engineer, Brigadier General Hugh J. Casey, who did his best to obtain additional fire equipment. By this time personnel casualties were light because the men sprinted for cover at the first alarm. Most of the losses occurred the last day when a bomb hit an incomplete shelter at Battery Geary and buried thirty-one of thirty-four men alive.

Although Malinta Tunnel was safe, morale there was lower than elsewhere on the island. Dust would fly and lights would flicker; the crowded multitude inside could hear the dull boom of exploding bombs. No shrapnel could get through, yet the tunnel dwellers felt helpless, trapped, stifled. Many would gladly have traded their safety for a chance to shoot back. But they could not do that, and so the men, some four or five thousand of them, and sixty-eight women, including nurses and seventeen civilians and army wives, would smile affectionately when young Arthur MacArthur, the General's four-year-old son, would stride through the tunnel shouting imperiously, "Air raid, air raid!" As long as he was there, one of them wrote later, ". . . we were convinced that all was well."

As January 7 dawned, the 60th's gunners, by their own admission, were "a little shook." Each well knew that if the Japs kept after the Rock long enough one of their bombs was likely to have his name on it. Then it would hardly matter whether its filler was old Ford engine parts, scrap from the United States, nails, or concrete (rumor had it the Japanese used all of these). But the only plane to appear that day was the customary "Dinah" reconnaissance plane which the men called "Photo Joe-san" and certain other vivid but less printable epithets. The relieved but cocky 60th was convinced it had driven away its foe. Not so. The 5th Air Fleet had been ordered to Burma to take on Claire Chennault's "Flying Tigers." It pulled out on January 14, leaving behind only a few fighters and light bombers to support the Bataan campaign.

Incomplete and scattered records credit the 60th with shooting down at least twenty-five enemy aircraft between December 29 and January 6, of which several were actually seen to crash. Unfortunately confirmation is impossible from Japanese sources, and it seems likely that if the pattern of the rest of the war applies, the 60th overstated its claims by at least 50 percent and perhaps much more. It would, however, be misleading to judge its performance on the basis of planes downed. Had it destroyed no aircraft the 60th still would have been accounted successful in its mission, for it kept the enemy planes so high they could not aim for specific installations, such as the Fort Mills power and cold storage plants, which escaped untouched. Aided by batteries on the lesser islands, particularly by Captain Stockton Bruns's Idaho on Fort Hughes, the 60th had saved the Rock from the fate of Clark Field and the Cavite Navy Yard. For its part Corregidor had shown a surprising ability to take it, and all concerned with its defense had earned the month of grace to follow before the Japanese resumed their offensive, this time with the long-dreaded siege artillery.

6 ☆ Retreat to Bataan

WITH MANILA in Japanese hands by January 2, and the air and sea under Japanese rule, Corregidor assumed the role envisaged years before in War Plan Orange. It became the guardian of the rear of a Filipino and American army battling on Bataan.

The Rock's artillery observers, rhythmically sweeping the China Sea with their powerful telescopes, could see but two U.S. Navy small craft patrolling off the marker buoys at the entrance to the mine fields. Only infrequently could they sight on the distant horizon a blockading Japanese destroyer. On January 7, the day after the departure of the Japanese bombers, they recorded their nearest plot, an enemy mine layer, at 39,080 yards, moving Seaward Defense Commander Paul Bunker to write in his diary, ". . . We could have paid some attention to her, had we a pair of sixteen inch guns in our make-up." But such modern weapons were reserved for places more important than the Rock, places such as New York, Hampton Roads, and San Francisco—places that never sighted an enemy.

A challenge did come on January 13, but not from seaward. On this day the Japanese boldly sailed a commandered steamer toward the stern of Fort Drum, the "concrete battleship," from the direction of Naic inside Manila Bay. It was probably an official party from General Homma's headquarters sight-seeing and testing American alertness. Normally, both of Drum's heavy turrets pointed westward into the China Sea; neither of the casemated 6-inch batteries bore directly astern, and although the upper turret, Battery Wilson, could traverse 360 degrees, the fort's cage mast on the stern blocked fire directly to the rear. The Japanese evidently realized this, for they were careful to keep the cage mast between themselves and Wilson's menacing 14-inch rifles as they drew nearer.

What they did not know was that Captain Sam Madison's gunners of Battery E of the 59th CA had anticipated such an eventuality. Just the day before they had emplaced on Drum's stern a long-stored 3-inch seacoast rifle on a pedestal mount. On observing the approaching Japanese, Major General George F. Moore, the Harbor Defense commander, telephoned Lieutenant Colonel Lewis S. Kirkpatrick, the fortress commander. When he learned that the "new" weapon, named Battery Hoyle, could be used, Moore ordered Kirkpatrick to open fire. Kirkpatrick had Captain Madison hastily assemble a five-man crew; the range was called down vocally from the depression range finder on the cage mast. At 9,000 yards, Hoyle opened up.

The first round was off in deflection, which was to be expected since the weapon had not been bore-sighted, but it sent the steamer into a hasty turnaround. The second fell nearer, and Hoyle came closer and closer with each shot until the seventh and eighth flung geysers of water over the ship. The ninth burst squarely on the lower deck. But the tenth fell short as the ship hurried out of range belching thick black smoke. The Japanese had learned their lesson. Never again did they approach Drum from the rear.

Although some on Corregidor regretted the "buck fever" that had led the aggressive Kirkpatrick to fire too soon and allow the steamer to escape, first blood in the battle had gone to the gunners of the Fortified Islands. They had effectively served notice to the Japanese of their guardian role, and everyone from General Moore on down felt good. Atop Morrison Hill on Corregidor Captain Rolly Ames reasoned with his Chicago gunners by means of the battery's news-sheet, the *Morrison Hill Gazette:* "Let us not think that Bataan is guarding our front door—we are guarding their back door! And together we are holding the whole damned house!"

It worked both ways. Corregidor and Bataan were mutually supporting positions. They must stand—or fall—together. Not for long could one outlive the other. And for many days in January, 1942, as a fierce battle raged in the jungle-clad peninsula, the fate of both wavered in the balance.

For the hungry and weary infantrymen—Filipino and American alike—straggling into Bataan, the Rock's ordeal by bombing in the first week of January had been a welcome respite. Had they suffered the full weight of enemy air attack during this period, a week they had used to regroup and reorganize, their miseries would have been compounded. Surprisingly, their morale was reasonably good despite the long retreat. The weaker ones had deserted, and as Colonel James V. Collier, MacArthur's assistant operations officer, put it, "The general feeling seemed to be we have run far enough; we'll stand now and take 'em on." By January 7 USAFFE Headquarters in Malinta Tunnel had settled the command problem. The west, or China Sea, side of the twenty-mile-wide peninsula would be the responsibility of General Wainwright's I Corps; the east, or Manila Bay, side would be defended by Major General George M. Parker's II Corps. In between the two Corps the supposedly impenetrable, jungle-covered mass of Mount Natib would block the Japanese. "I am on my main battle line," MacArthur radioed the War Department, "awaiting general attack."

He did not have to wait long. On January 9 his aggressive opposite number, General Homma, resumed his offensive. Attacking were the fresh troops of Lieutenant General Akira Nara's 65th Brigade. Rebuffed initially when they encountered the well-trained Philippine Scouts of the 57th Infantry Regiment, the Japanese shifted the focus of their attack, hitting at the west flank of Parker's II Corps line and turning it. On the other side of the peninsula, against Wainwright's I Corps, a Japanese battalion, demonstrating its skill at using jungle cover to advantage, slipped through American lines on January 19 and blocked the only road leading to the front suitable for heavy supplies and equipment. After several days of futile hammering at the dug-in foe, Wainwright realized that his position was untenable; he would have to abandon most of his artillery and retreat by trail. On the other side of the line General Parker's counterattacks with his best troops, the Scouts and Americans of the Philippine Division, had failed. His left flank had crumbled, and unless he, too, retreated, he might soon find Japanese infantry astride roads and trails deep in his rear.

By January 22 General MacArthur and his USAFFE staff realized that the first of their two defense lines on Bataan, the Abucay-Mauban line, could not be held. The roadblock had defeated Wainwright; Parker's left flank had collapsed. The high mass of Mount Natib physically separated the two corps, keeping them out of contact, further complicating command and logistics. The troops had fought well and hard, but although heavily outnumbered, their Japanese enemy had the complete initiative and had fought better. Retreat back to the second and final battle line, the Bagac-Orion line, was essential.

The next few days, between the twenty-third and the twenty-sixth, were among the most crucial of the entire Bataan campaign. MacArthur could have no assurance that Parker and Wainwright would be able to reorganize their men on the Bagac-Orion line. Once the Filipino reservists began retreating they might not stop until they had reached the edge of the North Channel two miles from Corregidor. MacArthur could not know that Nara's brigade had been badly cut up in the fighting, and he appears to have greatly overestimated the numbers of enemy troops thrown against him.

After consulting with his staff on January 24, the discouraged General concluded that Bataan was doomed and that a collapse of organized resistance probably was imminent. Summoning General Moore, he ordered his Harbor Defense commander to bolster Corregidor's food stocks from the depots on Bataan in the slender hope that somehow the fortress might hold out until July 1, when reinforcements from the States might arrive. He also told Moore that if Bataan fell he intended to transfer the Philippine Division to the Rock for beach defense.

To make room for the Philippine Division Moore in the next few days began to transfer ammunition stocked near Kindley Field to the 59th Coast Artillery's deserted Topside barracks. He also assigned nightly work details of its gunners to the chore of unloading and storing the food transferred from Bataan. Fortunately, these precautions did not prove necessary, for Parker and Wainwright managed to rally their exhausted men on their Bagac-Orion line. Weary and discouraged they were, but they were still in a fighting mood. As war correspondent Frank Hewlett spoke for them:

> We're the battling bastards of Bataan;
> No mama, no papa, no Uncle Sam;
> No aunts, no uncles, no nephews, no nieces;
> No rifles, no guns, or artillery pieces;
> . . . And nobody gives a damn.

They lived, as Lieutenant Henry Lee, the sensitive poet-soldier of the 31st Infantry wrote,

> Saved for hunger and wounds and heat
> For slow exhaustion and grim retreat
> For a wasted hope and a sure defeat. . . .

The chips were down. MacArthur radioed to General Marshall in Washington, ". . . All maneuvering possibilities will cease. I intend to fight it out to complete destruction."

The first threat, launched even before the Bagac-Orion line was fully manned, came from the flank, by sea. Imitating the highly successful operations in Malaya, General Homma dispatched a battalion by water around Wainwright's I Corps flank. Partly because of bad maps, partly because they ran into U.S.S. *PT-34,* a motor torpedo boat commanded by red-bearded Lieutenant John D. Bulkeley, the Japanese lost two barges loaded with men; they then split into two groups and missed their intended landing point. Fortunately for Wainwright, a provisional battalion of sailors from the U.S. Navy's section base at Mariveles was available, along with some grounded airmen, to contain the Japanese near the landing points. But the untrained men lacked the basic infantry fire and movement skills to exterminate the enemy in the dense jungle terrain.

One of the two groups, about three hundred strong, had landed only 14,000 yards from Corregidor, just within range of Battery Geary's eight huge 12-inch mortars. Their landing coincided with completion by Colonel Bunker and his Seaward Defense staff of a detailed fire plan to support the infantry with the mortars. For this purpose Geary had on hand about two hundred anti-personnel shells tipped with instantaneous fuzes, deadly to all exposed enemies within a bursting radius of five hundred yards. Its sister battery, four-gun Way, had three hundred more but lacked a crew; a map reproduction unit was occupying its bombproof magazines. Unfortunately, Geary was not yet fully combat ready. It had suffered a grave setback on January 6 when a bomb had collapsed an incomplete air raid shelter, suffocating most of its senior noncommissioned officers. Captain Ben E. King, its commander, had been working hard to train a new crop of key men, but this took time. Now, too soon, Geary would have to fire.

Even with the Japanese within range and the ground troops unable to destroy the enemy, the American high command refused to give Colonel Bunker permission to let Captain King open fire. On Sunday, January 25, Bunker noted in his diary, ". . . The decision is:—'Do nothing at present!' DAMN!" And he retired in frustration to the ruined front porch of his quarters nearby on Topside. Before long, since the untrained sailors and airmen still were unable to root out the Japanese outposts, USAFFE ordered them to pull back and Geary was allowed to participate.

On January 26 King's enthusiastic gunners lobbed nine huge shells, followed in the next two days by twenty-four more. Their inexperience showed up. The timing of the fire was so ragged and samples of manifest incompetence so many—several reports were received of "lanyard broken"—that the exasperated Colonel Bunker relieved Captain King, while recognizing that the failings were really not King's fault. Even so, thanks in part to the presence of an able observer, Lieutenant Dick Fullmer, on the scene to direct the gunners by field telephone, the fire was very accurate, many of the 670-pound shells bursting squarely on target. A wounded Japanese infantryman later informed his captors:

> We were terrified. We could not know where the big shells or bombs were coming from; they seemed to be falling from the sky. Before I was wounded, my head was going round and round, and I did not know what to do. Some of my companions jumped off the cliff to escape the terrible fire.

So ended the first firing at an enemy by major-caliber American seacoast artillery since the close of the Civil War. More firings would follow shortly, but with conspicuously less success than on this occasion.

The undaunted Japanese command elected to reinforce both of its isolated landing forces on the night of January 27. Even before they got ashore, these new elements were badly mauled by artillery, light naval forces from Corregidor, and the Far East Air Force's four remaining P-40's. Thereafter, the story of the "Battle of the Points," as this episode of the Bataan campaign has been called, is the story of a dirty, bloody, rifleman's fight to the finish. None of the Japanese would surrender; they had to be killed to a man. By mid-February the fight "to destruction" was over. Filipino and American losses were heavy, especially for the Scouts of the 57th Infantry, who had to be called in to destroy the bottled-up foe. But the Japanese losses were much greater in combat troops they could ill-afford to lose.

Over, too, was the threat to the Bagac-Orion line. On January 26 General Nara had struck again with his 65th Brigade at the II Corps, and although he had the good fortune to hit the line at the point where it was weakest, he could not break through. By early February his unit had been decimated.

On the western side of Bataan, in Wainwright's I Corps sector, the battle had gone equally badly for the Japanese 16th Division. Its attacking elements had managed to infiltrate the line on January 26, only to become bottled up in pockets. This fight degenerated into a Japanese attempt to relieve the pockets and a Filipino-American attempt to keep them contained. Some of the weary and emaciated Japanese managed to escape, but hundreds more were killed.

By February 8 it was General Homma rather than General MacArthur who was in serious trouble. His losses had been so great in dead, wounded, and seriously ill that he realized he must call off his offensive and retreat. By February 24, after his withdrawal far to the rear had been completed, his 16th Division, once nearly 14,000 strong, numbered but 712 effectives. Nara's 65th Brigade was down to only 1,000 men from its original 6,500, and many of these were wobbling from illness and weakness. Homma's combat strength numbered in companies instead of regiments.

MacArthur's men on the other hand were cocky and in good spirits. They had bested their fanatical enemy in stand-up fighting and were eager to take the offensive. The Filipino reservists now holding all of the line had learned how to fight the hard way and would have relished the opportunity to run the Japanese out of Bataan and Manila. They might have done so, for Homma lacked the manpower to stop them. To a man of MacArthur's aggressive temperament, the temptation to attack must have been great, but he rejected it for the more conservative strategy of building up his fixed defenses along the Bagac-Orion line while awaiting a renewed Japanese offensive. To attack, he may have concluded, would have depleted more rapidly his very slender food reserves.

The immediate threat to Bataan was over. It would take several weeks before Tokyo could dispatch more men and matériel to General Homma. A lull had set in on the peninsula, one that Corregidor—but not its sister islands—would share until March 24.

7 ☆ Dust, Heat and Hope

JANUARY's heavy air bombardments had left once-beautiful Corregidor scarred, mutilated, ugly. Green shoots sprouting from bomb-blasted jungle trees could not hide the craters that gaped everywhere; one could scarcely go twenty-five yards anywhere on the island without finding one. The golf course had been ploughed up and many of the wooden structures burned. It was now the dry season, and dust swirled and eddied about the shattered buildings, while nearby, Daisy Mae, the pet doe, still wistfully cropped grass. Wrote Paul Bunker, "What a sound is corrugated iron rattling in the wind that soughs through an empty and ruined barracks!"

Aside from a single light bombing on January 14, the Rock enjoyed an uneasy respite for a month after the departure of its tormentor, the Japanese 5th Air Group. Life settled into a dreary routine, as the tensions induced by the enemy bombing gradually abated. At Bunker's Seaward Defense headquarters, C-1 Station, the various telephone and voice radio circuits blended into a monotonous busyness. One defender of the island put the talk into verse.

> Test communication, Message understood
> Provide illumination, Modulation's good.
> Hearn, a met message; Crockett, you repeat!
> Ships in La Monja passage. Keep the station neat.
>
> Get the azimuth on that ship! Follow the beam!
> Someone, let the coffee drip. Who's got some cream?
> How 'bout giving me a ring? Fourteen calling Seven.
> Nope, we cannot see a thing. Azimuth three eleven.

On Valentine's Day, gazing at the still lovely tropical evening sky, many an officer and enlisted man could not help thinking of a loved one far away. And so the February 14 issue of Chicago Battery's *Morrison Hill Gazette* carried a poem, "To My Valentine."

While the bombers soar above
Come and be my jungle love.
Here beneath the absent moon
We'll enjoy a flashlight spoon.

Safe (?) from burst of bomb or shell
Be my Val— Oh, what the hell!
You're ten thousand miles away.
Feb. 14 is just a day.

Neither Chicago nor any other unit could escape the grim realities of war, even during a relative lull.

Like the 60th, the veteran 59th Coast Artillery Regiment manning the big guns mingled a cadre of old-timers with recruits. All were volunteers, most having requested duty in the Philippines. The 59th prided itself on being strictly "R.A." (Regular Army). The boss, Colonel Paul Delmont Bunker, was serving his second tour as its regimental commander, a tour he knew would be his last assignment before retirement. In terms of time in grade he was one of the dozen most senior colonels in the Army.

In his lifetime Bunker had become a legend. To thinning gray hair that once had been blond, a ruddy complexion, and a waxed mustache which he twirled, he combined a deep bass voice "that could scare the devil out of you." On only five feet ten or eleven inches of height, at sixty years of age, he easily carried 220 pounds. During his cadet days the West Point brass had had to widen the parallel bars in the gym to accommodate his tremendous shoulders. Twice he won Walter Camp All-America football honors, the first year at tackle, the second at halfback. "I could shut my eyes," wrote his classmate Douglas MacArthur, recalling their cadet days, "and see again that blond head racing, tearing, plunging—210 pounds of irresistible power. I could almost hear Quarterback Charley Daly's shrill voice barking, 'Bunker back.' " His massive build awed the Rock's enlisted men, who fervently believed the rumor that while a first classman at the Point he had slipped away one night to a nearby ring to box with and defeat Jack Johnson.

Bunker had the spit and polish of a Prussian officer. Long after others had abandoned the practice, he continued to wear the General Pershing–style high choke collar. Always he seemed to walk at attention. He demanded proper dress for his officers, including the regimental cummerbund for dinner. Yet he was convivial; after the dependents had gone home in the spring of 1941, Bunker frequently would assemble his officers around the piano in the Club to lead in singing the old Army campfire songs. His diary attests to his exceptional literary ability. Other of his wide interests included the fine arts, botany, zoology, the theater, higher mathematics, and the Bunker genealogy.

All of his career Bunker was a controversial figure. His outspoken nature and impatience with red tape did not always endear him to his superiors or to his subordinates and probably accounts in part for his being repeatedly passed over for brigadier general. Some feel that he was overly insistent on the use of coast artillery techniques in firing counterbattery. The mathematics of artillery fire fascinated him. He was convinced that if the range section had done its work properly, a good crew should place its first round at exactly the spot picked out by the observer. Of the wisdom of such a technique in firing at enemy ships, where the first shells must be "on," there can be no question. But in firing at enemy batteries on Bataan and Cavite his "Bunker system," as some called it, was less effective.

He scorned defeatism, knew no fear, and defied the overwhelming odds against him and his command. Despite heavy bombing and shelling he constantly carried out inspections with walking stick, campaign hat, and followed by his little dog, Colin. Legend has it that Colin once hid in a nearby ditch when shellfire grew hot, but Bunker chased him out with his walking stick, admonished Colin to be braver, and avowed that no blankety-blank Japanese was going to stop *him* from inspecting his batteries!

The 59th had its share of superior battery commanders serving under Bunker. Captain Harry Schenck of Wheeler was a "spark plug," the regiment's idea man, and Captain Herman Hauck of Crockett was its "tiger." During the bombing raids of early January, Hauck relished jumping into a battered old car, together with one of his gun commanders, Sergeant Carl Hill, for some "twilight requisitioning" amid the ruins of the buildings and nurse's quarters at Middleside. At such times, he knew, the guards would be deep in their foxholes. Most of the other battery commanders also were competent, West Point products. Many of the old-time first sergeants had learned their ABC's of military discipline by reading army regulations and ran taut outfits. Some of the enlisted buck sergeant gun commanders had served with their pieces so long they knew the idiosyncrasies of every operating part. As a result the batteries had a state of discipline, comradeship, tradition, and *esprit* virtually unknown in the draftee army that followed.

The two Scout outfits, the 91st and 92nd CA Regiments, commanded by Colonels Joseph P. Kohn and Octave De Carre, respectively, were in some respects superior to either the 59th or 60th. The officers, nearly all Americans, were able, and the enlisted men were professional Philippine Scouts, many of them in their thirties and forties, who had served on the Fortified Islands for many years.

The Scouts, writes Lieutenant Colonel John McM. Gulick, U.S.A.F. (Ret.), formerly of the 91st CA, ". . . completely outperformed the Americans." Not only were they "intensely loyal" and "highly trained," but were, ". . . I believe, somewhat aware of the failings of many Americans." Their literalness in repeating the same task in exactly the same way made them superior gunners. Under fire they showed courage and did precisely what they were told. Colonel Alfred J. D'Arezzo, U.S.A., then a captain in command of Battery D of the 92nd, insists, "You would have to stand them up to the best soldiers of any country." The only serious deficiency of the big-gun regiments—apart from obsolete equipment—was their lack of realistic training.

As men of action gunners both of the seacoast and antiaircraft batteries had only contempt for the people in Malinta Tunnel at Bottomside. They joked about the "DTS Medal"—for "distinguished tunnel service"—which should be awarded to the "thirty-five generals" alleged to be hidden in there. In truth, of course, the total of general officers on Corregidor, even allowing for recently promoted colonels, was far short of the rumored thirty-five.

Actually, life in Malinta Tunnel was not much better—and in some respects was worse—than at the batteries. The tunnel resembled a gigantic anthill, where day and night men swarmed in a "ceaseless, purposeful passing and repassing," glared on mercilessly by the supposedly healthful blue mercury vapor lights. One had no privacy, no place to go to escape from other people. Even the ladies of Corregidor, nurses and wives of officials, had to go through the doctors' quarters to reach their own in the hospital laterals.

The entire eight-hundred-foot length of the main tunnel was lined to a height of six feet with crates of all sizes and descriptions. Signs marked off each lateral: "Subsistence," "Harbor Defense," "USAFFE," "Hospital," "Commo." At the west portal, snuggled against the quarry wall, was the quartermaster mess, above which hung a net of cables and wire intended to snare any suicide-minded Japanese pilot. Perhaps the best place was the hospital mess at the tunnel opening emerging on the North Shore Road girdling Malinta Hill. The nurses took their breaks there, and if lucky, one might be able to talk with an in-the-flesh American female in the few minutes of relaxation she would have before going back to duty. The unlucky had to content themselves with pinups.

Life in the tunnel so depressed some men that they lost their lives by refusing to take shelter in its stifling safety. It was an unreal, molelike existence in which, as Carlos Romulo has written, "one moved, worked, tried to eat, tried to breathe, in a dream." Even though it was the dry season, nasty little black flies swarmed everywhere, bedbugs prickled the flesh like straw at night, and dust hung in a pall despite a twice-a-day mopping. These grievances were endurable, but the feeling of helplessness, of being unable to fight back, was not.

Psychologically, to remain in the tunnel for a considerable period of time was hazardous. Once a man became acclimated to its vitiating confinement and confident of its absolute security, he found it difficult to return to the dangerous life outside. Those who had to go out and in felt the impact most, and a few succumbed to "tunnelitis" and were reluctant to emerge.

Under the southwest corner of Malinta Hill, opening toward Bottomside, the Navy had its four tunnels, Affirm, Baker, Roger, and Queen, to which the 16th Naval District Headquarters had transferred from Manila. Perhaps because the Navy was used to living in confined spaces—such as submarines—its tunnels were somehow a bit more shipshape, more "sundown." Chow was a little better, too. Nevertheless, the same depression was there, if in somewhat different form. The best morale booster was the *Navy Evening Gopher,* another of the little newssheets, this one put out by Lieutenant Warwick Scott of Rear Admiral Francis W. Rockwell's 16th Naval District Staff. We have the Admiral's word for it that a poem appearing in the February 4 issue—which everyone suspected Scott himself had written—". . . was a masterpiece of what went on from day to day." It warrants reproducing, in part.

Tunnels, dust, heat, and flies
Everyone telling little white lies
Bombs, and craters, rotten roads
Army trucks shrapneled carrying loads

Marines and sailors, tattoes, khakis
Telephones, Boom-Boom, rotten lackeys
Horseshoes, poker, letter writing
Artillery fire, soldiers fighting

Raisins, rice, and Monkey Point
A nose forever out of joint
Refreshing showers, bridge, and chess
Canned beans, chili all in a mess

. . .

South Dock, North Dock, mine fields, oil
Working parties but not much toil
USAFFE's news and Littig's tan
Commander Cheek has gone to Bataan*

. . .

Bottomside, sandbags, coldstores, gas
Gopher, coding room, Sunday mass
And now that we've learned to love this Rock
Let's return to Manila, from the old North Dock

The sooner the better is what I say
Let's pack our grips and—ANCHORS AWEIGH!!!

The inauguration of Manuel Quezon for his second term as President of the Philippine Commonwealth on December 30 provided a strange break in the tunnel routine. The Harbor Defense adjutant, Colonel Louis J. Bowler, had set up a mess table and a few kitchen chairs on the dusty ground outside the west portal. A tarpaulin was hung with the United States and Philippine Commonwealth flags displayed. Then up marched the 92nd CA (PS) band, "spick and span as a set of new spoons," but without its instruments. The Japanese had destroyed them in the air raid of the day before. Fortunately, the Malinta Tunnel field organ was handy, and Virginia Bewley, the daughter of a Commonwealth government official who had elected to remain behind in Manila, played "Hail to the Chief," while the band furnished the military spit and polish with an expertise only the Philippine Scouts could muster.

The ceremony was simple, and though seeming pathetic, partook of a special dignity. President Quezon spoke first. "Ours is a great

* "Boom-Boom" was Tunnel Queen's mascot, a nondescript black-and-white demi–fox terrier. Lieutenant Littig was a member of Staff, Tunnel Queen, and Lieutenant Commander M. C. Cheek was the energetic and able District Intelligence Officer.

cause," he said. "We are fighting for human liberty and justice, for those principles of individual freedom which we all cherish and without which life would not be worth living. Indeed, we are fighting for our own independence. It is to maintain this independence, these liberties, and these freedoms . . . that we are sacrificing our lives and all that we possess."

MacArthur concluded the ceremony, reiterating in a low, firm voice his old theme of confidence in the infant Philippine government. Come what may, he predicted firmly, "ultimate triumph will be its reward."

On venturing into one of the laterals of Malinta Tunnel and threading his way gingerly past the plethora of desks in a vain attempt to locate the right niche, an unfamiliar visitor would gain the impression that Corregidor's nerve center was an organizational incubus. The Army's perceptive historian, Dr. Louis Morton, has termed the Rock's command structure "a dizzying pyramid of headquarters."

At the very top, but not in direct command of the Harbor Defenses, was Lieutenant General Douglas MacArthur, whose USAFFE headquarters occupied an entire lateral of the tunnel. He commanded not only all U.S. and Philippine forces, but theoretically all American troops in the Far East, including scattered units in Burma, China, and Australia. Preoccupied with many other matters, especially the decisive fight for Bataan and the necessity of obtaining reinforcements and supplies, MacArthur found little time even to inspect the Rock. After his departure for Australia in mid-March, Lieutenant General Jonathan M. Wainwright, who had commanded successively the Philippine Division, the North Luzon Force, and I Corps on Bataan, took charge of all U.S. forces in the Philippines (USFIP).

As part of the long-standing organization termed the Harbor Defenses of Manila and Subic Bays, Corregidor was under the direct charge of Major General George F. Moore, a capable, veteran coast artilleryman. An experienced reserve officer who saw Moore every day, Lieutenant Colonel George G. Maxfield, describes him as ". . . the exemplification of the officer and the gentleman." An extrovert with a keen sense of humor, tough when he had to be, perhaps a little too willing to accept the views of his subordinates, personally courageous, and mindful of his men, Moore was one of those rare persons who had no enemies. Many young graduates from Texas A. and M., where he had been R.O.T.C. commandant, had flocked to join him on Corregidor. His adjutant, Colonel Bowler, declares, "He was closer to his officers than any other general officer I have ever known."

One day in Malinta Tunnel after the fall of Bataan, Maxfield, who served as assistant fire marshal for Fort Mills, received notice of a fire on Topside. Because the shelling had become severe by that time, the officer of the day frequently did not permit the fire crew to go out, but this time he did. General Moore, standing nearby, heard the conversation and stepped forward to ask where the fire was. In some embarrassment Maxfield had to tell him it was Moore's own quarters. At this the general quietly countermanded the order. He had, he said, nothing in his quarters worth risking lives for.

In all, Moore had about 5,200 coast artillery troops organized for administrative purposes in four regiments, the 59th and 60th, composed of Americans, and the 91st and 92nd, composed of veteran Philippine Scouts. The Scout units also administered two so-called regiments of Filipino reservists, the 1st and 2nd CA (Philippine Army), which had been in training when war came and together mustered only 550 officers and men.

For tactical purposes Moore's men were organized into three commands: Seaward Defense, with responsibility for driving off enemy ships and replying to enemy siege artillery; Antiaircraft Defense, with responsibility for repelling air attacks; and Beach Defense, with responsibility for defeating enemy landings. Colonel Paul D. Bunker commanded Seaward Defense; Colonel Theodore M. Chase, Antiaircraft Defense; and Colonel Samuel L. Howard, U.S.M.C., Beach Defense, a responsibility of his 4th Marine Regiment and attached units. Each commander's headquarters was physically separated from the others—Bunker was at C-1 Station on Topside, the other two were in the tunnel, but General Moore's H Station was in a different lateral from Howard's command post. Coordination had to be by telephone with separate communications circuits for each command, an unwieldy practice decidedly inferior to the one developed later in the war of co-locating all organizations in a Joint Operations Center (J.O.C.) with unified communications.

On the whole, however, co-ordination was reasonably satisfactory, except between Seaward Defense and the Navy's Inshore Patrol. Between these organizations it was slow and cumbersome. Personality clashes may have been partly responsible, but most participants attribute the slowness to the neglect of joint operational co-operation between the Army and the Navy in peacetime and to the longstanding tradition of bitter interservice rivalry. As one officer has put it, neither service understood the other's problems. These explanations, of course, do not excuse a state of affairs which markedly lowered the combat potential of both the Harbor Defenses and the Navy's gunboats and P.T.'s.

After the evacuation of Manila had brought over MacArthur's headquarters and service troops, numbers of personnel on Corregidor averaged between 11,500 and 12,000, with another 400 on Fort Hughes, 200 on Fort Drum, 400 on Fort Frank, and perhaps 300 to 400 on detached duty on Bataan. General Moore thus commanded—or fed and sustained—about 13,500 troops and civilians, of whom only 5,700 coast artillerymen and 1,500 marines were combat troops. This was too few to man all of the seacoast batteries and less than half enough to man the beach defenses.

More than 6,000 personnel, including 2,000 civilians, served in noncombat supporting roles. MacArthur had a large staff; the hospital contributed several hundred more, including Filipino and American nurses; the Post Engineer, Quartermaster, Provost Marshal, Chemical Warfare, and sundry other establishments consumed a large number of officers and men and hundreds of civilian employees; the Navy added an additional 2,000. While most of these people as individuals had legitimate reasons for being on Corregidor, having been ordered there, many had lost their staff and support functions when Manila and Cavite fell, which meant they were little more than supernumeraries, eating precious food, contributing little, administering paper commands that no longer existed. Some charge that Corregidor had too many elderly staff officers making useless plans and curbing initiative, but this would be difficult to substantiate. Nevertheless, there can be little doubt that the fortress was long on support people, however essential their services might have been in peacetime, and short on trained fighters. Exactly the contretemps had developed that a Defense Board in 1910 had warned against and in its planning had striven to avoid: there were far too many "useless mouths."

One of the favorite occupations of any soldier or sailor is peddling rumors. The most popular fables on the Rock were those predicting the imminent arrival of a convoy from the States with reinforcements. General MacArthur himself had given these substance on January 15 in a message to his entire command, which stated unequivocally: "Help is on the way from the United States. . . . Thousands of troops and hundreds of planes are being dispatched." He did not predict when they would arrive, but adding, "Our supplies are ample," he exhorted his men to hold out until aid came. Most personnel on Bataan and Corregidor, commissioned and enlisted alike, believed him.

Sergeant Hopkins, a realist in almost everything else, admitted, "I think so myself," after hearing others argue that it was certain a convoy was en route. But as time went on, and especially after Singapore fell on February 15, he and many others grew skeptical. On February 22, after hearing a rumor that some of the "older generals" in the tunnel favored surrendering Corregidor if Bataan were lost, the doughty sergeant exploded: "Personally, I don't think that the Rock could hold out long after Bataan fell, but my golly! Why the hell surrender? We can make the Nips wish to hell they had been sent up against some easy place!" Yet he concluded his entry with the grim prediction that defiladed Japanese artillery and dive bombers eventually would blast Corregidor to pieces.

A few learned the score when a submarine arrived direct from Hawaii in early February. From its crew they heard of the tremendous damage suffered by the battleships at Pearl Harbor and knew that Japan controlled the seas. This meant no convoy could get through, a fact most were wise enough to keep to themselves so as to preserve morale.

Given their desperate circumstances it was fortunate that most of Corregidor's defenders worked so hard that they ended each day physically tired and grateful for sleep. Morale was lower among those who had the least to do and the most time to ruminate—as in the tunnels. Elsewhere, "ceaseless work was the rule." Even at the antiaircraft batteries—by now well splinterproofed—maintenance, tunnel-digging, and housekeeping kept everyone busy. On the beaches the 4th Marines built, with a few hand tools, a complex system of defenses against the inevitable day when Bataan would fall and the Rock would stand alone. They strung wire, mined beaches, sited machine guns, dug trenches, emplaced their M-1916 37 mm. and British-model 75 mm. guns in splinterproofed and camouflaged pillboxes, and even rigged wooden chutes to slide surplus Air Corps fragmentation bombs over the cliffs onto the beaches below.

Many units joined the tunnel-digging craze. Two large and several smaller projects absorbed the attention of Major Robert B. Lothrop and his Fort Mills Post Engineers. The most important was the tunnel housing Colonel Bunker's C-1 Station, located near Battery Wheeler. Work began in December just before hostilities and was completed in February. Lothrop also resumed the Middleside Harbor Defense Command tunnel, which had been started in 1921. Designed as a ten-by-twelve-foot bore six hundred feet long, it was abandoned after some 235 feet of rock had been removed, when the Five-Power Treaty was signed. It was not fully complete at the time of the surrender and consequently never was used by General Moore for his headquarters, but ammunition was stored in it, and it also served as an excellent personnel shelter. The busy Major's lesser projects included digging personnel shelters for Batteries Monja, Hanna, Sunset, and Rock Point, which he completed sufficiently to provide shelter for the crews.

With Lothrop's blessing and advice, all of the antiaircraft batteries began tunnels to provide crew protection and ammunition storage. Those of Chicago, Denver, and Mobile ultimately saved many lives when all three units took a terrific battering after Bataan's fall. Other units, particularly the marines in exposed beach defense posts, began impromptu tunnels with shoring obtained by "twilight requisitioning" from wrecked quarters and buildings. Perhaps the most important of these was one begun by Lieutenant Edward F. Ritter, Jr., a young Navy doctor stationed in James ravine with the marines; he had the assistance of a 59th CA man, an ex-miner. A U-shaped affair, this tunnel was blasted from solid rock and used as an aid station and shelter by dozens of marines stationed in this viciously shelled spot.

An engineer officer of General Moore's staff, Colonel Lloyd E. Mielenz, has estimated that the total length of all the wartime tunnels equaled the length of all tunnels completed in the peacetime years.

On February 16 Captain Achille Tisdelle, a headquarters officer, recorded that "the damned Nips have got a new propaganda program that does not help our morale any. The men joke happily, but underneath they are disquieted. KZRH in Manila plays American songs to American soldiers on Bataan and Corregidor at 2145 hours every night. Theme song 'Ships that never come in' followed by popular records."

"Ships that never come in." The Japanese had chosen their theme song well. MacArthur had realized from the beginning that the length of his resistance would depend on the amount of supplies and reinforcements reaching him. The War Department, while sympathetic with his predicament, knew it could not send substantial aid in view of Japan's naval superiority in the Pacific.

In early January the War Plans Division of the General Staff solemnly reviewed the problem, only to conclude that MacArthur's command could not hold out for the three months' time it would take to mount a large-scale relief expedition. Ship passage to Australia—a necessary stopping place—alone would consume six precious weeks. Protection for a force of several Army divisions would require seven to nine battleships, five to seven aircraft carriers, fifty destroyers and sixty submarines, plus a fleet of auxiliaries that did not then exist. Unless the war against Germany and Italy was to be abandoned, and the Russians left to their fate, it was beyond the combined resources of the United States and Great Britain even to assemble such a force.

On January 4, the same day the War Plans Division gave its pessimistic report, MacArthur recommended developing a blockade-running system to evade the Japanese stranglehold about the Philippines. He even suggested the use of submarines to slip in supplies. His message was well received in the War Department, which already had dispatched two officers to Australia with funds to initiate just such a program. Chief of Staff General George C. Marshall strove in every way he reasonably could to back them. Regardless of the strategic situation, or the impossibility of sending large-scale reinforcements, Marshall recognized the moral and political necessity of getting at least something through to MacArthur. "Use your funds without stint," he instructed the officers. "Call for more if required. . . . Arrange for advance payments, partial payments for unsuccessful [blockade-running] efforts, and large bonus for actual delivery. . . . Organize groups of bold and resourceful men. . . ."

It certainly took bold and resourceful men to attempt so desperate a voyage as the one through the Japanese-patrolled passages and channeled waterways leading from Australia to Manila Bay. Even a ship lucky enough to get through could expect certain destruction by bombing on arrival. Little wonder crews proved hard to find, and that only three ships succeeded in getting from Australia to the southern Philippines, where their cargo was unloaded for transshipment to Corregidor in smaller vessels. Several other ships were sunk.

The use of submarines was considered and rejected. Nearly all naval men dismissed submarine transport as a waste of resources, since by their very nature subs make poor transports. Without its torpedoes a standard fleet submarine could carry thirty to forty tons of small packaged items, a bagatelle compared to the daily needs of the troops on Bataan. Submarines, both doctrine and common sense had it, were better employed sending the enemy's troop transports and supply ships to the bottom.

One significant exception was made. In response to an urgent plea from General Moore, via General MacArthur, the submarine *Trout,* commanded by Commander Frank W. Fenno, was loaded with 2,750 rounds of mechanically fuzed 3-inch antiaircraft ammunition and dispatched directly across the Pacific to Corregidor. There its precious cargo was unloaded on February 3 and 4, sent to Chicago Battery, and replaced with another of far greater monetary value. The gold reserves and some of the silver of the Philippine treasury made excellent ballast for *Trout,* and the sub sailed homeward laden with nearly $10,000,000 in bullion. Other submarines occasionally called at Corregidor to replenish torpedoes and fuel, and some took out aviators and other key personnel needed elsewhere, but no concerted attempt was made to use submarines for evacuation purposes.

While Washington was trying to organize a blockade-running system from Australia, General MacArthur had initiated one of his own within the Philippines. Several thousand tons of food were stored at the Army depot at Cebu city, and MacArthur hoped by means of coastal vessels to smuggle it to Bataan. Only three ships of more than a dozen, however, managed to get through. The *Legaspi,* a small interisland steamer, made two trips in February, but was sunk by a Japanese gunboat while attempting a third on the first of March. The *Princessa,* another interislander, made it from Cebu on February 21, and the *Elcano* got through at the end of the month from Mindanao. After that every ship sent was lost. By mid-March a halt was called, although several loaded steamers were waiting off Cebu, which as yet the Japanese had not occupied. Consequently, only about a thousand of the ten thousand tons of food at Cebu reached Bataan. This was enough to support the troops for about four days.

MacArthur also tried blockade-running in the vicinity of Manila Bay itself. He had agents in southern Luzon collect rice for transport overland by native cart to a secret storage place near Looc Cove on the Cavite shore. From there it was loaded into two four-hundred-ton motor ships and run across by night to Bataan. In this manner some 1,600 tons of rice was accumulated.

Altogether, the blockade-running project probably was not worth the cost in ships. As Major Tisdelle confessed, after seeing the foodstuffs arrive from the *Legaspi,* "Cases of food piled on the docks look very big but won't scratch the surface for what we will need; and unless we can get command of the air and bring in an actual convoy we are lost."

Well did General MacArthur recognize that grim fact! As time went on his pleas to General Marshall in Washington grew more and more desperate. Two sympathetic biographers have gone so far as to assert that ". . . for the most part, MacArthur fought the battle of Bataan with radio messages to Washington; his real fight was to try to get reinforcements. . . ." He even encouraged newsmen to write articles stressing the critical need for supplies. When in early February a disillusioned President Quezon, heartsick at the frightful physical condition of his Filipino reservists on Bataan, talked of accepting a Japanese "offer" of independence in return for a Philippine surrender, MacArthur passed Quezon's idea to Washington with a qualified endorsement—probably not because he agreed with it—but because he saw it as a useful means to bring further pressure on General Marshall.

In truth Marshall had done his best. The only plausible strategy for the United States in those disastrous months was the one Marshall pursued: to build a secure supply line to Australia, to create a base there, and then to attempt to check the Japanese advance in the Netherlands East Indies, supporting the Philippines as best he could by blockade-running. As it turned out, even this was too difficult. The Netherlands East Indies fell easily, and only two timely naval victories, the Battles of the Coral Sea and Midway, prevented the loss of all of New Guinea and, probably, steppingstone islands to Australia as well.

By early February everyone "in the know" in Washington realized that Bataan was doomed and that Corregidor's fall also was inevitable—as, from the beginning of American rule in the Philippines, the more perceptive planners had realized would happen in the event of war with Japan.

The original Orange War Plan had called for occupying the Pico de Loro hills of Cavite Province with an infantry regiment to keep the Japanese at arm's length. During the retreat to Bataan, MacArthur evidently decided this provision was impractical, for no troops were sent. On January 10 General Homma's men began occupying the entire Cavite shore line without opposition.

On January 15, lookouts sighted dust clouds to the southeast on the Cavite shore road. Thirty-power field glasses could not reveal what was moving, and so Colonel Louis Bowler, General Moore's adjutant, borrowed a fifty-five-power telescope. Through this instrument he could barely make out a motor column turning into the jungle between Sapong and Ternate about twelve miles from the Rock. Although Bowler had no way of knowing it, the vehicles belonged to a small Japanese artillery unit of two 150 mm. and four 100 mm. guns under the command of Major Toshinori Kondo. It had orders "to secretly deploy" and "prepare for fire missions" against the Fortified Islands.

Paul Bunker immediately bid to interdict the road and pepper the area of observed activity, but USAFFE demurred, apparently at the request of President Quezon, who feared indiscriminate artillery fire would cause needless loss of life among the civilian populace of Cavite Province. The frustrated Colonel could only retort in his diary, "But you can't make a cake without breaking up eggs."

In the meantime Captain Richard G. Ivey of the 60th CA, who commanded a small concealed aircraft warning (AAIS) detachment located atop Pico de Loro Mountain, had made contact with one Captain Rueda of the Philippine Constabulary. Rueda had not surrendered his three hundred men when the Japanese moved into

In the beginning, Corregidor served as a lighthouse station. The lighthouse was started in 1835 and completed in 1853. On a clear day it could be seen from 33 miles away. (*U.S. Army photograph*)

Corregidor's 8-inch muzzle-loading guns failed to prevent Admiral Dewey from entering Manila Bay. After the occupation of the Rock sailors from the U.S.S. *McCulloch* destroyed the weapons, but Corregidor was soon to be re-armed. (*Photo courtesy, U.S. Naval Institute*)

Before the war Corregidor was a community with such comforts as a movie theater, swimming pool, golf course and the trolley line, shown here. The trains ran on a regular schedule between Kindley Field and Topside and had first, second and third-class seats. (*U.S. Army photograph*)

Open to the skies were many of the batteries, such as Hearn (shown here), which looked like giant bullseyes to the pilots of attacking planes. (*Photograph courtesy Corps of Engineers*)

The "concrete battleship," Fort Drum, was the result of a brilliant engineering idea. Its guns went on firing to the end of the battle in 1942. (*Left, Air Force photograph; right, U.S. Army photograph*)

Firing the great 14-inch disappearing rifles demanded strength and excellent timing. The men trained constantly, as here at Battery Woodruff on Caballo Island (Fort Hughes). (*U.S. Army photograph*)

Some of the islands' weapons. Top, 3-inch antiaircraft guns of Denver Battery on Point Corregidor. Center, the giant 14-inch disappearing rifles of Battery Greer on Carabao Island (Fort Frank). Bottom, Battery Geary's M-1908 mortars. (*U.S. Army photographs, courtesy Col. Reilley E. McGarraugh*)

In the last days of peace, the troops of Corregidor were sharp and ready. On June 18, 1941 they marched in review on the parade ground. Shown in the background is the massive barracks building. War was six months away. (*U.S. Army photograph*)

As the battle raged, the work of running the garrison went on in the tunnels amid heat, dust, flies and dwindling hope. This photo, taken out on May 3, 1942, by the last submarine to stop at Corregidor, shows the finance office in Malinta Tunnel. Further back was the Signal Corps Message Center. (*U.S. Army photograph*)

Hidden behind the hills of Bataan, Japanese artillery battered the islands. This photograph, taken on May 4, 1942, shows a Japanese 150 mm. gun firing in defilade in the last stages of the bombardment. (*Japanese 14th Army photograph*)

The defiance of Corregidor's defenders was exemplified by Battery Way, the wreckage of which is here examined by Americans after the Rock's recapture. Major William Massello and his crew from Erie Battery kept the M-1890 mortar at far right firing to the end. Of the 90-man battery crew, 75 percent became casualties. (*U.S. Army photograph*)

General Jonathan M.
("Skinny") Wainwright

Colonel Paul D. Bunker

General George F. Moore

HE WEATHER

The Tribune

5 Centavos
4 Pages

R XVIII — MANILA, PHILIPPINES, FRIDAY, MAY 8, 1942 — NUMBER

CORREGIDOR FALLS

ieneral Wainwright Orders
ntire USAFFE to Surrender

roops Must
isarm, Give
p in 4 Days

Instructions
To Officers, Men
Read Over Radio

ORDERING the remaining USAFFE forces throughout the Philippines to surrender is Lt. General Jonathan M. Wainwright, left, commanding general of the American and Philippine Forces. The order was given over the radio last night. A Japanese Army officer is seated at the right.

Japan Force
Occupy Ent
Stronghold

Tokyo Imperial
Headquarters M
Announcement

PNB Emergency Notes Banned

People Asked To Display Nippon Flag

Eye-Witness Tells of "Fall"

The Manila Tribune, May 8, 1942.
General Wainwright, watched by a
Japanese officer, announces the fall.

Occupying Corregidor, Japanese troops cross the parade ground and head for the now shattered barracks. Below, more troops bring equipment onto the island and clear some of the wreckage. (*Japanese 14th Army photographs*)

Posed beside one of Corregidor's guns, Japanese soldiers shout, "Banzai!" in celebration of their victory. This widely circulated photograph exemplified the fanatical confidence of the so-far victorious Japanese. (*Japanese 14th Army photograph*)

Corregidor's nurses were lined up at the entrance to Malinta Tunnel for a propaganda photograph. When told to smile, they refused. Left to right, Vivian Weisblatt, Adele Forman, Jeanne Kennedy, Peggy Greenwalt, Eunice Young, Dorothy McCann and Eleanor Goren. (*Japanese 14th Army photograph*)

Gaunt and weary American and Filipino prisoners stood before Malinta Tunnel just after the surrender. In the foreground, Japanese officers prepare to march them to the 92nd Garage area. (*Japanese 14th Army photograph*)

Prelude to recapture was a series of shattering air attacks. Here bombs dropped by Seventh Air Force B-24 Liberators blast Topside. At right, a stick of thousand-pound bombs hits Japanese gun emplacements. (*U.S. Air Force photograph*)

The drop zones on Corregidor were small and often perilously close to the cliffs. A C-47 drops supplies onto the cratered, chute-littered field. Battery Wheeler lies wrecked at right. (*U.S. Army photograph*)

As the paratroopers landed, their buddies on the ground watched closely so as not to be hit. Many paratroopers became casualties without seeing actual combat. (*U.S. Army photograph*)

Shortly after the paratroops began their operation, landing ships moved toward "Black Beach." Chutes could still be seen floating downward as this LCT moved into position. (*U.S. Navy photograph*)

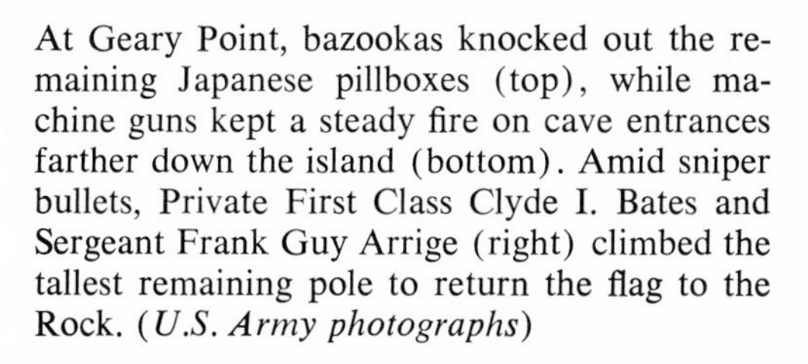

At Geary Point, bazookas knocked out the remaining Japanese pillboxes (top), while machine guns kept a steady fire on cave entrances farther down the island (bottom). Amid sniper bullets, Private First Class Clyde I. Bates and Sergeant Frank Guy Arrige (right) climbed the tallest remaining pole to return the flag to the Rock. (*U.S. Army photographs*)

After a week, the Americans were still fighting to secure Malinta Hill. Moving up from the rocky beach, Company L of the 34th Regiment advanced cautiously through the ravine on the north side of the hill.

On his return to the Rock, General MacArthur congratulated the commanders who had led the recapture, including Colonel George M. Jones (wearing helmet), Lieutenant General Walter Kreuger (standing to Jones' right) and Lieutenant General Richard K. Sutherland (beside MacArthur). (*U.S. Army photograph*)

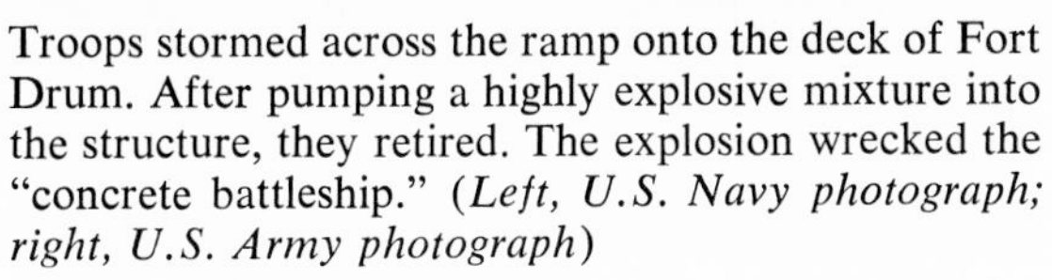

Troops stormed across the ramp onto the deck of Fort Drum. After pumping a highly explosive mixture into the structure, they retired. The explosion wrecked the "concrete battleship." (*Left, U.S. Navy photograph; right, U.S. Army photograph*)

The remains of M-1908 mortar Battery Kohler on Fort Frank testify to the punishment suffered by the Fortified Islands in the two battles. (*U.S. Army photograph*)

"I see that the old flagpole still stands. . . . Hoist the colors to its peak and let no enemy ever haul them down." Once again American soldiers saluted the Stars and Stripes on the parade ground. It was March 2, 1945. (*U.S. Army photograph*)

Cavite Province; instead he had dispersed them where he could round them up on a few days' notice. On about January 24 one of his men spotted the Japanese emplacing their artillery and Ivey radioed to Corregidor a detailed report on Kondo's strength and dispositions.

Two days later, after slipping by night to Fort Frank in a banca, Ivey and Rueda went to Corregidor and urged MacArthur's staff to use Rueda and his men as guerrillas to harass the Japanese. Colonel Charles A. Willoughby, General MacArthur's intelligence officer, turned down this suggestion on the ground that certain reprisal against Filipino civilians would result. Willoughby similarly rejected a proposal by General Moore to use regular USAFFE troops for this purpose.

Although Ivey, Rueda, and Moore were disappointed, Colonel Willoughby's decision was wise. The struggle for Bataan was touch and go at this stage, and if the word should spread among the Filipino reservists holding most of the front that the Japanese were slaughtering civilians, their morale might give way. Also, the opposition of Quezon had to be considered. MacArthur hardly could risk his entire command to destroy a few artillery pieces, so Kondo continued to dig in without harassment.

On January 31 USAFFE had a change of heart. Moore and Bunker received permission to open fire; Colonel Napoleon Boudreau, now commanding Fort Frank, had the 12-inch mortars of Battery Koehler roaring by 5:42 that evening. The veteran Scouts of the 92nd, although they had not fired the eight weapons for several years, were "on" with their first bursts, and a hill near the village of Ternate suspected of harboring a supply tunnel was blasted with thirty of the huge shells. Kirkpatrick on Drum joined with the 6-inch rifles of casemated Battery Roberts. His bursts were short at first, but Captain Madison's gunners soon were "on" and shifted to high-explosive antipersonnel shells. Nevertheless, as Bunker noted, the firing was several days too late. Already, Kondo's men were well dug in and awaiting their own orders to fire.

8 ☆ The First Bombardment

WORD of Major Kondo's move into Cavite Province had quickly spread among the Corregidor garrison, generating heated debate among the officers and men as to whether a Japanese shell fired from Cavite could reach them. The "wise money" was against the possibility. At about 8 A.M. on February 6, Kondo abruptly ended the debate by opening up with his four 100 mm. (4-inch) guns. His first round fell on Topside, and some shells made liars of the optimists by sailing clear over the six-hundred-foot heights to land in the North Channel beyond. Kondo's modern 4-inchers, firing at a range of over ten miles, could outrange every weapon on the Rock except the two long-range 12-inch rifles of Batteries Smith and Hearn!

Kondo continued shelling at one-minute intervals until eleven o'clock. For the most part he pummeled Frank and Drum, hitting the concrete battleship a hundred times with but superficial damage. From time to time he shifted to the Rock, cratering the Kindley Field area and filling several of Mobile's tents with holes, and also to ships anchored in the south harbor between Corregidor and Fort Hughes. The aggressive Kirkpatrick on Drum countered with his 3-incher, Battery Hoyle, and then with his casemated 6-inchers of Battery Roberts. Boudreau on Frank replied with his mortars, losing a Scout killed outright and Captain Robert J. White, Koehler's commander, who was fatally wounded when a huge projectile burst just after clearing the mortar tube. A number of others were injured.

Everyone attempted, but nobody succeeded, in getting a good fix on Kondo's guns, which were defiladed in valleys. Colonel Octave De Carre, the 92nd's commander, searched long through spotting telescopes until his eyes ached but saw nothing. The only chance observers might have had was to spot the gun flashes at the moment of fire. But Kondo had thought of that, and on this morning, as became his custom, he fired with the bright sun at his back, ceasing fire when it rose high. His powder was smokeless, and as a deception he sent up smoke rings from dummy positions. Other units tried to help the artillery spotters but most of their efforts were "useless," according to Colonel Bunker, "and led to no positive locations of Jap guns."

Battle experience had confirmed the worst expectations of prewar pessimists. Even the bursts of the awesome 12-inch mortar shells, lethal to a radius of five hundred yards, could avail nothing unless the spotters could glimpse the enemy. On the other hand, it was clear that Kondo could do little damage with small-caliber artillery. Drum's thick sides were barely scratched; the damage at Corregidor and Frank was negligible and casualties were few. Kondo had been sent with a boy's tools to do a man's job.

In the days following, until mid-March when Homma finally decided to reinforce him, Major Kondo did his best. On February 8 he began using his two 150 mm. guns in addition to his four 100's, and in midmonth, when he received a pair of 150 mm. howitzers, he intensified his fire so as to shut off the supplies trickling to Bataan from across the bay.

Moore and Bunker tried everything to find Kondo. In the hope of defeating the glow of the sun they placed spotters at widely separated positions, but the Japanese guns were so deep in the forested valleys that only occasionally could a dim flash be seen. Most of the American firing was done from maps, with Bunker selecting spots ". . . where indications led us to believe the Jap guns *might* be."

These difficulties finally induced General Moore to use Captain Dick Ivey and his AAIS detail. Ivey took with him two courageous American civilians—Backus and Ganfield, who had been hiding out with Captain Rueda—two Filipino guides, and a portable radio transmitter, and slipped back to the Cavite shore by night. He found a good spot overlooking Ternate from 5,000 yards, where he could hear Kondo's guns and observe Japanese troops passing in trucks along the road, but still could not actually see the pieces or spot their flashes through the heavy jungle growth. This forced him to rely principally on sound to direct Fort Frank's fire.

With Ivey on the radio and Colonel Bunker monitoring via telephone, Battery Frank North's four 155 mm. guns opened up. Ivey slowly brought the fire left, a degree at a time, until the Scout gunners received the welcome "Hit, Hit," from him. Six quick salvos scored four more hits. A mollified Bunker wrote in his diary that evening, "I guess *that* Japanese gun position is now no good." Ivey, however, was much less sure. He was, he confesses ruefully, ". . . never certain whether we had hit an enemy gun position or not."

The next day, February 9, Moore persuaded MacArthur to authorize more risky tactics. The Far East Air Force on Bataan still had a few carefully hoarded aircraft, including a half-dozen fast P-40 fighters and a slow Stearman biplane trainer of the Philippine Air Force. The Filipino hero, Captain Jesus Villamor, who earlier in the campaign had repeatedly risked his life flying an antique Boeing P-26 against Zeros a hundred miles an hour faster, volunteered to pilot the trainer over the Ternate area and photograph Kondo's positions. The P-40's would fly escort.

As his partner for this extremely risky mission Villamor had another volunteer, Master Sergeant Juan V. Abanes, who had joined the Philippine Air Corps at its inception in the mid-1930's. Abanes would sit in the front seat and operate the cumbersome camera while Villamor flew the beat-up trainer from the student's seat in the rear.

After the morning haze and cloudiness had burned off, the six P-40's roared off Bataan's Cabcaben airstrip. Villamor waited until the dust settled, then took off, climbing as rapidly as the straining engine would allow to 7,000 feet. His plan was to take just enough pictures of the Ternate area for a minimum coverage, and then hightail it for home.

Villamor began his run, watching anxiously for the enemy, but all he saw was the formation of P-40's. Emboldened, he tapped Abanes on the shoulder at the end of the run, and back the old plane went, crisscrossing the Ternate area until Abanes had exposed all 110 frames in the camera. Still no sign of enemy fighters. Then Villamor decided to give the troops on the Rock a thrill by flying over on his way back to Cabcaben. He dropped to about 3,500 feet, and flew a few jaunty figure eights, waving to the men below. Straightening out, he finally headed across the North Channel for Cabcaben.

It was not until he was about to swing into his landing pattern that Villamor suddenly noticed the P-40 escort drop their noses and dart ahead. Sensing trouble, he dove the trainer, forgetting completely that Colonel Curtis L. Lambert, his engineering officer, had warned him not to: "Its wings are too weak and won't stand it!" Leveling off just above the strip, preparing to touch down, Villamor finally understood why he had not seen the Japanese fighters; instead of pursuing him they had been circling over Cabcaben, waiting for him to come back to his only airfield. Already the enemy leader was diving toward the other end of the field, guns winking from nose and wings.

Just as his wheels touched, Villamor saw little spouts of dust sweep rapidly toward him. He kicked rudder, and as he ground-looped the trainer violently to the right, he heard the bullets rip his left wing. Straightening the plane, he spotted more dust spouts as the leader's wing man dove. This time Villamor kicked the plane violently left, as bullets clipped the other wing. Gunning toward a clump of trees he and Abanes leaped out and took cover in foxholes. From there they watched a swirling dogfight erupt over Manila Bay. Villamor saw two Japanese Zeros fall, and the American fighter pilots claimed two more, but one of the six precious P-40's was lost and another heavily damaged. The daring of Villamor, Abanes and the other pilots had paid off, but at too great a cost. With the element of surprise gone a repeat mission was out of the question.

This was all the more regrettable since the next day's artillery duel yielded the only really gratifying results obtained during the bombardment. Firing from data derived from the photographs and with Captain Ivey helping out with his radio, Fort Frank's Scouts scored several direct hits on Kondo's emplacements and set fire to a barracks. Afterward Kondo withdrew to an area further from the beach. Dodging Jap patrols, Ivey, Backus, and Ganfield returned to Fort Frank.

A few days later Ivey volunteered to try again. Kondo was in action once more from new positions, and the situation had reverted to what it had been before. This time Ivey took along Sergeant Boyd and Corporal Bob Morrison, both from the 60th CA, and two Philippine Scouts to furnish protection. On February 14 the team spotted fire without incident, with Morrison doing the observing, Ivey and Boyd working the radio, and the two Scouts on lookout on either flank.

When they tried again the next day from another location, a Japanese patrol ambushed the party, either killing or capturing Morrison, who never was heard from again, and forced the others to flee. Ivey and the rest made their way individually to a prearranged rendezvous point and so escaped. Loss of the radio made it certain that the Japanese had discovered the spotting activity and would patrol vigorously to stop it. Ivey's usefulness had ended. General Moore now could do no more than give him a well-earned Distinguished Service Cross and assign him to a post in the tunnel.

When Kondo intensified his shelling in mid-February he also concentrated on his nearest target, Fort Frank. With a top only two hundred feet wide and all batteries connected by bombproof tunnels, Fort Frank proved difficult to hit and strongly resistant to fire. The obsolescent pre–World War I "concrete artillery" on all of the islands withstood prolonged shelling and bombing and numerous direct hits surprisingly well.

As a harassment measure the Japanese on February 16 severed the water pipeline connecting Frank's water tanks to Calumpit dam and reservoir on the Cavite mainland, forcing Boudreau to begin operating his sea-water distillation plant. On the twentieth Boudreau dispatched a volunteer party of seventeen men to repair the water pipe. They reached the dam safely, but were attacked by a Japanese patrol while working. This time the Japanese suffered. Private James D. Elkins of the 60th, sent along with the Scouts as "shotgun," sprayed them with such heavy fire from his automatic rifle that they all fled leaving at least ten dead behind. Only one Scout was wounded, but the water pipe remained cut and the angry Japanese relieved their frustration by burning the barrios of Calumpang and Patungan that night. A few days later another party repaired the pipe without molestation.

On February 22 Kondo suddenly stopped firing; a quiet spell began which continued until March 15. The Americans fondly believed that their morning "serenades" had silenced Kondo, but the major was merely awaiting new orders and reinforcements. Frank had suffered a number of casualties but had no guns out of action. Drum was chipped and dented but its fighting capacity was unimpaired. On Corregidor and Hughes the shells had been merely a nuisance. "It was surprising to me," wrote Colonel Stephen M. Mellnik, "how quickly we lost the fear of being shelled." The men soon learned to ignore the fire unless it was falling in their vicinity.

While Kondo had been firing, worried officials in Washington, D.C., had been considering the fate of General MacArthur. If Bataan and Corregidor fell, as it seemed certain they must, there was little point in handing over to the Japanese America's most noted soldier, whose talents could be useful elsewhere. President Roosevelt responded on February 22 by ordering MacArthur to leave Corregidor and proceed to Australia. The General himself realized the wisdom of this but delayed his departure until the last minute. When he finally decided to go on March 10 it was almost too late. The Japanese had tightened their blockade so closely he decided against waiting five days for a submarine and instead took the risky decision to run the gauntlet by PT boat.

When the time came for the MacArthur party to embark aboard

four PT's of John D. Bulkeley's Torpedo Boat Squadron Three waiting at the North Dock, MacArthur turned to George Moore, who had come to see him off. "Keep the flag flying," he said, firmly shaking Moore's hand, "I am coming back." His gamble paid off; all four PT's successfully evaded the blockading Japanese warships, and MacArthur reached Mindanao Island on March 14. There he and his party motored to Del Monte airfield, which was still in American hands, and flew on to Australia aboard a pair of B-17's.

For most of Corregidor's garrison the news of MacArthur's departure seemed a ray of hope. They hoped their former commander would use his massive influence to get aid to them. Had they known the real circumstances, they probably would have taken MacArthur's departure for what it really was, a token of doom.

Another such token was a decision in early March to dispose of the silver reserves of the Philippine Commonwealth stored in the government vault at Middleside. An area between Corregidor and Fort Hughes was surveyed and the decision made to dump the silver—in the form of sixteen million pesos worth fifty cents apiece—into the bay. Packed in wooden whiskey boxes, at three thousand coins per box, the silver was much too heavy and bulky to evacuate by submarine or to bury on land.

The work parties had a lark at first, skipping the coins across the water, but the "lark" soon became routine heavy labor; the men grunted, sweated, and cursed as they heaved the three-hundred-pound boxes overboard. Finally, they dispatched the remainder of the nearly 350 tons by sinking the barges on which the boxes were loaded. About half of the coinage was later recovered in 1942 by the Japanese who used captured U.S. Navy men and Moro pearl divers; and by the U.S. Seventh Fleet in 1945–1946, using net tenders with dragging gear. But to this day the other half lies widely scattered over the bottom.

In early March Filipino agents slipped to the mainland by Colonel Willoughby, MacArthur's G-2, returned with disquieting news. The

Japanese, they reported, were preparing new artillery positions in the Pico de Loro hills, much closer to Fort Frank. These were intended for Colonel Masayoshi Hayakawa's 1st Heavy Artillery Regiment (reinforced), a much stronger outfit than Kondo's and armed with ten of the most powerful field pieces in the Japanese Army, squat, ugly 240 mm. (9.4-inch) howitzers. Although these iron-wheeled cannon appeared obsolete at first glance, they had greater range and power than the famed 11-inch howitzers that had shattered Port Arthur in the Russo-Japanese War and were well-suited to the destructive task at hand. Their crews knew their business and the precise location of each of their targets.

While Hayakawa was digging in his pieces—no small task, for each required a hole as big as the Imperial Palace—Homma's headquarters used a blunt form of psychological warfare. A Filipino civilian, a former Scout discharged before the war for suspected Sakdalista (agrarian radical) leanings, carried a message to Frank. Couched in ominous terms, it read:

> Surrender Carabao [Fort Frank] and save lives, the whole area along the coastline of Cavite Province is now a Japanese Military Reservation; large guns in large numbers are being massed there; Carabao will be reduced by our mighty artillery fire, likewise Drum; after reduction of Carabao and Drum our invincible artillery will pound Corregidor into submission, batter it, weaken it, preparatory to a final assault by crack Japanese landing troops. Be wise, surrender now and receive preferential treatment

Colonel Boudreau realized that the Japanese probably meant exactly what they said. Frank's vulnerability and probable early loss had long been recognized in prewar planning. He passed the message to General Moore, intensified the alert of his beach defenses, and defiantly answered Homma's propaganda by dropping some 12-inch mortar shells into the Pico de Loro area where the battery construction was reported.

While Boudreau fired Bunker worried. He had plenty of delay-fuze, deck-piercing, 12-inch projectiles for use against ships, but too few with instantaneous fuzes for use against land targets. On February 27 he had suggested removing the 0.05 second delay pellet from the fuze of the deck-piercing projectile, thus converting it into a nearly instantaneous one for antipersonnel use. After deliberate consideration General Moore consented and work began. Ordnance could laboriously modify only twenty-five rounds a day, but the results were worth the effort.

On the ides of March Hayakawa opened up with a single ranging shot, then with another, and then with a burst of four. After that, joined by Kondo's smaller pieces, he hailed shells on all of the harbor forts. Tremendous blasts from the shells hitting Drum and Frank made it obvious that he was using guns larger than 150 mm. One round smashed through the armored shield of Battery Roberts on Drum, bursting inside the casemate with a low order of detonation and filling the concrete battleship with smoke and fumes. Luckily, the crew was not at the gun, no fire started, and there were no serious casualties. From the base of the projectile, which was recovered intact, Kirkpatrick's men ascertained that the Japanese were using the 240's. Hayakawa continued his barrage until the sun rose so high as to make the gun flashes visible to the Americans; then he stopped, to resume after dark with flashless powder.

He had hurt Boudreau badly. Battery Frank North had two 155 mm. guns destroyed and the other two damaged but repairable. Battery Ermita (four 3-inch AA) suffered similarly. The cable and derrick used to hoist supplies from the beach were knocked out, and seven of eight mortars at Battery Koehler were damaged. Over five hundred shells had struck the island, mostly of 240 mm. caliber, each weighing over four hundred pounds; yet personnel casualties were slight thanks to the bombproof tunnel system.

At Drum the shell which penetrated the casemate at Roberts did the most damage, putting one of the 6-inch rifles temporarily out of action. Shells struck repeatedly on the sides, tops, and faces of the 14-inch turrets without harm, justifying the insistence of the fortresses' designers on all-around heavy armor. Nevertheless, the shock was not a comfortable experience. As Albert L. Corn remembers it, "The noise was terrific. Like being in an iron barrel with someone striking it with a large hammer." On one occasion Colonel Kirkpatrick was talking over the telephone to General Moore's operations officer (G-3), Colonel William C. Braly. There was a pause. "Pardon the interruption, Colonel," said Kirkpatrick, "that last one bounced the phone right off the desk."

Shells striking the concrete deck did surprisingly little harm, although a 240 mm. round would leave a crater two to four inches deep and eighteen to twenty-four inches in diameter. Another hit in the same place, however, would blast out a good-sized chunk, evidently because of the weakening of the structure by the first hit. But after repair of the 6-inch weapon at Roberts and patching of the casemate, the concrete battleship was ready to shoot again. Forts Mills and Hughes received little damage; hits there were mostly from Major Kondo's smaller guns.

Counterbattery fire was distressingly ineffective. Once again the brilliant morning sun had blinded Bunker's spotters. Battery Craighill's 12-inch mortars at Hughes silenced a 240 which was hammering Drum, only to draw the enmity of another which accurately dropped two projectiles into one of the twin mortar pits. Paul Bunker was angry and worried. He knew that even if General Moore could obtain permission to send out an invaluable P-40 on a reconnaissance mission, ". . . the damn Japs will move."

The next morning, March 16, Hayakawa again gave Frank and Drum a merciless beating. Koehler on Frank had a narrow escape. A 240 mm. shell struck the junction of the vertical wall and floor of one of its mortar pits, penetrated eighteen inches of concrete, and detonated beneath the battery's powder room, breaking up the concrete floor and hurling sixty filled powder cans about. Miraculously, none of them exploded or caught fire.

Corregidor's Battery Hearn (12-inch long-range gun) and Hughes's Craighill (12-inch mortars) and Woodruff (14-inch gun) provided most of the counterbattery, while Frank and Drum lay doggo. For the next several days, much the same pattern was repeated, with the

Japanese firing less and Frank and Drum replying just enough to show they were still in commission. Frank's beach defense 75's also peppered Japanese patrols spotted moving about in the nearby hills looking for Dick Ivey. Both forts doubled their nightly beach defense details anticipating a landing attempt.

It was well they did, because Homma was planning just such a move, utilizing the two thousand men of a reconnaissance regiment that he had sent in with the Hayakawa Detachment to halt MacArthur's rice smuggling details. But on March 22 he changed his mind and ordered Hayakawa to transfer to Bataan to support the offensive scheduled to begin in early April.

The shelling of March 21 was therefore Hayakawa's going-away present and the end of Drum and Frank's ordeal, although when executing it he probably assumed it was a prelude to invasion. Several hundred shells struck Frank, the principal target, with Koehler's mortars and Crofton's 14-inch gun bearing the brunt. Ill fortune cost the gallant Scouts dearly even though Boudreau kept them under shelter all day. In early afternoon a heavy projectile struck the bombproof tunnel at an L where it was weakest; the shell crashed through, and burst with a high order of detonation amid a group of men lined up near a dispensary for yellow-fever shots, killing twenty-eight outright and wounding another forty-six, of whom three died later, a frightful disaster for so small a garrison.

Drum had no one killed or seriously injured, but a shell striking a seam on one of the turrets opened a crack four inches wide and eighteen inches long. Its crew hastily welded a piece of iron over the slit to keep out fragments, and fortunately no shell struck that spot again. Unnumbered hits had whittled away eight feet of concrete from alongside the upper and lower casemates of Battery Roberts, and every square foot of their insides was dented and torn. Two duds striking one of the 6-inch guns dented the barrel just enough to make firing the piece unsafe. Atop the fort the two 3-inch antiaircraft guns jacked to the concrete deck were blasted away, but surprisingly the 60-inch searchlight with its steel mirror still was repairable.

Drum's men proved tough, for despite the severe concussion and continual rocking of the "ship" from the hits outside, Sam Madison's Battery E had no cases of combat fatigue. As former Private First Class Charles A. Cobb put it years later, these were "tough guys" who prided themselves on being hard and not showing fear. Cobb himself was wounded slightly when a shell fragment bounced down the barrel of one of the 14-inch guns, came out the open breech, and struck him on the arm; but he carried on. With others he also courted death by repeatedly going outside his turret to help recalibrate the rifles after hits on the tubes had knocked them out of alignment.

As ordered on March 22 the Hayakawa Detachment abruptly ceased fire and packed its equipment to go to Bataan. The reconnaissance regiment also pulled out, leaving forty-five bancas that it had collected for a landing attempt lying on the beach. Colonel Boudreau destroyed them later with his beach defense 75's. The harbor forts had another breather, but not for long; two days later, on March 24, the bombers came back. General Homma was beginning his final offensive to conquer Bataan and the Rock.

9 ☆ The Fall of Bataan

FROM mid-January to mid-March the antiaircraft crews on Corregidor had had few targets except for the elusive Photo Joe, who was too fast and agile for them to hit. One day they had nearly fired on a flight of eighteen "heavy bombers" until someone identified the target at the last moment as high flying pelicans. While on the alert near their guns and instruments the crews played poker and bridge. Others enthusiastically rolled the "galloping dominoes," although it probably occurred to many that it made little difference whether they won or lost. At Chicago, Corporal Richard W. Bartz opened the "Bartz Memorial Library" with books donated by the chaplain. Several men of Chicago Battery had harmonicas, another a guitar, which, with a jug added, sufficed for a "mountain music" orchestra.

Meanwhile, Colonel Val Foster and several other officers, knowing well that the Japanese would be back, had concocted a scheme they hoped would give the enemy a rude jolt. The high-angle mortars of Batteries Geary and Craighill could loft a shell to the altitude of the Japanese planes, and it seemed theoretically feasible to explode a salvo reasonably close to an attacking flight. Sergeant Hopkins was quite taken with the idea. "It is eminently practicable," he wrote in his notebook. "What a surprise for the Japs if ever 600 lbs. of TNT goes off under their whole flight of planes! And if four or eight guns fire at once!"

Hopkins' enthusiasm was justified, but when Craighill at Hughes fired a test round with a 3-inch mechanical fuze installed, it failed to detonate and nearly hit Fort Drum instead. Either the primer charge in the fuze was too weak or the shock of the discharge had failed to arm it. The powder time train fuze would not work either, and the problem of getting a shell to burst remained unsolved.

In their second aerial offensive the Japanese pursued the same general strategy as in their first: to strike Corregidor a powerful enough blow "to demoralize the enemy" (perhaps they thought Wainwright less gritty than MacArthur) preliminary to a renewed ground offensive on Bataan. On March 21 at Clark Field, now the main Japanese air base, Army and Navy staff officers of two recently arrived Army air regiments, the 60th and 62nd, and of two Navy squadrons, planned a joint attack. They would hit Corregidor hard between March 25 and 28 with sixty Army "Sallys" and twenty-four twin-engine Navy "Bettys," fast new Mitsubishi G4MI's. After the 28th most of the bombers would shift their attention to Bataan in preparation for the ground offensive, with one squadron continuing to bomb Corregidor by day and night to maintain the pressure.

Early on the twenty-fourth the "Sallys" roared from Clark Field and swung over Corregidor at 9:23 A.M., alternating their attacks with the "Bettys" until 4:20 in the afternoon. The short distance enabled each plane to fly two or three missions that day. Prudently, they stayed very high, from 8,350 to 9,150 yards, forcing Colonel Chase to rely on Boston and Chicago with their mechanical fuzes for most of the firing. The two batteries claimed six planes, and although the Japanese recorded no losses, ground observers on the Rock saw two bombers disintegrate in mid-air. The 60th's revised total of aircraft claimed rose to sixty-four planes, a respectable sum even if divided twice or thrice. Damage was not great although seventy-one tons of bombs fell. One gun of Battery Wheeler took a hit on the racer but was repairable. Another bomb hit the north end of Topside Barracks and exploded the ammunition stored there since January, demolishing that end of the barracks. Casualties were light.

That night at 11:15 P.M. the Japanese tried their first night raid, using three medium bombers of the 60th Air Regiment to drop incendiaries in Cheney ravine. Subsequent night attacks failed, for the big 60-inch searchlights of Batteries Albany and Erie brilliantly illuminated the planes, confusing the pilots and blinding the bombardiers, forcing them to salvo their loads at random. The antiaircraft guns fired but seldom hit, although Chicago optimistically claimed one night flyer.

The next day, March 25, the Japanese struck in daylight with about fifty bombers and repeated this performance through the twenty-eighth. Thereafter the scale of the attacks sharply diminished until April 2, when all planes shifted to Bataan to support the opening of the ground offensive. By the last two days of the heavy attacks, the twenty-seventh and twenty-eighth, the Japanese had developed such a healthy respect for the 60th that they raised their bombing altitudes to as high as 10,000 yards (30,000 feet), from which their accuracy became so poor the bombardiers frequently missed the island altogether. Even so, the 60th's gunners picked off one bomber at 27,300 feet, a remarkable achievement for optically directed 3-inch antiaircraft.

In view of this Japanese caution the gun crews had to rub their eyes at 5:00 P.M. on March 30 when two "Sallys" approached Corregidor at only 22,500 feet. They bided their time, and then all the batteries fired at once, shooting down one of the planes in a brusque fire action that lasted only seconds. The other plane, smoking and losing height, disappeared over Bataan, as hundreds of watchers on the Rock cheered frantically. "The blazing plane did just like they do in the movies," wrote Rolly Ames. "It twirled like a blazing toy and fell in the North Channel between Bottomside and Cabcaben Point. What a sight! Never knew murder could be so pleasant." For the Japanese it was quite unpleasant. Excited chattering on their voice radio circuits immediately afterward indicated an unusual concern. Scratch one incautious party of sight-seeing, high-level visitors?

In terms of military effectiveness this second Japanese air offensive failed as completely as had the first. Corregidor had suffered little

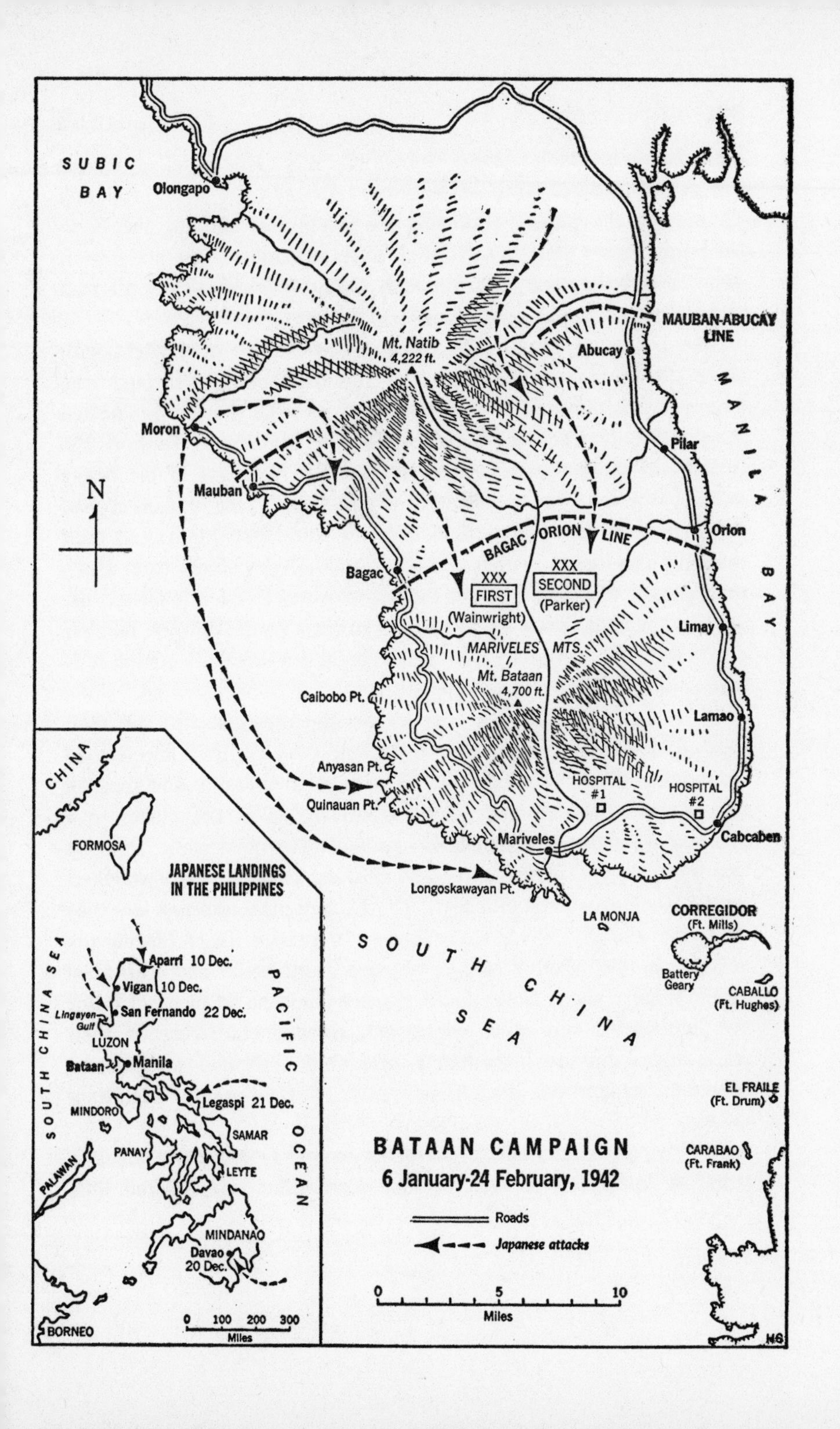
SUBIC BAY
Olongapo
MAUBAN-ABUCAY LINE
Mt. Natib
4,222 ft.
Abucay
MANILA BAY
Moron
Pilar
Mauban
N
Orion
BAGAC ORION LINE
XXX
SECOND
(Parker)
XXX
FIRST
(Wainwright)
Bagac
Limay
MARIVELES MTS.
Mt. Bataan
4,700 ft.
Caibobo Pt.
Lamao
Anyasan Pt.
Quinauan Pt.
HOSPITAL
#1
HOSPITAL
#2
Cabcaben
Mariveles
Longoskawayan Pt.
LA MONJA
CORREGIDOR
(Ft. Mills)
Battery
Geary
CABALLO
(Ft. Hughes)
SOUTH CHINA SEA
EL FRAILE
(Ft. Drum)
CARABAO
(Ft. Frank)
BATAAN CAMPAIGN
6 January-24 February, 1942
Roads
Japanese attacks
0
5
10
Miles
CHINA
FORMOSA
JAPANESE LANDINGS
IN THE PHILIPPINES
SOUTH CHINA SEA
Aparri 10 Dec.
Vigan 10 Dec.
Lingayen Gulf
San Fernando 22 Dec.
LUZON
Bataan
Manila
PACIFIC OCEAN
Legaspi 21 Dec.
MINDORO
SAMAR
PANAY
LEYTE
PALAWAN
MINDANAO
Davao
20 Dec.
BORNEO
0
100
200
300
Miles

additional harm. Chicago, for example, was hit directly on March 26 and 28 by missiles landing within the gun square. Nobody was hurt although the height finder was knocked out of calibration by the shock of one bomb landing ten feet behind it and another four feet ahead of it. Rolly Ames's gunners had had the unusual satisfaction of seeing their shells destroy one of the planes that had bombed them. They knew it to be the culprit, for they had seen it drop its load and had tracked its screeching bombs into their battery area.

Once again the 60th gunners had saved the Rock. Unless and until the Japanese could attack from lower altitudes, aiming directly for such key installations as the Fort Mills power plant, which was miraculously still intact, serious military damage could not be inflicted. But that time was coming—and soon.

By the beginning of March the food shortage on Bataan had become a much deadlier foe than the Japanese. MacArthur's delay in December in ordering Plan Orange put into effect, and the consequent inability of his quartermasters to stock Bataan, had led to a situation that was beginning to seriously debilitate the troops. From January 5 the men had been losing weight steadily on half rations and had been supplementing their slender meals with whatever they could forage. By early March most of the carabao roaming the Bataan Peninsula had been found and slaughtered, the horses of the 26th Cavalry had met a like fate, and even the ugly iguana lizards were growing scarce as the men hunted them down. Rice—very little of it—bolstered by a bit of canned salmon, comprised the meager fare. The quinine supply was low, and the malaria rate already was disastrously high.

Several coast artillery batteries were on Bataan acting as antiaircraft, coast defense, and field artillery units. Some had been withdrawn from Fort Wint at the mouth of Subic Bay; others had been assigned from Corregidor to bolster the defenses in accord with the Orange Plan. All suffered equally with their infantry brethren.

Captain Aaron A. Abston's gunners of Battery Globe, claimants of fifteen enemy aircraft while defending the Mariveles area, took to foraging when their victuals ran short. "I still wonder," muses Corporal Clarence M. Graham, "who put the hairy monkey hand in our monkey soup." Captain Robert A. Lawler's Scouts of Battery B of the 92nd CA were serving as heavy field artillery gunners in support of the II Corps. By early March Lawler was delirious with malaria much of the time, and only four of more than a hundred men in his battery had the strength to lift the ninety-eight-pound shells to the breeches of the 155's. One was Lawler's husky executive officer, blond Lieutenant Ed Kalbfleish, who had to act as gunner himself.

Food and quinine: the "Battling Bastards" needed these more than reinforcements, more than ammunition. But their only outside contact was with Corregidor, and the Rock had little to spare.

The Corregidor garrison had also gone on half rations after January 5, eating but two meals a day. Some units managed to supplement this ration with food recovered from barges and sunken ships scattered about the island's shores. A barge load of dried fruit helped to balance the diet, as did wheat germ mixed with rice. Until the end most of the units received occasional small amounts of coffee, ham, powdered milk, and jam, items which helped greatly to sustain morale. The marines discovered a rich prize, a stock of whiskey aboard President Quezon's half-sunken yacht, the *Casiana,* as well as aboard a barge, labeled the *Barleycorn,* which was sunk in ten feet of water. Many and mysterious were the deals that followed until the MP's caught on.

The diet was far from adequate. Although much less slowly than their comrades on Bataan, the hard-working men lost weight steadily, especially after a three-eighths ration went into effect on March 1. One quartermaster officer described his supper the next day as consisting of ". . . one slice of bread, one slice corn beef, cup of tea, rice, and that my friend is what we now call a good chow—about a third ration." An exotic item had found its way into the menu earlier, on February 14, when six mules were butchered and served to the garrison. "Strangely," wrote the officer, "it went over in a big way."

A shortage of cigarettes caused more gripes than the food. By March 10 the ration was down to a pack a week.

When General Wainwright took over in mid-March as supreme commander from General MacArthur, he hoped at first to revive his predecessor's plan to smuggle food to Bataan from the depot at Cebu. A quick review of past operations, however, showed that the dispatching of additional coasters would be suicidal against a strengthened Japanese blockade. Wainwright therefore proposed to MacArthur, now in Melbourne, a plan for a co-ordinated bombing attack and supply run to disrupt the enemy's blockade long enough to bring in a convoy. His idea was that MacArthur would dispatch a force of bombers to still-unoccupied Del Monte field on Mindanao. From there the planes would mount two days of attacks on the Japanese small craft guarding the key passages between Cebu and Manila Bay and also blast airfields, including the major Japanese base at Clark Field. In the confusion, Wainwright hoped, a convoy of coastal vessels could slip through from Cebu.

Days passed and no aircraft arrived at Del Monte from Australia. To mount even a modest attack force was totally beyond the capacity of the Army Air Force. From Washington, Chief of Staff Marshall offered what encouragement he could. "My hourly concern," he cabled Wainwright in trying to cheer him up, "is what we can do to help you. . . ." He approved of Wainwright's plan and ordered additional measures: airlift of quinine to Mindanao; use of fleet submarines for food shipments (the Navy reluctantly consenting); and the dispatch of a large, fast ship laden with balanced rations directly across the Pacific from Hawaii. But to no avail; *nothing* could be done either from Washington or Melbourne to relieve the defenders of Bataan and Corregidor.

In late March, knowing that Bataan's resistance now was desperately limited, Wainwright began shipping food from Corregidor to Bataan. But he dared not send too much, for extravagant distribution of the Rock's foodstuffs would only shorten the length of over-all resistance of his command without appreciably aiding the Bataan defenders. As it was, his calculation ran close; on its surrender Corregidor had but six weeks of foodstuffs left at the three-eighths ration allowance, an amount that would have sustained Bataan for about a week.

Japanese combat strength revived in inverse proportion to Filipino-American decline. The High Command in Tokyo, disturbed at Homma's failure to break through on Bataan, agreed to refill the depleted ranks of his 16th Division and the 65th Brigade, and also to dispatch from Shanghai the entire 4th Infantry Division and from Central China a detachment of four thousand troops from the 21st Division under Major General Kameichiro Nagano. Assured of these reinforcements, Homma's 14th Army Headquarters began drafting plans for a powerful new offensive.

After a lull lasting from mid-February the Japanese struck again on April 3. Behind a thunderous artillery and air barrage, they easily broke through Wainwright's II Corps on the Manila Bay side of the front, partly because the defenders found themselves too weak and ill to adjust their positions in the jungles. Similarly, though hit not as hard, his I Corps, on the China Sea side of the peninsula, could not move to their comrades' aid. By the next day the retreat was becoming a rout, and four days later, by April 8, all organized resistance virtually had come to an end. One of Corregidor's long-range 12-inch batteries, Hearn, fired road interdiction when the enemy neared, but without effect. As the Japanese approached Cabcaben, Bataan's commander, Major General Edward King, sadly concluded he had no alternative to surrender. Thus 79,500 men, the largest force in American military history to succumb to an enemy, put down their arms. The "Battling Bastards" drained their cup of gall under worse circumstances than the prewar pessimists had expected. Now the garrison of the Rock must accept the proffered cup.

Already General Moore had suffered a sharp disappointment, for the Philippine Division had failed to escape and reinforce him. When it became clear that Bataan was falling, he had taken up with General Wainwright's USFIP staff the withdrawal of the division in accord with the Orange War Plan. Unfortunately, issuance of the necessary orders bogged down in the staff (a conspicuous point of weakness throughout the campaign), and the American 31st and Philippine Scout 45th and 57th Infantry Regiments became so enmeshed in the confused fighting they could not get free. Consequently, the 4th Marines failed to receive the reinforcements they so badly needed for beach defense, although it is open to question how much the sick and starved Bataan troops could have helped.

In extracting units under his own command Moore was more successful. Batteries Globe and Erie, manning 3-inch guns and searchlights respectively, escaped, although with only a portion of their equipment. Battery Cebu's Scouts of the 91st CA, under Captain Jack Gulick, the son of the former Coast Artillery chief, also manning 3-inch guns, made it to safety, but Lawler's B 91st passed into captivity with their 155's.

Fortunately, the nurses from the two general hospitals escaped by an eyelash what easily could have been a fate worse than death, a fate many of their British sisters-in-mercy had suffered at Hong Kong and Singapore. Alerted on the evening of April 8 by Colonel Wibb E. Cooper, the chief surgeon on Corregidor, the young ladies clambered into trucks and witnessed nightmarish scenes and delays as ammunition dumps crackled and exploded close along the road. Starving men begging them for food were all the more pitiable, since, as Mrs. Bruce Walcher (then Lieutenant Peggy Greenwalt) recalls, ". . . one knew that they were going to be taken prisoner the next day." At about 5:00 A.M., after a trip punctuated by numerous halts, she and her fellow nurses from Hospital No. 2 arrived at Mariveles, only to find the expected boats not there. These had left a few minutes before with the nurses from Hospital No. 1. Lieutenant Josie Nesbitt, the chief nurse, went back to headquarters to phone Corregidor for more, while the miserable and weary girls huddled under what shelter they could find.

At about 10:00 A.M. a lone engineer launch operated by a Negro soldier arrived to circle and pick up a few of the nurses at a time—because of the bombing—until all, Filipino and American, had managed to crowd aboard. "Do you think we'll make it to Corregidor, Josie?" Peggy Greenwalt asked. "Well," her boss replied, "God has been looking after us so far." And He continued to favor them. Although Japanese planes were overhead much of the time, they did not strafe the launch, which arrived at the North Dock after a three-hour trip delayed by much dodging and circling in the North Channel.

One of several vessels the nurses' launch passed was Commander Alan McCracken's gunboat *Mindanao,* which had a boat out rescuing swimmers and survivors in smaller craft near the shore. By early afternoon it had sixty aboard. At 3:30 P.M. Japanese artillery began firing on the water from the tip of Bataan, and the *Mindanao,* "shooting in all directions," pulled out around the headland of Corregidor, accompanied by a tug, which took a hit near the funnel, and a score of other craft. Arriving in the south harbor after dark, McCracken outfitted the sixty half-starved soldiers in the dress whites of his crew and sent them ashore. Visiting Tunnel Queen later that same evening, he found that the fight at sea was over for himself and his men. He, his executive officer, Lieutenant David Nash, and all of his crew, together with the crews of the other two gunboats, the *Oahu* and *Luzon,* had been assigned to shore duty at Fort Hughes. There they lived—as Lieutenant Nash disgustedly put it—a "helluva life" amid dust, flies, and dirt for the remainder of the siege, courageously firing Battery Craighill's four long-range mortars.

Altogether, about 2,300 soldiers, sailors, and civilians, Filipino and American, managed to flee the caldron on Bataan. Several small noncombat service units totaling about five hundred men came en masse without authorization. About 1,800 others crossed the two miles of the North Channel by small boat, raft, bamboo pole, and swimming. Not many were trained combat soldiers, and although they were assigned to the beach defenses and various construction projects, most of them were, as General Moore has put it, "a dead load." Moreover, they brought to the Rock the dread cerebral malaria which had taken a heavy toll on Bataan and soon would cost the Japanese dear. Some of the more dispirited drifted to Malinta Tunnel to become a severe disciplinary and morale problem. As Lieutenant Maude Williams, a former civilian nurse serving in the hospital, wrote:

> These men, whether Filipinos or Americans, were frankly tired of war. Gaunt, unshaven, dirty, wrapped in sullen despair, they squatted silently in the tunnel curbs by day. By night they stretched out on their scraps of blanket or on the bare cement, across the paths of trucks and cars. . . . Yet it was impossible to clear them out for they had a certain tired stubbornness which defied command or insult. . . .

To the awed garrison of the Rock the night of April 8 and 9 was unforgettable. Gigantic explosions, casting up flame and vivid colors thousands of feet into the air, rent the sky as demolition teams put the torch to the big fuel and ammunition dumps on Bataan. Nature added to this man-made hell, jolting southern Bataan and Corregidor just after midnight with a sharp earthquake. The next morning the artillery observers at M Prime West, peering through the smoke and mist, spotted long columns of troops in blue fatigue uniforms marching northeast in a column of fours along the Cabcaben road. The "March of Death" was underway to the hell-camps of O'Donnell and Cabanatuan.

10 ☆ Corregidor at Bay

WITH BATAAN in their hands the Japanese lost no time in shifting their attention to the Rock. The reckless crew of a battery of 75's rushed to a paddy field near Cabcaben at 4:00 P.M. on April 9 to set up their pieces in plain view of the Rock's observers. They opened fire before Battery Kysor's 155's could get the range; but the Scout gunners corrected quickly and flung men and guns into the air with a direct hit. Unfortunately, several American prisoners forced to remain near the Japanese guns were killed and injured, but Colonel Bunker was right when he called the episode ". . . a crucial point in our operations—a milestone." The test anticipated since 1908 was at hand: How would Corregidor fare against batteries located less than three miles away in defiladed positions?

The first two days were "no contest." Japanese fire was light and, in order to give the Japanese time to clear Bataan of its thousands of prisoners of war, General Wainwright would not allow Corregidor's guns to reply. The exasperated Paul Bunker exclaimed, "Haven't the brass learned *anything?* They pulled the same boner months ago, when we wanted to interdict the Cavite roads and thus delay the Japs. . . . The Termites [his term for staff officers in the tunnel] later squalled when the Jap artillery opened up."

In truth, Wainwright's order, which stemmed from his sense of compassion, made little difference to the battle and doubtless saved lives. Moreover, after permitting searching fire to begin on April 12, he continued to insist that great care be taken to spare the two thousand American and six thousand Filipino patients still in Bataan

Hospital No. 2, which the Japanese had completely ringed with artillery. Maps were issued clearly marking the hospital, and so far as is known the only loss of life occurred on April 22 when several stray rounds struck in the wards and mess hall, killing or wounding a score of patients.

During the several days it took to emplace his artillery, General Homma, who was anxious to take Corregidor as quickly as possible —probably because he feared, with reason, that Tokyo would relieve him if he didn't—relied on his bombers to carry the offensive. And, at first, the Rock fared well against the renewed attack. The 60th and 62nd Air Regiments, supported by the two squadrons of naval "Bettys," roared in on the morning of April 9 for what their air crews thought was "a very successful and effective attack." In truth they did little damage, aside from disabling temporarily the controlled mine field with a hit on the mining casemate. Still flying very high to escape the 60th CA's sharpshooters, they continued the pace until the twelfth when General Homma shifted them to targets in the central Philippines. One squadron continued to attack daily until the twenty-eighth, yet only after the Japanese artillery had put Chicago and Denver virtually out of commission did they reduce their bombing altitudes.

On April 13 hope surged briefly through the Rock's garrison. The word spread quickly: an American plane, a B-17, had been seen over Corregidor! Perhaps the long-awaited convoy, with a carrier, was just over the horizon! Perhaps gleaming new P-40's soon would swoop down to land on Kindley Field, which Company A of the 803rd Engineers was laboring hard to lengthen to four thousand feet, filling in bomb and shell holes as rapidly as the Japanese made them. Confirmation seemed to come—in part—from the San Francisco radio that evening which boasted that American planes had "counter-attacked" in the Philippines.

It was true that an American plane had overflown the Rock. Ten B-25 medium bombers and three B-17's had landed the day before at Del Monte, Mindanao, from which the B-25's had flown to attack shipping and the heavy bombers to attack Clark Field. The six remaining P-40's and P-35's at Del Monte had strafed the Japanese fighter squadron based nearby at Davao. But only General Wainwright and a few staff officers knew the bitter truth: the striking force was the one promised weeks before, to make possible the blockade run of a convoy laden with food from Cebu. It had arrived much too late. Bataan was gone; Cebu had fallen on the tenth; and by this time, the thirteenth, its warehouses with their once-precious stores lay in smoking embers, fired to keep them out of Japanese hands. The air strikes, therefore, had been no more than a pinprick, a minor nuisance to the Japanese.

In the days that followed, Corregidor's garrison paid less and less attention to the many bombers overhead, not because they had become inured to them, but because they had learned to respect the Japanese artillery so much more. Recalls Lieutenant Colonel John McM. Gulick, "I have never seen anything like it except the movies of the U.S. pre-landing bombardments. We dreaded the Japanese artillery much more than their aerial effort." Wrote Colonel Stephen M. Mellnik, a single day's heavy shelling did ". . . more damage than all the bombing put together."

For the artillery bombardment of Corregidor, the Japanese assembled their first team, the best in His Imperial Majesty's Army. An intelligence regiment of 675 men arrived with flash and sound gear capable of giving the enemy gunners precise ranges to observed targets. They were supplemented by a squadron of observation planes and the 1st Balloon Company of 150 men with an observation balloon. When the disgusted Americans sighted this obsolete but effective contrivance rising over Bataan on April 10, they dubbed it "Peeping Tom," and ardently wished for a P-40 to shoot it down. Altogether, before the campaign ended, the Japanese massed a total of 116 guns in eighteen batteries. These included forty-six 150 mm. guns and howitzers, twenty-eight 100 mm. guns and howitzers, and thirty-two 75's; but the weapons that caused by far the most damage were the same ten 240 mm. howitzers used earlier by Colonel Hayakawa against Forts Drum and Frank. Although the 75's and some of the

100's began firing sooner, most of the weapons did not begin until April 12. Probably because of the lengthy interval needed to get them ready, the 240's did not open up until April 18.

The first real artillery duel developed on April 12. That day "Peeping Tom" rose early and the atmosphere soon reverberated from the bursts of Japanese shells and bombs. Battery Geary, now under the command of Captain Thomas W. Davis, III, delivered a prompt and devastating reply after Major Harry Julian and Captain Harry Schenck had spotted some of the Japanese gun flashes with their ranging gear. The great 670-pound mortar projectiles smashed first on an artillery concentration near Lokanin Point, destroying a battery, then on another battery and an ammunition dump, and finally on a group of tanks of the Japanese 7th Tank Regiment, which—perhaps deceived by the lack of American fire hitherto—had brazenly parked in plain sight of American observers. The big shells burst squarely among them, setting several afire and scattering the survivors.

As the morning wore on, more and more Japanese guns came into action and the issue of the battle turned. Inexperience told on the crews of Bunker's 6-inch and 155 mm. batteries. They were unaccustomed to "live" targets and lacked equipment as sophisticated as the Japanese flash and sound gear. Their officers had difficulty making the necessary range corrections, allowing the Japanese to hit first. This drove the American and Scout gunners to cover, silenced the guns, and resulted in some loss of life. Two men perished at Battery Kysor (two 155's) and others elsewhere. Direct hits on mounts disabled many pieces for extended periods. Henceforth, only heroic work by the Harbor Defense Ordnance Department under Colonel Edwin F. Barry kept the "concrete artillery" operating. After eating his tough carabao dinner that evening, Colonel Bunker penciled ruefully in his diary, "Our guns and emplacements are very vulnerable. It is not going to be so good when the Japs start using against us those ten 240 mm. guns which, we are told, are coming down from the north."

Even before the 240's arrived, Batteries Grubbs (two 10-inch),

Morrison (two 6-inch), James (four 3-inch), Rock Point (two 155 mm.), and Hamilton (two 155 mm.) all were knocked out, greatly reducing the firepower Bunker could direct against Bataan. Kysor, too, was shelled out, with five killed and fifteen wounded from a hit that flipped one of its two 155's onto its back. Some weapons of these batteries were repaired later, but their crews could not freely use them. The Japanese would immediately drive the gunners to cover with a hail of accurate counterbattery as soon as they opened fire. The 12-inch long-range guns of Smith and Hearn, standing naked and vulnerable on their great circular "bull's-eyes" of concrete, lay hidden under great piles of brush, silent and useless for counterbattery, although unmolested by the enemy, who seemed unaware of their location. Geary continued firing, but its mortars had begun to run low on instantaneously fuzed projectiles and had to be used sparingly. In addition, as the Japanese began using howitzers, direct hits in its pits became frequent and casualties mounted.

Craighill's 12-inch mortars on Fort Hughes provided substantial help, as the battery's designers had hoped, but also drew fierce counterbattery whenever they fired. Only one weapon was permanently knocked out, from a hit in the upper pit that stripped the trunnion bolts holding down the mortar. One man was seriously injured by a shell fragment that cut his throat. The *Mindanao* sailors manning the mortars performed heroically, supervised by Sergeant Joe West, a dried-up wisp of a man, whom Colonel Valentine P. Foster, then Fort Hughes commander, describes as ". . . that rare type of older N.C.O. who knew his duties and did them well." At first the sailors could get off six rounds before Japanese fire smothered them, then five, then four, and by the end of the siege just one. Yet even a single shell was often effective, for it would sometimes catch enemy troops in the open. Even so, the duel between Craighill and the enemy was tragically unequal; like all the other batteries, its gunners could be seen but could not see. Only turreted Drum with the great 14-inch rifles of Battery Wilson, and casemated Monja on Corregidor with its two 155 mm. could fire unimpeded.

Unfortunately, Monja at extreme traverse could bear only to the middle of Mariveles Harbor, not far enough to hit the Japanese batteries near Cabcaben. Still, Captain Frank W. Bovee and his Scout gunners had plenty of targets. Each weapon fired at least fifteen hundred rounds, and toward the end of the siege the gun tubes were so worn the crews could see their shells tumbling in flight. Monja was immune because one of its guns was mounted in a casemate and the other in a defiladed cut. Japanese shells struck the cliff above and the water below but could not reach the gun positions. Had all of the north shore batteries been converted to this type of installation—as had been proposed in peacetime, but not carried out for lack of funds—the drama of the siege might well have had a different script, though not a different outcome.

Despite the frustration of engaging in an unequal duel, the Rock's garrison did not lose spirit. Morale sagged somewhat—less at the batteries than in the tunnel—but all performed their duties. The men's pride showed vividly on April 16 when a Japanese shell fragment cut the halyard on the hundred-foot flagpole before the ruins of post headquarters on the Topside parade ground; the Stars and Stripes began to fall, in "Skinny" Wainwright's words, "slowly, terribly," to the ground. To many soldiers of the later GI Army such an incident might have been regarded as a bad omen or humiliation but not something to risk one's neck about. But to Captain Arthur E. Huff and two men from his Boston Battery of the 60th it was unthinkable that the colors should touch the ground. They raced from cover, gathered in the flag as it fell, repaired the halyard on the spot, and sent the flag back up.

For the most part the Japanese bombing and shelling did not cause heavy casualties during April. Even open foxholes provided a large measure of safety, as did bomb craters. Those who stayed under cover were fairly secure, even when shells or bombs exploded close by, but he who panicked, jumped up, and ran became an excellent candidate for the Fort Mills cemetery below Kindley Field. Many men had close calls. While Corporal Myron H. Hayes of Battery

Cheney was in a machine-gun pit a large bomb landed alongside him without doing serious harm. Also without injury, Sergeant Don V. Hart of Battery Wheeler was blown thirty feet while walking from Geary back to his unit, although he was wounded four times on other occasions during the siege.

Several tragic episodes caused most of April's losses. Against orders a group of Filipino gunners of Battery A of the 1st Philippine Army CA, manning Battery James, had dug a large unreinforced tunnel into the cliffside to their rear. Taking shelter there instead of in the battery's concrete bombproofs, forty-two suffocated on April 15 when heavy Japanese fire collapsed the cliff overhanging the tunnel mouth. Chaplain Herman Baumann, who ministered to them, recalls that when rescuers dug through to the men, they found them sitting in natural positions along the sides of the tunnel. "They looked asleep, but they were dead."

The next day, on April 16, a shell burst in the dining hall of Headquarters Battery of the 60th. This explosion killed five and wounded fourteen, including Lieutenant Louis P. Lutich, who lost a leg. It also injured Corregidor's senior citizen, Enrico Romero Martinez, who had come to the Philippines from Spain in 1896 with reinforcements sent to fight Aguinaldo's guerrillas. He had joined the Americans as an interpreter after Dewey's conquest, and since 1905 had been on the Rock as a construction engineer with the post engineers. He remembered them all; correspondent John Hersey writes:

> He could tell you about every American general who had been out there—about Jack Pershing, about the good father, Leonard Wood, about MacArthur the older one, and MacArthur the younger one. He could tell you about the time when Corregidor was just a grassy island, and about the first time the first battery fired its guns at a target towed by old Captain Charley Olsen, the transport master.

Now Martinez lay wounded by a shell fragment, with hundreds of others, inside the bowels of the Rock he knew so well.

The hospital held more than wounded men; it also had malarial cases induced by infected men who had come over when Bataan fell.

Liberal applications of quinine reduced the threat, and by the end of April the danger of an epidemic had passed.

So had a danger of another sort—for the Japanese. Their combat losses in breaking through on Bataan had been very light, but they had been gravely concerned in early April how to slip their barges needed for the amphibious landing past the fortresses' big guns. On the eleventh, evidently less concerned than the Army, the Navy in broad daylight brazenly tried to sail through the North Channel into Manila Bay a half-dozen forty-two-foot barges. Although—in Colonel Bunker's critical opinion—the 155 mm. and 6-inch batteries were slow in reacting, they damaged at least two badly and turned back the others. This incident angered General Homma's headquarters, which feared that the Navy's rashness had lessened its chances of slipping through the barges of its own 22nd and 23rd Engineer Regiments.

On the night of April 14 Homma tested out Bunker's observers by passing through a few under cover of an artillery barrage fired to drown out the sound of their motors. This scheme evidently worked, for the American records and diaries show no indication that they were seen or heard. Most of the remainder slipped through uneventfully in the same manner on the nights of the sixteenth and seventeenth.

However, the Japanese had used a tactic on the fourteenth which should have tipped off the Americans. They began shelling the Rock's searchlights the instant they came on, so heavily as to arouse General Moore at H Station and Colonel Bunker at C-1. Bunker decided to test the Japanese reflexes; he ordered his No. 1 light flicked on for only fifteen seconds, with its operator racing full tilt down the bombproof tunnel for cover as soon as he had snapped off the light. Yet before he could turn the corner into the bombproof L twenty yards away, where the searchlight recessed when not in use, Japanese shells landed close by, damaging the light. "Which proved," Bunker concluded, "that the Japs had their guns loaded, laid, and men at the lanyards with orders to shoot instantly when the light showed."

Even had Bunker asked himself why, and somehow managed to

use his lights that night, an incident on the twentieth, after the Japanese had ended their special anti-searchlight alert, strongly suggests that his gunners could not have stopped the passage of the barges. At about 10:00 P.M. the Japanese slipped through a boat towing a pair of others. Batteries Monja and Sunset fired and missed, and an utterly disgusted Bunker wrote, "That was that!" He discovered the reason the next morning after calling on the carpet Colonel Joseph P. Kohn, commander of the 91st CA, and his executive officer, Lieutenant Colonel Floyd E. Mitchell. The artillery spotters had first sighted the boats visually in the moonpath without the aid of searchlights, but when the gun pointers tried to pick them up through their telescopes, the "execrable" quality of the old optical sights of the 155's prevented them from seeing anything. The No. 1 light, which had been repaired, chose that moment to suffer a power failure, and Numbers 3 and 4 were so slow in getting on the target that the barges soon pulled out of range of the No. 3 light. In the meantime the 155's tried to "range in" on the intersection of the two searchlight beams with "rotten results." Barrage fire was impossible because so many guns were out of action, "so the Japs sailed calmly past," lamented Bunker. "We were helpless!"

This time it was a tow, but next time it could as easily be a flotilla of landing craft headed for the Rock. What then? George Moore was not pleased by the prospect and neither was "Skinny" Wainwright. They therefore arranged to set up two "roving lights," a pair of spare antiaircraft searchlights manned by crews from Battery Erie of the 60th. Each light was allocated a series of positions, with its commander under orders to man one at nightfall and pull back under cover at daybreak. With their aid Bunker's men were more successful. On the night of April 22 they illuminated Hornos Point so frequently that enemy movement was impossible. But it was already too late; the landing barges were in the bay.

On April 18 Paul Bunker did not need a report from his intelligence officer to tell him that the dreaded Japanese 240's had finally gone into action. Thunderous blasts from the vicinity of Battery Geary told him that Homma had thrown his Sunday punch. These weapons, he knew, posed a deadly menace to every installation on Corregidor and Fort Hughes except the Malinta Tunnel, and some officers were worried about that. Even the seventy feet of rock over the hospital laterals, they feared, might cave in under the impact of the four-hundred-pound projectiles.

Colonel William C. (Bill) Braly, Moore's active and intelligent operations officer, realized at once that their arrival doomed all of the fixed installations. He therefore suggested and Moore quickly approved establishing several single-gun "roving" 155 batteries. A half-dozen guns were withdrawn from their fixed installations, hitched to prime movers, and assigned a series of positions defiladed from Bataan. Each was designated by the officer in command. Braly's idea was that a "roving" battery would emplace its gun at night and fire counterbattery the following day. Experience quickly showed that it could usually get away between twenty and fifty rounds before the Japanese could figure out its approximate location and begin a "search" for it. Then the crew would take to foxholes and sweat out the enemy barrage.

Although the work was dangerous, casualties were light among the Scouts from the 91st and 92nd Regiments who formed the crews. One unit, for example, would set up its piece, yell, "Count your men, Tojo," and then blaze away. "How they kept from being blown off the island, I'll never understand," writes C. W. Montgomery, then a machine gunner with Mobile Battery.

The chief drawback of the roving batteries was the relatively flat trajectory of the 155 mm. gun. With an elevation of about 30 degrees, a 155 could not touch the reverse slopes of the deeper ravines on Bataan. For reasons best known to themselves, however, the Japanese had placed many batteries alongside the roads near Cabcaben, where they had foliage cover but were not in defilade. To reach the better-protected Japanese weapons the Scouts needed 155 howitzers with a high trajectory, or better yet, those twelve 240 mm.

howitzers that had turned back in mid-ocean on February 22, 1922, after the United States had decided to sign the Five-Power Treaty.

Japanese use of 240's led to some epic artillery duels, duels in which the roving batteries hotly engaged. A mighty exchange occurred on April 22 when the Japanese opened up on their favorite target, Battery Geary, and used the occasion to drop several additional rounds squarely at the entrance to Bunker's C-1 tunnel. "So we got mad," the doughty Colonel wrote, "and started our first dress rehearsal of our Retaliation Shoot!" This carefully planned affair was designed to cause the Japanese the maximum possible annoyance and damage. The great rifles of Drum lofted ten 1,660-pound shells into Cabcaben; Geary fired ten 670-pounders at two different targets; the sailors manning Craighill let loose ten of the same at a Japanese battery spotted south of Cabcaben; and two roving batteries fired fifty ninety-eight-pound projectiles apiece at still another Japanese battery. Then everyone ducked, expecting a counterbarrage. But the Japanese were disinclined to play games, probably because 14th Army Headquarters had not included such sport in the daily fire plan.

On April 24, however, it evidently had. When Bunker's men tried a "serenade" just after dinner, during the normally quiet period of the day, hoping to catch the Japanese gunners napping in their hammocks above ground, the enemy responded with an angry fusillade at Geary, causing a casualty.

This duel served as a warm-up for the hottest one of the month, beginning about three o'clock in the afternoon. The Japanese had continued shooting in desultory fashion but suddenly intensified their fire and began to pepper Geary once more with the 240's. Next they shifted to nearby Crockett, a 12-inch disappearing battery that faced directly away from Bataan—a strange decision, since it could not be of harm to them. The crew had anticipated this eventuality and had fortified their backside with oil drums filled with earth, the better to avoid catching shell fragments in embarrassing locations. The heavy Japanese shells quickly tore this barrier to pieces and began to land directly within the battery. Exploding with blinding flashes, the shells sent steel fragments ricocheting viciously about the concrete walls, killing or wounding several men, knocking the number one gun permanently out of action, wrecking the shot hoists, and starting a fire in the power passages of the battery. Fortunately, the crew and some marines extinguished the fire before it could reach the magazine. Although some of Crockett's excited gunners at first believed their battery had been "blown to hell" and so reported to Colonel Bunker, the Japanese stopped just short of doing so.

For this Crockett's gunners could thank the 14-inch rifles of Battery Wilson on Drum. The roving batteries had tried and failed to silence the 240's, and Geary and Craighill were smothered and silenced by smaller weapons as soon as they had opened fire. That left only Drum, which just in time drove the Japanese gunners into foxholes with a rain of massive projectiles. Had Manila enjoyed a temperate climate Crockett would have perished, for Wilson's rifles could not have reached the Japanese at well over twenty thousand yards range. But with the fort continually buttoned up in the tropic heat and the exhaust fans seldom in use, the temperature inside the concrete battleship had been rising slowly at a uniform rate. By this time it was over a hundred degrees. This, of course, was hard on Sam Madison's crew, who could do nothing about it but sweat, but it had an unexpected bonus. The propellent powder in the magazines warmed up along with everything else, and as a consequence exploded with greater vehemence, producing a higher muzzle velocity and corresponding increase in the flight distance of the shells. Instead of barely reaching the Bataan shore, Wilson's rifles could fire to Cabcaben and even beyond, putting the enemy 240's within effective range.

Battery Crockett's ordeal produced one of those incredible episodes that sprinkle the annals of warfare. A 59th Coast Artillery surgeon, Captain Lester I. Fox, was manning his battalion aid station at the battery when the Japanese opened up. After fire had broken out in the hoist room and several men had been wounded, Fox was busy giving aid. More shells crashed through, breaking his leg, but as he recalled it years later, ". . . I hopped around on my other leg and was able to organize the remaining men in the battery to put out the fires that were threatening the powder magazine." Still more shells hit, ". . . ripping off part of my right elbow and producing many soft tissue wounds scattered throughout the right side of my body." The others fled the compartment, shells continued to explode, ". . . and I was wounded repeatedly; in the right eyebrow, losing the sight of my right eye, fracturing several ribs, and generally making me very mad." Although it seems impossible, this tough doctor survived to be carried to the Malinta hospital after the shelling, and from there to pass into captivity as a patient when the Rock surrendered.

The duel of April 24 dealt Battery Denver on Water Tank Hill a cruel blow by taking the life of its rough and tough old soldier, First Sergeant Dewey Brady. Still unaware of his promotion to second lieutenant just that morning, Brady was at his usual lookout completely exposed atop one of the water towers on the hill when a 240 mm. shell fragment almost severed his leg. One of his buck sergeants climbed up to help him but received a growled, "For Christ's sake get back to your guns. Those —— —— slant eyes can't kill me with just one of these things." But then another hit him, tearing him almost to pieces. Still, he had a final revenge. "They might kill me," he had habitually told his men when they would reproach him for remaining exposed, "but they can't keep me from stinking."

Also for six young marines of Company D of the 1st Battalion, 4th Marines, this day was fatal. A shell crashed through and exploded the ammunition in a splinterproof magazine at Engineer Point where they had taken refuge.

The day's memorable duel closed tragically at 9:58 in the evening when the Japanese lobbed two 240 mm. rounds, aimed with diabolical foresight, at the west portal of Malinta Tunnel, where a large number of men had been gathering nightly, in violation of standing orders, for a final smoke before hitting the sack. Without so much as a warning whistle the two great projectiles struck, one a dud, the other bursting squarely among the men, killing fourteen and wounding seventy. Lieutenant Juanita Redmond, one of the nurses evacuated from Bataan, has described the macabre result.

> We worked all that night, and I wish I could forget those endless, harrowing hours. Hours of giving injections, anesthetizing, ripping off clothes, stitching gaping wounds, of amputations, sterilizing instruments, bandaging, settling the treated patients in their beds, covering the wounded that we cannot save.

She continues to describe individual cases: the headless corpse; the boy with the leg hanging by shreds; pieces of ugly shrapnel jutting from even uglier wounds—the true face of war from which she and her sister nurses could not turn.

Raised in a land where "face" means much, Japan's unit commanders were ill-disposed to risk disgrace by recording their losses in detail. Consequently there is no documentary record of precisely how much damage Bunker and his men inflicted in this duel of April 24 and earlier. We do have a postwar tabulation by Colonel Hiromitsu Hashimoto, who commanded an artillery unit during the campaign. He records a total of twenty-five 240 mm. and 150 mm. pieces as "damaged" during the Corregidor operation, either by enemy fire or by premature bursts of their own shells. If this figure is meaningful, we may reasonably assume that most damage accrued in April prior to the heavy pre-invasion bombardments which gravely weakened the American reply. Both Japanese and American evidence suggests that Bunker's gunners did at least as well and perhaps a bit better than one would have anticipated under the circumstances.

With a Japanese landing on the Rock a foregone conclusion and most of his batteries silenced, George Moore was understandably anxious to learn, if he could, when the enemy was coming. But because nearly all of the Navy's small craft were out of service and because co-operation between the Inshore Patrol and the Seaward Defense Command had not been satisfactory, he finally decided to use an Army boat for reconnaissance duty. In mid-April he ordered

Lieutenant James Seater to equip the Engineer launch *Nighthawk* with machine guns and a 37 mm. cannon manned by six Army gunner volunteers, and to patrol by night a goodly distance up the Manila Bay side of the Bataan Peninsula. He wanted to know where the Japanese were concentrating their landing barges; if they were so foolish as to base them too close, he could ruin them with a night barrage of high-explosive shells from Smith and Hearn, his two long-range 12-inch batteries.

After making several trips without sighting anything, Seater and his men sighted off Limay a larger two-decker craft approximately 120 feet in length, formerly a customs boat of the Commonwealth government. The Japanese crew was busily signaling to shore, unconcerned at the presence of the *Nighthawk* pulling up alongside. Charging his heavy gun, Corporal Jolly, a Bataan escapee from the 31st Infantry, at once chopped down the men moving about on the deck; Seater joined immediately, firing the 37 mm. cannon, as did the other machine gunners. The surprised Japanese—engineers of the 22nd Regiment entrusted with the chore of arming captured vessels—replied gamely, hitting Sergeant Raleigh D. Vermillion of Battery Kingston in the arm and Sergeant Clyde E. Winters of Battery Mobile in the thigh. Winters nevertheless continued to fire his .50. Caught flat-footed, the enemy had no chance, and after their fire ceased, Lieutenant Seater jumped aboard the riddled, burning, and drifting craft, to find thirty dead and no other sign of life. Anxious to gather what intelligence he could, he affixed a tow to his prize, dragged a wounded Japanese from the water with a boat hook, and started back to Corregidor. When four more enemy boats appeared, Seater had to cut the tow and run for it, trading bursts with the enemy with his light cannon and Winters' .50. The Japanese broke off the chase as the *Nighthawk* rounded Cabcaben Point in range and sight of Corregidor, but on his arrival at South Dock well after daylight, Seater found to his dismay his prisoner missing and the Filipino boat crew deadpan and silent as to his fate. He had either jumped overboard or—equally likely—had been pitched overside by the Filipinos.

As in other instances during the campaign, a daring and imaginative tactical success resulted in strategic failure. Seater had spotted no landing barges, and from henceforth Moore could expect the Japanese to escort their landing craft rehearsing for the assault on the Rock. The *Nighthawk*'s usefulness had ended and Moore was blinded.

With the surrender of Bataan, "Skinny" Wainwright realized that the end was near for Corregidor, America's "keep" in the Far East. His remaining duty, as he now saw it, was to tie up the Japanese for as long as possible. His need for supplies assumed far less importance; the Rock could use a few more mechanical fuzes for the 60th's guns, but this was about all. Enough food remained to hold out until the end of June, but a crucial shortage of diesel fuel, needed to operate the electric water-pumping system, could not be remedied. Even if a convoy or a single supply ship somehow could get through, it could not unload in the teeth of the enemy's artillery. Wainwright's concern became twofold: to preserve the morale and fighting spirit of his men as best he could, and to try to arrange for the evacuation by submarine of selected personnel, including intelligence specialists, grounded aviators, and nurses. When the diesel oil ran out in mid-May and his pumps could no longer draw water from the wells, he would surrender unless the enemy had overrun him first. After hearing of the announcement over the radio of his promotion to Lieutenant General and receiving the congratulations of one of the ladies in the tunnel, he replied graciously but wryly, "It is an empty honor, Madam. I know *why* I am being promoted."

By April Wainwright's only reasonably continuous lifeline had consisted of the two Philippine Army observation planes based at Kindley Field and a few tattered civilian craft. These flew back and forth to Mindanao, staging through an airfield at Mindoro still in American hands and landing by night as one of Corregidor's searchlights dipped briefly over the Kindley airstrip. Major Bill Bradford flew several of these hazardous missions, evacuating among others several Air Corps officers and the Rock's war correspondents, Frank

Hewlett and Dean Schedler. By the end of the month this life line was cut; the Japanese had seized the Mindoro staging field. Bradford flew the last trip, and on his arrival in Australia on May 5, the day before Corregidor surrendered, he revealed that he had urged Wainwright to escape with him. But "Skinny" had replied, "I have been with my men from the start, and if captured I will share their lot."

In keeping with his efforts to maintain the morale of his men, Wainwright spent as much time with them as he could. Daily he visited the hospital laterals, and his lean figure, supported by a cane, frequently could be seen outside the tunnel. Calmer Ersness remembers, "Skinny, as we all called him, and as he preferred to be called, would walk into a group of G.I.'s and bum a match or a cigarette and sit down and bat the breeze with them."

Of General Wainwright, his former Chief Engineer of the North Luzon Force and later of the I Philippine Corps on Bataan, Colonel Harry A. Skerry has written, "His was a true soldier's philosophy and the utter hopelessness of the situation did not cloud his judgement or deter him. . . . He was a human sort of individual, kind and thoughtful of his associates and yet demanding a very high performance of duty." Wainwright chose to stick it out, to stay with his men, even though in retrospect, it would have been far better for him and for them had he flown out with Bradford. His relentless foes would take advantage of his position and newly acquired rank to make his last duty, that of surrendering the Rock, the most painful and shattering of his life.

11 ☆ The Brutal Overture

WEDNESDAY, APRIL 29, 1942, was an important Japanese holiday, the birthday of the deified Emperor Hirohito. Knowledge of this began to filter among the Americans in advance, and all expected their foe to stage a rousing "celebration." Their foe did more than that; he began, this day, his intensive pre-invasion bombardment by land and by air of all the harbor forts. As one victim put it, the Japanese threw over everything in the next seven days, even "the kitchen sink." The Rock's ordeal by steel and fire, its week of hell, had begun.

The Japanese began their brutal celebration at 7:25 A.M., when the first bombers droned overhead. Five minutes later the balloon, "Peeping Tom," rose jerkily, to the accompaniment of measured shelling from a lone gun. Within the next hour the big 240's were firing—their gunners stripped to the waist and sweating as they hoisted the heavy shells—plastering Geary and Crockett, making it too dangerous for Bunker's men to respond with their standard "retaliation shoot"; still, most of the batteries in commission, including sailor-crewed Craighill on Hughes, individually got away a few rounds before the noon hour. On and on the hellish bombardment continued. To awed marine Carl Allen on the beaches, it crackled sometimes "like the fire of machine guns."

Combining practicality with malevolence, the Japanese did their best to rid themselves of troublesome Fort Drum that day, repeatedly sending light, glide-attacking bombers after it. As in previous attacks most of the bombs dropped into the water, but in the early afternoon one heavy missile glanced from the turret face of Battery Marshall onto a gun tube. Instead of exploding it smashed open, scattering TNT over the deck but doing no damage other than to knock the 14-inch rifle out of alignment. Once again the attackers had failed.

This aside, the bombardment of April 29 was far and away the heaviest Corregidor and Fort Hughes had endured to date. The light and heavy bombers flew eighty-three sorties and dropped a record 106 tons of bombs. The artillery fired a vast quantity of shells and wrought tremendous material damage, although casualties were not high. By midmorning, fires had erupted all over the Rock, and smoke towered three thousand feet from two gasoline blazes at Kindley Field. Broken trees and branches, ripped by blast and shrapnel, lay everywhere.

Because much of the bombing and shelling was aimed at Malinta Hill, damage there was greatest. The Japanese could not resist the notion that bombardment of the hill could destroy or demoralize "the American command post" inside. In this, too, the enemy failed, as in the attack of December 29, but he blasted from the solid rock three 75 mm. beach defense guns emplaced facing Bataan. He also wrecked the quadruple 1.1 inch pom-pom on the top of the hill and damaged the adjacent tunnel for No. 8 searchlight—in which the pom-pom crew had taken refuge—roasting to death Lieutenant Stanley O. Friedline, the platoon commander, and five of his men. A great 240 mm. shell had plunged from a steep angle squarely down the tunnel's ventilation shaft into the gasoline tank of the searchlight's 25 kw. generator.

For his fellow officers and many of the men of Battery Mobile, the death of young Stan Friedline was hard to accept. They had regarded him as so fine and promising an officer and gentleman they scarcely could believe afterward that he was gone.

Life beneath this concentrated blasting was miserable. In the hospital laterals bottles and small items crashed from the shelves as the rock and concrete walls of Malinta Tunnel vibrated and shook.

Dust rose in a choking cloud, forcing the nurses to cover the patients' and their own faces with wet gauze. In such times of bombardment, Lieutenant Maude D. Williams recorded in her diary, the face of the chief nurse, Ann Mealer, would glow "a beautiful pink." Yet, Mrs. Williams added, ". . . she is apparently calm and certainly proficient." Not all the Rock's heroes were men, although like the rest they, too, wore GI coveralls.

Elsewhere on the island the shells blasted and burned most of the remaining wooden buildings, damaged the height-finders of all of the antiaircraft batteries, cut their data transmission lines, and exploded several more ammunition dumps. Hard-hit Battery Geary had several mortars knocked out of action and its pits littered with debris and dirt. Watching the smoke towering from all over the island, the Japanese were convinced—with reason—that they had given their Divinity a suitable birthday present. But they suffered some cost in doing so. A pair of light bombers from the 16th Regiment went down, and several batteries were silenced, especially by the fire of Drum's turrets, Battery Craighill, the roving batteries, and Battery Way's four old 12-inch 1890-model mortars.

This was Way's first major action. Prior to the fall of Bataan it had continued unmanned for want of a crew, with the Harbor Defense Mapping Service making use of its bombproofs. Afterward a detail of about a hundred men from Battery Erie of the 60th, under Major William Massello, Jr. ("Wild Bill," some of the men called him), and Captain Frederick A. Miller, spent some days reconditioning its guns, which had not been fired for several years. By April 28 it had three of them proof-fired in time for Hirohito's birthday. Because Way was new to them, the Japanese gunners failed to hit it that day. The next day, however, aided by aerial photographs, they had refined their firing data and retaliated ferociously with a concentration of a hundred 240 mm. shells. Henceforth Way was punished as severely as Geary.

With fury the Japanese continued their barrage during the next two days. By May 1 they had Godfrey Ames's exposed Chicago virtually out of commission, forcing Colonel Chase to transfer its precious mechanically fuzed ammunition to other batteries. On their hillside facing Bataan, Ames's men huddled miserably in their battery tunnel. On leaving it to cross the battery area, which from time to time some had to do, they felt as conspicuous as if they were naked on Broadway, with a sniper shooting at them. Even small groups drew enemy fire. On its exposed ridge top, Denver, too, lay silent, without fire control for its guns, its tired and dispirited men unable to move about.

On May 2, the fourth day of the bombardment, the Japanese intensified their fire, though to the defenders it hardly seemed possible. During one incredible five-hour period they rained twelve 240 mm. shells per minute, a total of 3,600 rounds, onto the Geary-Crockett area at Topside. To their horror First Lieutenant Harry C. Minsker, the pit officer of Battery Geary, and his commanding officer, Captain Thomas W. Davis, III, realized that the shells were gradually eating their way through the extremely thick but unreinforced concrete sides of two of the magazines. From his command post several hundred feet away, Davis could actually follow the big shells with his eyes as they arched over his head to smack viciously against the concrete and blast out great chunks.

Already Geary was badly mauled. Pit A—containing its best weapons, four M-1908 12-inch mortars—was inoperative and several of the crew had been killed, but the gunners had continued in action from the other pit, B, containing four M-1890 mortars which they were manning for the first time. Anticipating the possibility of an explosion, Davis several days previously had requested permission to empty the magazines of the inoperative pit to prevent a blast that would destroy Geary. Headquarters, probably not understanding the imminence of the danger, had refused his request on the ground of conserving ammunition. In the interest of preserving his command, Davis went ahead without orders and had completely emptied the left magazine of all its powder charges and had partially emptied the center magazine between the pits when the Japanese began the day's violent shelling, forcing his men under cover.

Finally it happened. At 4:27 P.M. a 240 mm. shell crashed through the side of the weakened center magazine to explode among 1,600 sixty-two-pound full section powder charges. A Gargantuan blast shook the Rock, knocking Sergeant Carl Hill and several others at nearby Battery Crockett sprawling while squat thirteen-ton mortars tumbled like pebbles. One from Pit A flew 150 yards through the air to land muzzle down on the golf course. Two others catapulted across Pit B and under the concrete gallery, collapsing it atop them. Where the center magazine had been, a large crater now gaped. Debris, mingled with unexploded 12-inch shells, pelted down all over the island. A man died at Globe close by when a projectile struck a 3-inch gun, wrecked it, and glanced onto him. Already hard-hit by a bomb that had killed eleven and wounded a like number on April 30, Globe had thirty-four additional men injured. Nevertheless, its gritty men, led by Captain Aaron A. Abston, were among the first to reach Geary to carry out rescue operations. Others came running from Crockett, and even from Bunker's C-1 tunnel a half-mile distant. Fortunately, the elated Japanese stopped their shelling immediately after the blast, or they would have rung up a much greater tally.

Because of the foresight of Davis and Minsker, only six were killed and six injured of Geary's sixty-man pit crew. When the shelling began, the two officers had concentrated most of the men in the safest place they could find, the far chamber of the three comprising the right magazine. The outer chamber collapsed under the blast but did not explode, the middle chamber partially caved in, trapping several men who had to be dug out, but the third remained intact. All those killed or injured were in the two nearest the explosion. Minsker suffered a mangled leg but did not lose it. Everyone was badly shaken. A sergeant of the battery, recalls Captain Davis, a veteran of big-gun duels in France, "took off" and ran aimlessly for a hundred yards before recovering his senses and returning to apologize to his commander.

Geary was done for. All its mortars were destroyed; and before this unforgettable day had ended, Way had lost two of its three serviceable pieces. The Japanese shells fell on Way at such an angle that they landed only on the far side of the four-gun pit, irreparably damaging the two mortars on that side. They could not hit the other piece directly, and Way remained operational with one gun, which of necessity was silent most of the time. In a single day's shelling the Japanese had virtually eliminated Corregidor's most effective counterbattery weapons—the mortars—which had been counted on for so many years as the answer to Japanese howitzer fire from Bataan.

On May 3 the violent barrage continued, its only tolerable feature being that it slackened during the night to give the hard-working Japanese gunners rest and their American antagonists a respite. Counterbattery fire was pitifully limited and without success. An impatient Massello had to lay low at Way; Craighill's sailors could get away only a few rounds before being smothered. In what Lieutenant Nash termed "nice shooting" the Japanese gunners dropped five 240 mm. rounds squarely into the pits. Strangely, at this juncture they hurt nobody. As on previous days the roving batteries and the indestructible Monja and Drum had to furnish the bulk of the opposition. General Wainwright radioed to General MacArthur in Melbourne at the close of the day, "Situation here is fast becoming desperate."

On May 4 the Japanese artillery, which this time had continued a desultory harassment throughout the night, again increased its intensity of fire, hammering an estimated sixteen thousand rounds on Corregidor in the next twenty-four hours. This terrible day the enemy gunners ominously shifted their aim from the batteries and searchlights to the beach defenses along the entire northern shore. The marines, especially those of the 1st Battalion located from the base of Malinta Hill eastward, took a horrible beating, as did their fellows in exposed James ravine. From his foxhole at Monkey Point, Dayton L. Drachenberg, a slender, intense Air Corps lieutenant attached to the battalion, listened in fear and awe. "The island shook as the big shells landed," he remembers, "as if the victim of a continuous earthquake, with trees, limbs, rocks, and other debris crashing and flying in all directions." Lieutenant Colonel Curtis T. Beecher, the 1st Battalion commander, went down to Malinta Tunnel hospital in the afternoon from his command post on Malinta Hill to see how some of his wounded were faring and encountered his B Company commander, Major Paul Brown, in the corridor. Brown said he was on his way back to his command post but acted so strangely Beecher called a doctor to look at him. The doctor confirmed what Beecher had suspected; Brown was suffering from severe concussion—shell shock, in World War I terminology—after having twice been buried in foxholes. And so when late in the afternoon a shell killed Major Harry Lang, the commander of Company A, Beecher had lost two of his three key subordinates. Over-all, however, casualties for the marines were surprisingly light, considering that the only cover for most was foxholes. But the unremitting bombardment was telling on their morale. It took all the courage the bravest could muster to stay near the beaches. Some fled inland to seek safer cover, but most remained.

By 3:00 P.M. of May 4 the heaviest general artillery bombardment of the campaign was under way. Nearly every Japanese gun, from 75 to 240 mm., was firing "a continuous drum-fire of bursting shells." Only the roving batteries, Monja, and the 14-inch rifles of Drum replied, but it was hopeless.

12 ☆ The Final Bombardment

HAD GENERAL HOMMA CHOSEN he need not have invaded Corregidor at all. Even had there been no shortage of oil for pumping water, Corregidor's food stocks would have lasted only until the end of June. But the impatient Japanese commander had no intention of merely starving the American garrison into submission. To attack was more glorious, more in keeping with the Bushido spirit, and a good if risky way to build one's reputation.

During their trek down the Bataan Peninsula, one of the worst malarial areas in the world, the Japanese contracted the disease in greater and greater numbers. A few days after Bataan fell, an epidemic of cerebral malaria was raging full force; fifty thousand troops were sick, and about five hundred perished before the pestilence abated. Corregidor's continuing resistance thus cost the Japanese more casualties from illness than they had suffered from all causes during the entire Bataan campaign. On many occasions the awesome Japanese batteries could muster but half their men; four-gun batteries could fire only two pieces, two-gun batteries only one. The infantrymen of the 4th Division, encamped awaiting the landing, suffered equally; only the arrival by air of 300,000 quinine tablets brought the disease under sufficient control by late April to allow these fever-weakened troops to proceed with the necessary amphibious training.

General Homma's resources for the attack were not lavish. The 4th Division, commanded by Lieutenant General Kenzo Kitano, was considered the worst in the Imperial Japanese Army by some 14th Army staff officers, since it was poorly equipped in comparison to most of the other units and lacked amphibious experience. Only eleven thousand strong, it had but three instead of four infantry companies in each battalion. Moreover, the number of landing craft Homma had on hand was insufficient to boat more than two battalions—about two thousand men—simultaneously. Since the Americans were estimated to have between five and ten thousand men on Corregidor—in fact there were about fifteen thousand—the 4th Division's landing force would be heavily outnumbered.

In view of his numerical weakness, General Homma decided to use deception to surprise his foe, even though his artillerymen, confident of the damage they had inflicted, predicted the infantry would stroll ashore unopposed. To lull Wainwright into thinking that he would have an extended period of grace, Homma had his headquarters in Manila busily pretend to concentrate on occupation problems, referring publicly to Corregidor with the propaganda line, "Time will settle everything." On the Emperor's birthday, when the pre-invasion bombardments began—bombardments which not only tipped his hand but revealed the landing site—he staged a big parade in the Philippine capital, announcing to the press afterward that he was assuming personal command of mop-up operations on Mindanao. Instead he drove to Bataan to supervise the 4th Division's amphibious training. This elaborate hocus-pocus was unsuccessful, for Generals Wainwright and Moore paid no attention to it.

In sharp contrast, Homma's invasion plan, issued on April 28, was simple and well adapted to the tactical situation and to the want of amphibious training by the 4th Division. Because of the shortage of landing craft, it called for separate landings at 11:00 P.M. on two successive nights, the first with two thousand men on the Rock's vulnerable tail, supported by a reinforcing battalion at 4:00 A.M., and the second on the beaches below Topside's north shore, with a total of four thousand men landing in three successive waves. Logistics were simple; every man would stagger ashore under a heavy pack containing enough food, water, ammunition, and other supplies to sustain him several days. Eleven in the evening was chosen as H hour because tidal conditions were favorable and because the moon would rise about an hour after the landing barges grounded, giving the benefit of an approach during maximum darkness and fair visibility to the infantry shortly afterward.

The plan of the first landing unit, the A unit, made up of the 1st and 2nd Battalions of the 61st Infantry Regiment under the command of Colonel Gempachi Sato, was to seize by the early morning of May 6 the Rock's entire tail, Malinta Hill, and Bottomside. The next evening the second unit, the B unit, would land its four battalions in waves, attack Topside by way of James ravine, and link up with the A unit in the Middleside region. Afterward, both would mop up, calling in other units of the 4th Division as needed.

As any good military plan should, Homma's provided for an alternative in case a hitch developed. If the defenses on Topside proved too strong, or if the A unit ran into stubborn resistance about Malinta Hill, the second landing would be canceled and the B unit would land instead on the already secured tail. Since Corregidor's beach defenses were appraised as "not yet strong," Homma's staff considered this possibility unlikely and thought that an early American surrender was more probable. In that event only the bearer of a white flag of truce from Wainwright himself would be recognized and 14th Army Headquarters would be notified at once. Hostilities would *not* be terminated; the attack would go on until Homma ordered it stopped.

The 4th Division carried on amphibious training several miles down the Bataan coast, with fever-weakened troops, from April 29 through the second of May. Then it pulled back to its bivouac area near Orion to make final preparations. The officers indoctrinated the men with great care, telling them they were the "human bullets"—the vanguard of His Imperial Majesty—who would give their lives, if necessary, that those who followed might triumph in glory. A Japanese warrior had no more sacred or rewarding privilege than to participate in the initial, suicidal first wave of an attack. This quasi-medieval fanaticism was in keeping with the samurai spirit and was accepted completely by the peasant-soldiers. They needed this fanaticism, for as "human bullets" they also would become "human targets." As their national anthem put it,

> Across the sea
> Corpses in the water;
> Across the mountain
> Corpses heaped on the field.
> I shall die only for the Emperor;
> I shall never look back.

The Japanese were quite correct in their estimate that Corregidor's beach defenses were "not yet strong." The failure of the Philippine Division to reach Corregidor had left Colonel Howard's Beach Defense Command with too few trained infantry to fulfill its mission. Altogether, Howard had about 3,900 officers and men of whom only 1,500 were marines, members of his own 4th Marine Regiment. The remainder were from several score units of the Army, Navy, Philippine Army, and Philippine Scouts. Except for a handful of Bataan survivors, who were in poor physical condition, some aging World War I veterans, and a few leathernecks who had fought in Nicaragua in the 1920s, none had had prior combat experience. Even the marines had not trained in the field as a unit for years. Their prewar station had been Shanghai, where they had served as garrison troops.

All of Howard's men had rifles and a respectable total of 225 .30 and .50 caliber machine guns as well as twenty light M-1916 37 mm. cannon, but they were woefully short of other support weapons. Their few converted Stokes mortars had no sights, they had no field howitzers, and their only antitank weapon was the "Molotov cocktail," a bottle of gasoline and oil with an igniting fuze. Ominously, there was no plan to support them with fire from seacoast batteries on Corregidor or the other forts.

For antiboat defense Howard had one 155 mm. gun, twenty-three British-type 75's of indifferent quality with large spoked wheels, a pair of Navy 3-inch landing guns, and three Navy 3-pounders. With the exception of the sailors who manned the Navy guns, all of the gunners were Scouts of the 91st and 92nd Coast Artillery Regiments. In the aggregate the guns totaled a respectable number, but when scattered in pairs all around Corregidor, they were spread quite thin, and along the north shore Japanese fire had knocked out all of them. Only on the extreme tail of the island two 75 mm. guns remained intact facing Bataan. These survived because of their location and because their commander, Lieutenant Ray G. Lawrence, U.S.A., had been ordered by General Moore not to reveal his position by firing back during the pre-invasion bombardment.

Colonel Howard had devised his defense plan at a time when the greatest threat to the Rock came from outside Manila Bay rather than from Bataan. Consequently, the bulk of his men were on Topside. There he had concentrated 2,035 men of the 2nd and 3rd Battalions, mainly in James, Cheney, and Ramsay ravines, backing them up with his regimental reserve of about six hundred officers and men stationed in Government ravine at Middleside. Only one battalion, his 1st, under Lieutenant Colonel Curtis T. Beecher, defended the entire tail of the island from Malinta Hill eastward. For reasons best known to himself Howard did not change his dispositions after Bataan's fall, even though it now was obvious the Japanese probably would mount from inside the bay, striking at his vulnerable 1st Battalion.

With over ten thousand yards of traversable beach to defend, and possessing neither a defense in depth nor a usable reserve, the 1st Battalion was a hollow shell. Once through its thinly manned lines the Japanese would encounter little opposition. It had only fifty-three officers and 1,024 men, and of these but twenty officers and 367 men were marines. The remainder consisted of Filipino aviation cadets, miscellaneous American and Filipino survivors of Bataan, Company A of the 803rd Engineers, 240 veteran Scouts of the 91st and 92nd CA Regiments manning the surviving beach defense guns, and even a number of retired Filipino mess boys of the U.S. Navy who had been recalled to active duty when war came.

Along the shattered north shore, where all wire and beach defenses had been destroyed, Beecher had merely a reinforced company and a platoon from battalion headquarters, commanded by Captain Lewis H. Pickup. Just three platoons guarded the area where the Japanese actually landed, from North Point eastward to the tip of the tail. The other side of the island was defended by Company B under a young lieutenant, Alan S. Manning, who twice had been wounded by the bombardment, while the weapons company, D, under Captain Noel E. Castle, disposed its machine guns and 37's on either side of the tail. Beecher had a small battalion reserve under Lieutenant Robert F. Jenkins, Jr., but since it was occupying positions above possible landing beaches on either side of Malinta Hill, he had to leave it in place; consequently it never saw action.

All the members of the 1st Battalion were groggy from concussion and lack of sleep. Seven of the officers had been killed or wounded, including, as we have seen, the commanders of Companies A and B, whom Pickup and Manning had replaced. Many had suffered close calls; it was not uncommon for a marine or G.I. to have his rifle smashed from his hands by a shell fragment. Patches covered shrapnel holes in the jackets of some of the water-cooled machine guns. Considering the ferocity of the bombardment the wonder is not that units became entangled and the beach defense line ragged and intermittent as the men sought the deepest holes they could find; the wonder is that they remained on the exposed tail at all. Three days before the landing Beecher warned Colonel Howard that his command's battered condition made it "extremely unlikely" that he could beat off a Japanese attack.

To mount a counterattack if the Japanese won a lodgment Colonel Howard could muster only his ill-equipped reserve armed with Enfield rifles and Lewis machine guns. His two companies of headquarters troops, Companies O and P, totaling thirty-two officers and

276 men under Major Max W. Shaeffer, U.S.M.C., formed one-half of the reserve. This half was called the Regimental Reserve. The other half, commanded by Major Francis H. (Joe) Williams, U.S.M.C., consisted of 275 officers and men grandiloquently designated the 4th Battalion, 4th Marines. Both units were stationed along steep trails in Government ravine at Middleside, defiladed from the murderous Japanese artillery on Bataan.

Consisting mostly of veteran sailors, petty officers in the higher grades from the Navy's section base at Mariveles and the scuttled submarine tender U.S.S. *Canopus,* 4th Battalion was led by a heterogeneous collection of Navy and Army officers, of whom a few had seen combat on Bataan. First Lieutenant Otis E. Saalman, U.S.A., formerly of the Scout 57th Infantry, was perhaps the most experienced. Boasting that it was the "highest paid marine unit in the world," because of the lucrative salaries of its enlisted specialists, the battalion also had the highest lettered companies anyone had ever heard of: Q, R, S, and T. The men "trained" by plinking at debris in the bay with their rifles and listening to lectures on combat tactics during lulls in the bombardment. All took the meager indoctrination seriously. "The chips were down," wrote Captain Harold E. Dalness, U.S.A., commanding Company R, "and there was no horseplay."

Each man had an Enfield rifle, but there were not enough helmets, cartridge belts, or canteens to go around. The equipment of Frank Gomez was typical.

> I had a World War I helmet, a white piece of line for my belt, a safety pin that was to hold my canteen to the line. A Filipino sailor gave me a big horse blanket. I stripped my gas mask bag. . . . That was my ditty bag, just room for a change of clothing, soap, if any, and a few canned goods, like salmon or dry chocolate (unsweetened).

Effective use was not made of the coast artillery units, even though all had small arms and machine guns for their men and had trained as infantry and at counter-landing assignments. Instead of pulling them from their positions as their batteries were silenced, headquarters left them in place and merely assigned each a defense mission in its vicinity. It alerted four batteries for use as reserves on call of General Moore. In view of the heavy shelling, it may be that headquarters concluded that to do more would be impossible.

With his customary thoroughness Captain Ames of Battery Chicago had prepared a line of defenses across the forward slope of Morrison Hill, making certain by drills carried out under fire that each man would occupy his assigned foxhole when the order came to man the line. Denver, on the other hand, occupying what turned out to be the key to the American defense, a position atop Water Tank Hill, a ridge running west from Kindley Field, was so demoralized following the death of First Sergeant Dewey Brady on April 24, that its morale temporarily had collapsed. To revive the stricken battery Colonel Chase had assigned to command on May 1 Ames's able "exec," Captain Paul R. Cornwall, but time was too short for the young officer to restore the battery completely even though morale improved. Consequently, Cornwall was unable to carry out in full the defense plan, which called for Denver to establish a defense line across the crest of its hill, tying into the marine beach defenses on either side. He did, however, establish some positions across the top of the ridge near the two water towers and on a shoulder of the hill, admonishing the men to do their best should the Japanese attack.

As the morning of May 5 dawned, even the few remaining optimists sensed the inevitable end. No convoy from the States could help now. "A continuous pall of dust and debris hung over everything," wrote Captain Jack Gulick. "There was a feeling of doom mingled with wonder." To Lieutenant Commander T. C. Parker the whole island seemed ". . . beaten and burned to a crisp. It resembled a sponge. . . ."

By now most of the fixed installations either were out of action or useless because of Japanese fire. The antiaircraft batteries were silent from cumulative damage to data transmission lines, weapons, directors, and height finders. Batteries Flint and Chicago each had one antiaircraft gun operative; Denver had none. The others, unable to direct their fire, lay silent. The unopposed Japanese pilots dipped so low that helpless observers on the ground could see them thumb their noses as they flew by. To be sure, most of the damage was repairable, but Corregidor needed a respite from the fierce shelling before much could be done.

Already General Moore had been deprived of a commander's most essential need—his power to communicate rapidly with his units. After April 29 all telephone lines on the island were regularly cut after a few hours, forcing reliance on runners until repair crews could fix them. This means of conveying orders was dangerous, slow, and unreliable. Crossing Bottomside on foot in the vicinity of the wrecked power plant was a particularly hazardous venture. Captain Rolly Ames of Battery Chicago traversed it nightly to have a wound dressed in the Tunnel. Although the Japanese slackened their fire at night, Ames still termed the area a "nasty place" where "one felt positively in the spotlight for artillery batteries on Bataan." The once-jungle-covered road along the north shore of the island was a seared, whitened scar along ground blasted bare. The time was rapidly approaching when repair of wire communications would be impossible, when movement would cease above ground by both day and night.

Getting enough water even for drinking purposes was already a serious problem for the more exposed units, especially Beecher's marines and attached troops on the tail. Chicago, with positions facing Bataan, had to manhandle its water from Middleside in cumbersome twelve-inch powder cans from a well equipped with its own pump. Mobile, with its platoons scattered along the tail and on Kindley Field, being refused water at Malinta Tunnel, had to send its only remaining truck to the well Chicago was using. Even Malinta Tunnel was running critically short; reserve stocks from which the post hospital drew had dwindled from a total of three million gallons on April 10 to but a few days' supply at normal consumption rates. Showers had stopped in the hospital on April 15, and the principal source of additional water for the entire tunnel complex was a well near the east portal served by a pump operated by a coughing diesel motor.

Corregidor still had plenty of water in the ground; the trick was to get it out. Most of the wells had auxiliary pumps and continued to supply water, although the Fort Mills power plant had been inoperative since the first week in April. But by May 5 the supply of diesel oil was sufficient for only another week of pumping operations.

Feeding the men outside the tunnels had become as difficult as getting them water. The marines, their attached troops, and the crews of the antiaircraft and roving gun batteries ate frugally twice a day, once shortly after dark when the shelling slackened, and again before dawn in the morning. Rice, bolstered by a little canned salmon and a few tidbits, was the ration. As Colonel Bunker, a dedicated meat-and-potatoes man, noted, "This rice diet fills you *temporarily* but it doesn't stick to your ribs." Some had less even than that. A section of Battery Mobile near Kindley Field had one can of tomatoes apiece per man in a thirty-six-hour period, supplemented by a monkey or two they found and killed.

By May 5 virtually all of the naval vessels were out of commission. Commander McCracken's leaking *Mindanao* finally sank. The strafers had done her in. Other smaller craft were immobilized by a lack of bunker oil, the one major supply item to run out completely during the campaign. General Moore feared that when the Japanese landed he might get no warning and was reduced to positioning two small craft six hundred yards offshore of the east and west ends of the island to signal with a vertical sweep of their searchlights when the enemy came. "Damn that full moon!" he exclaimed on the evening of May 5 to Colonel Braly, his operations officer, "they'll probably come tonight." The night before, General Wainwright had estimated to General Marshall in Washington that if the Japanese landed, his chances of beating them off were "somewhat less than even."

A few lucky men and women had left the Rock. On April 29 two PBY's from Australia had glided in during darkness and alighted in the bay between Corregidor and Fort Hughes. To drown out their engines the crews of several naval launches had operated their motors without mufflers, making a terrific racket. With the Japanese unsuspecting, the PBY's took off safely with fifty passengers, including radio intercept specialists General MacArthur had specifically asked for, and several nurses. One made it to Australia, but the other hit a log on Lake Lanao on Mindanao, its staging point, and was disabled. The water runway ordinarily used had come under shell fire and the PBY's were forced into swamps. The damaged PBY later got away but its passengers eventually fell into Japanese hands.

The last submarine, the *Spearfish,* slipped in on the night of May 3 through a new passage swept in the Navy's contact mine field between Corregidor and the Cavite shore. It carried out fourteen more nurses, as many as could be accommodated, in addition to a few other carefully selected personnel. Colonel Irwin, General Wainwright's operations officer, and Colonel Hoyle, who had commanded the 45th Infantry on Bataan, went out, as did Colonel Jenks, the USFIP finance officer, Colonel Hill, the Inspector General, and Colonel Savage, the air officer. All these men held locked within themselves and within the records that accompanied them experience too precious to lose. General Moore offered Colonel Louis J. Bowler a berth on the sub, but the gentlemanly adjutant demurred. "No," he said, "send a nurse."

A complete roster of those still alive went, along with a list of recent promotions. In this way "Skinny" Wainwright and George Moore did their best for their men. Had promotion orders not gone, many would not have received credit, and the allotments of their dependents through three long years of captivity would have been substantially less.

What kept those going who stayed behind? The men themselves wondered. Considering the terrific punishment the Rock was taking and the weariness of the exposed units, cases of combat fatigue were surprisingly few. Colonel Wibb E. Cooper, the chief surgeon, and his fellow medical officers believed that this was because there was no escape from reality, no place to hide. What is more surprising is that morale held up adequately, although a decline became noticeable in the last few days when even the most sanguine finally realized that help would not come.

The combat leaders, commissioned and noncommissioned, were professional soldiers. War was their business, and so long as they could fight they would fight. Their men were for the most part volunteers, in the Philippines because they had elected to be. They took fierce pride in unit and country. The majority of the men on Corregidor did not then and do not now believe their sacrifice was in vain. Many remain certain that their stand saved Australia from Japanese invasion and was therefore militarily worth it. But they paid heavily in blood; by May 5 the casualty figure stood at about a thousand killed and wounded since the war began, and the worst was to come.

On May 5, 1942, the Japanese took all four of the Fortified Islands of Manila Bay under heavy fire, concentrating most of the day on the batteries, probably as a deception measure. Planes roared constantly overhead at low altitudes without reply from the antiaircraft guns. Nevertheless, at General Wainwright's command, George Moore at 12:30 P.M. ordered Paul Bunker to fire a co-ordinated counterbattery with everything he had left. Crofton (14-inch gun) on Frank, Wilson (14-inch turret) on Drum, and Way (one 12-inch mortar), Cheney (one 12-inch gun), Wheeler (one 12-inch gun), and roving batteries Wright, Rose, and Gulick, all on Corregidor, roared defiance simultaneously, exploding three ammunition dumps and silencing several Japanese batteries, at least temporarily. A pinprick this was, a fine gesture of defiance, by men who knew their hours of freedom were numbered.

Air raid number 300 sounded at 2:47 P.M. with Fort Hughes the target. Dropping very low, the Japanese pilots were accurate, filling Craighill's mortar pits with debris and inflicting several casualties. By 6:30 P.M. all the harbor forts were being pounded "terrifically," and an ominous change had taken place in the fire directed at Corregidor.

The Japanese had begun to shell the tail and beaches of the north shore, obviously in a pre-invasion bombardment. At 9:00 P.M. Colonel Howard ordered the beach defenses manned, the shelling having grown more intense rather than slackening, as it usually did after nightfall. The tip-off came at about 9:30 from the sound locators of the 60th's searchlight units. Amid the din of bursting shells their great mechanical ears picked up the unmistakable sound of many landing barges warming up in the vicinity of Limay. The operators flashed the word to the air defense headquarters, and from there Colonel Chase relayed it to H Station, General Moore's command post. At 10:30 Moore warned Colonel Howard, "Enemy landing attack indicated." The issue now was joined; the Japanese soon would be on their way.

13 ☆ The Fight for the Beaches

AT DUSK on the evening of May 5 the two thousand heavily laden infantrymen of Colonel Sato's 1st and 2nd Battalions, 61st Infantry, clambered awkwardly into their landing barges, which were drawn up along the beaches of Lamao on the east coast of Bataan—out of range of Fort Drum's rifles. A few minutes later they were jolting across choppy waters for their line of departure from whence the plan called for them to drive ahead and ground on the tail of Corregidor at exactly 11:00 P.M. Overhead the shells of the massed artillery shrieked toward the defense lines of Company A. Observers on Fort Hughes watched transfixed as the entire tail of the island appeared to turn into a vast sheet of flames, which gradually became obscured by rising dust and smoke.

The inexperienced coxswains from Colonel Ogawa's 21st Engineer Regiment were having trouble with their barges. Because of Corregidor's distinctive silhouette, they had expected to have no difficulty finding their assigned beaches, but as they approached, familiar landmarks blended into the shore line or disappeared in the dust and smoke. Moreover, the barges had arrived in reverse order at the line of departure, forcing Colonel Sato to send those carrying the 2nd Battalion across the rear of those containing the 1st, even though this meant the 2nd would arrive almost an hour after the 1st had grounded. Finally, to complete a sequence of errors, an unanticipated current swept the barges well east of their intended landing beaches, bringing the infantrymen ashore from North Point eastward to the tip of the tail. This put them thousands of yards further from Malinta

Hill, their daylight objective. It also brought them into point-blank range of Lieutenant Lawrence's concealed weapons on the curling tail, which could not have borne on the enemy had Sato's men landed, as planned, further to the west.

Shortly before 11:00 P.M. the bombardment suddenly reached its peak of intensity as the enemy gunners poured in white phosphorus shells that seared ground already stripped bare of vegetation. To the defenders the barrage seemed "unbelievably worse." Then it abruptly shifted westward, away from the landing beaches toward Malinta Hill, giving the hard-pressed Marines and GIs of A and D Companies a chance to shake the earth and debris from their backs and come up for air.

Looking toward the North Channel at about 11:10 P.M. the men of Sergeant John F. Hamrich's squad of Company A, stationed near Cavalry Point, spotted dim shapes approaching on the water. "Here they come!" someone yelled. A shot roared, then another, a machine gun began to stutter, and soon up and down the beaches A and D Companies and Lawrence's Scouts were blazing away with everything they had, .30 and .50 caliber machine guns, 75's, M-1916 37's, rifles, even pistols.

"I saw what I took to be a row of men standing along the side of a boat with their head and shoulders above the edge of the boat," writes Lloyd A. Ponder, an Air Corps man attached to Company A. "The machine guns opened up . . . and the heads and shoulders fell over like dominoes falling down." Again and again he fired his 1903 Springfield, which "felt like a mule kicking," until it grew so hot it oozed cosmoline.

A platoon of Mobile Battery under Lieutenant Thomas A. Hackett, stationed on Kindley Field, poured out murder from their heavy antiaircraft machine guns. It was hard for the gunners to see at first with the moon still set and no searchlights operating, but the glow of their tracers streaking over the water soon provided enough light to aim. The Japanese on the left flank who landed in front of Lawrence were virtually annihilated. The young officer commanded in all eighty-two men, including marines, Scouts, and ten attached escapees from Bataan. They were armed with two 75's, two 37 mm. subcaliber guns on machine-gun mounts, and two .50 and two .30 caliber machine guns. They also had rifles for every man, eight Browning automatic rifles, and several thousand hand grenades. To supplement this heavy collection of firepower—which was good by World War II or any other standard—they had improvised chutes extending over the tops of the low, precipitous cliffs from which Air Corps twenty-five pound fragmentation bombs could be slid to detonate on the beaches below.

When he heard the motors of the Japanese barges approaching, Lawrence ordered his beach defense searchlight turned on and illuminated the barges a hundred yards out. Small arms fire quickly shot out the light but not before all hands had a good look at the enemy. As elsewhere the glow of tracers soon provided illumination. The 75's—which had been ordered to remain discreetly silent during the bombardment—plinked off barges like ripe fruit, while those barges that grounded were riddled by the 37's and machine guns. At the beginning of the action Lawrence found Corporal Navarro, the gun commander of the number one 75, peering through his gunsight in puzzlement. "Sir, I cannot see them through my sight. The light is out." Lawrence pointed down the barrel and yelled, "Use it like a shotgun, you're shooting ducks on the pond, now." Navarro and his men then fired with the speed and precision of their best peacetime drills, blasting barge after barge. "We heard the Japanese crying for mercy," Lawrence recalls, "telling us to cease fire, they were Filipinos." His men responded with a rain of hand grenades and fragmentation bombs onto the beach below. If any of the Japanese of the first wave who grounded in front of Lawrence managed to survive, they did so only by slipping along the beach to the westward, away from the death pouring from above.

How many barges sank in this first wave and how many of Sato's "human bullets" lost their lives never will be known. But the Japanese, who had been expecting an easy landing, were shocked at their losses. Lieutenant Mochizuki, who later came ashore with the 2nd Battalion, told a Japanese Domei news agency correspondent that the landing was "a dreadful massacre" and that only 30 percent of the men reached shore safely. Nevertheless, except in front of Lawrence, they won enough scattered footholds to consolidate a beachhead.

At North Point proper, coming in against positions held by Gunnery Sergeant John Mercurio's 2nd Platoon of A Company, the invaders had an easier time of it—but not by much. Of necessity Mercurio's resistance was spotty because so many of his men had left their exposed beach positions to seek better shelter inland from the enemy's shell fire. A few barges, including the one that carried Colonel Sato, slipped ashore unseen and unopposed; others met savage resistance, as when Gunnery Sergeant Dudley of Company D actually lifted up the trails of his 37 mm. gun, so that the weapon could fire below its normal level of depression at the barges below.

When the Japanese climbed from the beach Mercurio's marines and soldiers fought with valor, although for most it was their first taste of combat. Gunnery Sergeant "Tex" Haines took on single-handed a party of invaders coming up a ravine. After emptying two pistols at them, he picked up the rifle of a dead buddy and emptied that. Then, cradling a machine gun with a mount damaged by shrapnel, he advanced against the enemy, stopping only to fit a new belt to the gun. He fired two belts of ammunition before a Japanese threw a grenade which wounded him horribly, putting out an eye. Eventually Mercurio's men had to retreat, filtering westward through the darkness to safer ground. Despite very heavy losses the Japanese had gotten ashore and had won a firm hold along most of the northern edge of Kindley Field. On the cliff below the western edge of the field a surviving knot of about twenty 803rd Engineers continued to hold out.

While A Company was locked in battle, Mobile's 3rd Platoon had been helping out with its antiaircraft machine guns, the first section from a position on the southwest corner of the airfield opposite the Japanese, the second section from a position on a little ridge on the same side, about halfway down the runway.

Two of the second section gunners, Ralph W. Middlebrooks and Cloyd W. Montgomery, for some time kept the Japanese from crossing the lower end of Kindley Field. Lieutenant Hackett, the platoon commander, kept yelling, "For God's sakes, Montgomery, don't let them cross that airfield." Montgomery did his best. He, Middlebrooks, and the others dug up the tripods of their heavy weapons and aimed the guns below their normal level of depression directly onto the field; but in a short time the Japanese, alternately crawling and rushing at them across the field, forced them to slip away from the gun pits to avoid capture. They became separated, but most escaped either to Battery Denver's positions on Water Tank Hill or to the Navy's Radio Intercept Tunnel on Monkey Point. Sergeant Odas A. Greer lugged a .30 caliber machine gun with him and used it until he was too badly wounded to fight on.

The 3rd Platoon's first section was even less fortunate. Early in the action, while the gunners still were firing at the landing barges, a shell burst at the edge of the pits, wounding several men. Lieutenant Kenneth W. Ramsay loaded them into a truck and sent them on toward Malinta Tunnel by way of the South Shore Road, then took the remaining men and pulled back to the Radio Intercept Tunnel on Monkey Point, where some dozens of strayed and confused soldiers and marines were gathering.

Unfortunately, his retirement induced Mobile's 2nd Platoon to retreat. Located on the east end of the ridge above Kindley Field, a key position, the 2nd Platoon might have blocked Sato's westward advance had it stood and fought. As the truck carrying the wounded from the 3rd Platoon passed, the platoon commander jumped to the conclusion that the tail of the Rock was being evacuated, and in accord with prearranged plans ordered his men to withdraw hundreds of yards westward to an old concrete infantry trench near the east portal of Malinta Tunnel, built during World War I and intended as a final line of resistance. There the platoon set up, suffered through periodic enemy barrages, and waited for an enemy that never came.

By about midnight, perhaps a little before, perhaps a little after, Sato's 1st Battalion had succeeded in knocking out most of the resistance along the landing beaches, with the exception of the Rock's tail eastward of the airfield, which was still held firmly by Lawrence. Lieutenant William F. Harris, U.S.M.C., commanding the 1st Platoon of Company A, also was holding out with his men between Cavalry and Infantry Points, as was the little band of aviation engineers of the 803rd, even though Sato's men were cutting in behind them. A small group of Japanese had dug in on the airfield to contain the Americans concentrated near the Radio Intercept Tunnel at Monkey Point. The main body, with Sato in the lead, had begun a cautious advance along the shell-pocked North Shore Road toward the high ground of Water Tank Hill. It moved slowly, shooting up flares as it went, to signal its position to the artillery on Bataan.

At about this same time the landing barges of the 2nd Battalion left their line of departure in the North Channel and started for shore. They paid heavily for their delay. Sighted while much further out than their predecessors, they were enveloped in a murderous cross fire from what appeared to Japanese observers on Bataan to be a hundred guns raining red-hot steel.

Massello's Battery Way went into action, as did Craighill and two beach defense 75's and Battery Idaho on Fort Hughes. Captain Stockton D. Bruns's Idaho gunners fired their 3-inch antiaircraft pieces below normal depression, spraying the water with deadly shrapnel and lashing the North Channel into a froth. Fragments pattered about the twenty isolated 803rd Engineers as they too blazed away "with everything we had," while Japanese to their flanks and rear lobbed grenades and mortar shells at them.

On the extreme tail, Lieutenant Lawrence's men were busily mopping up isolated Japanese snipers on the beaches below and clearing their gun pits of spent cartridges when they sighted the second wave of barges approaching. They opened up at five hundred yards, and in Lawrence's words, "I doubt if any reached the shore. I'm sure we sank at least a dozen offshore." After daylight he counted twenty-two half-sunk landing craft and four others drifting fully loaded with sixty dead Japanese in each. Hundreds of bodies in orange-colored life jackets floated in the water, giving the sharks and barracudas a feast. "We of course," Lawrence continues, "were in good spirits. I had one dead Philippine Scout and one wounded, both from small arms."

In contrast the shaken survivors of the Japanese 2nd Battalion who had reached the beach were in very low spirits. "Most of us," one said later, "just kept still—half-leaning, half-lying against the slope—just waiting, hoping that reinforcements would arrive." Few managed to get off the beaches until daylight, and Sato's 1st Battalion had to carry on the fight with little reinforcement until the dawn brought the landing of a reinforcing battalion.

The antiaircraft gunners of Denver first heard the Japanese were ashore from the 3rd Platoon of Mobile Battery as it passed by along the South Shore Road. Paul Cornwall at once mustered his tired men, many of whom had just fallen into numbed sleep in the shelter of two power-plant tunnels located below the gun square on the sheltered south slope of Water Tank Hill. Recognizing their condition and their lack of training, he gave them a realistic order: to man their assigned positions across the top of the ridge; to hold out as long as they could; and then to follow their own best judgment. The men, many of whom were so lightheaded they moved as in a dream, drew their small arms and prepared to do their best.

The fighting which followed was so confused no clear picture emerges, but probably not long after midnight the Denver boys—those who did not drift to the rear—found themselves heavily engaged with Sato's leading elements in a concentrated fire fight in the vicinity of the two water towers. The Japanese climbed the hill to the north from the Bataan side, keeping well clear of the mouth of the battery's tunnel, in which nine sharpshooting marines had taken shelter behind a barricade of railroad ties. Denver's .50 caliber machine gun, sited near the water towers, drove them to cover with a vicious fusillade until it grew so hot it jammed. Then the men fought with rifles, rocks, and even fists until driven back down the hill to the vicinity of the streetcar station behind the ashes of the 92nd CA barracks. There some of them joined with Scouts and marines to form a strong point. Others fled westward to Malinta Tunnel.

Denver, however, still had a Parthian shot for the enemy after First Lieutenant Robert W. Perkins rallied some of the men near the car station. He and Private First Class Luz Cisneros led back up the hill a small party which included Privates Halford M. Shirley, Herbert R. Gordon and Ellis W. Slater. Managing to slip past the Japanese located near the water towers, they worked their way along the top of the ridge, tossing grenades into Denver's gun pits as they went. The group killed a Japanese sniper who had tied himself to a tree and then retired southward down the hill to Battery Maxwell Keyes on the south shore. Almost singlehanded they had temporarily cleared the top of the ridge, inflicting considerable loss on the enemy. But they did not try to hold the ground.

Thus Denver was beaten despite scattered, heroic resistance. By 1:30 or 2:00 A.M., Sato held all but the forward slope of Water Tank Hill and was well-entrenched in Denver's splinterproof positions. His infantry had survived frightful losses to take the high ground. The fight for Corregidor had become a stalemate: Sato lacked the manpower to advance further; his disorganized foes could do no more than take precarious cover below Water Tank Hill on the cratered ground, pelted by machine-gun fire and shrapnel.

The command post of Captain Pickup, C.O. of Company A of the marines, was several hundred yards west of the landing point. Consequently, Pickup was unaware that the Japanese had gotten ashore until after midnight when men from his 1st Platoon enlightened him. Like many others, he had seen some of the Japanese barges appear to turn back and had assumed his men had defeated the landing. On learning that the Japanese were advancing along the North Shore Road, and knowing that the defense plan called for Denver to hold a line across Water Tank Hill, he at once ordered Marine Gunner H. M. Ferrell, commanding D Company's mortars, to go up to Denver and investigate. This Ferrell did in company with Corporal O. O. Morris. They were actually into the battery positions before they heard voices "not American" and dropped hastily to the ground. Morris crawled up closer and came back to whisper that Denver had "Japs all over it" digging in. Returning to Pickup's command post, and finding the captain absent for the moment, Ferrell began sending men from his own mortar squads up along the north side of the ridge. His intent was to keep the enemy off the backs of A Company scattered along the beaches below.

On Ferrell's return, Pickup was disturbed by his report but was disinclined to pull Company A from the beaches to deal with what might be only a few Japanese. His main concern was to plug the "hole" through which the invaders had gotten ashore. Although artillery from 14-inch rifles to 75 mm. guns was intact and could have borne on the tail, neither a fire plan nor communications existed to zero them in. Pickup had to do the job on his own. He was grateful, therefore, when his fellow marine, Captain Noel E. Castle, commanding Company D, agreed to take some of his men and a few stragglers up to Denver and drive out the enemy. Innocent of what they were in for, and with Castle walking upright in the lead a few yards ahead, the small party started along a road leading toward the hill, but when they neared the road junction immediately in front of the hill, the "pings" of machine-gun bullets sent them diving for cover. Ahead, Castle plunged dead in the road.

This disaster and the obvious strength of the Japanese greatly alarmed Pickup and also Colonel Beecher's adjutant, Captain Golland L. Clark, Jr., U.S.M.C., who had arrived from Malinta Tunnel to find out what was happening. The two captains still did not dare to strip the beach defenses, but rounded up every spare man they could find and rushed them toward Water Tank Hill. Within a few minutes they had a line of sorts, about two platoons in number, scattered across the road on the north or Bataan side of the hill.

On the other, the Cavite, side, unknown at first to the marine captains, Lieutenant Colonel Lloyd W. Biggs of the 92nd Coast Artillery had been organizing a line of defense with stragglers from Denver Battery, some stray marines, and his own Philippine Scouts of

Batteries E and F, who had been manning batteries and beach defense 75's on the south shore. At 12:30 A.M. he had dispatched a runner to General Moore reporting that he had formed a line across the top of the ridge below Water Tank Hill, tied in with the marines. Nevertheless, the line was dangerously thin and the situation critical. The GIs, Scouts, and marines holding before Water Tank Hill urgently needed help if Sato was to be kept from his obvious objective, Malinta Tunnel, and Wainwright's headquarters.

Back in the tunnel Colonel Howard had not learned of the Japanese landing until 11:47, a half hour after the event. Then he at once had ordered his Regimental Reserve under Major Schaeffer to come down to the tunnel and had alerted the 4th Battalion, which for the time being remained in Government ravine. General Moore for his part had alerted Batteries B, C, D, and H, of the 59th CA, manning Wheeler, Crockett, Cheney, and Geary, to form as infantry. Neither had dared to do more, for the probability existed that the Japanese might land on Topside at dawn. If that happened Howard and Moore wanted reserves available there, too.

A situation had developed that would have been ludicrous had it not been so serious. With something like fifteen thousand personnel on Corregidor, with perhaps four or five thousand of these concentrated in the Malinta and Navy tunnel systems, Howard and Moore found themselves unable to scrape together a reserve greater than ten understrength infantry companies, six marine and four Army, with none adequately equipped with supporting weapons, to oppose perhaps a thousand Japanese. At this point the Rock had a surfeit of technicians, administrators, and even nurses; it needed fighters.

Urgent pleas from Beecher convinced Howard at about 2:00 A.M., or perhaps a few minutes earlier, that it was time to commit Schaeffer's Regimental Reserve, Company O under Captain Robert Chambers, Jr., and Company P under a rugged marine first lieutenant with the appropriate name of William F. Hogaboom, who already had proved his valor on Bataan in the "Battle of the Points." Guided by Beecher's adjutant, the ubiquitous Captain Clark, Schaeffer's men moved out of the east portal of the tunnel, formed as skirmishers, and started for Water Tank Hill about 750 yards away. They had not gone far when several of them fired on shadowy forms on a ridge to the left, only to have an explosion of "sulphurous oaths" identify the targets as "friendly." The voices belonged to Captain James R. Holmes and Second Lieutenant William F. (Bull) King of Mobile Battery, supervising their defense line in the concrete infantry trench. King, who had a voice "like a great big bullfrog," had been commissioned on April 17, 1942. Prior to this he had enjoyed his reputation as the roughest, toughest, meanest first sergeant on the Rock.

About halfway to the combat area misfortune struck. The two companies fell under one of the periodic artillery barrages the enemy was rolling back and forth between Bottomside and Water Tank Hill. Although the marines took shelter in bomb craters, they were badly hurt. Hogaboom's Company P came through in fair shape, but Chambers' Company O was decimated. Many men in all three of its platoons were killed or wounded, including eight in Quartermaster Clerk Frank W. Ferguson's 1st and all but five in Quartermaster Sergeant John E. Haskin's 3rd.

On his arrival at the extemporary American line, Major Schaeffer took command and began to organize a counterattack. This was very difficult because the individual platoons of his reserve had lost contact, and men from a dozen units, Filipino and American, were all jumbled together. The moon, so bright one could read a newspaper by it, illumined terrain features at some distance but also exposed the men to Sato's machine gunners on the brow of Water Tank Hill. Consequently, the attack of the Regimental Reserve consisted of a series of isolated forays by small knots of men armed only with hand weapons and without the aid of co-ordinated supporting fire. Several platoons did manage to crawl to within thirty yards of Sato's perimeter, and they stayed there near enough to prevent the Japanese from using their artillery on Bataan for fire support. But their audacity also prevented Gunner Ferrell from using his Stokes mortars —the ones without sights. Ferrell went back to direct their fire, but could not get them registered and had to give up after twenty rounds. No means existed to zero in the roving batteries or beach defense 75's on Topside. All communication lines were out.

Since some kind of support weapon seemed indispensable to root the Japanese from their snug positions in Denver's sandbagged gun pits, Captain Chambers attempted to obtain one of the portable 37 mm. guns from the beach defenses, only to be told that the threat of additional landings made sparing the weapon impossible. That left only hand grenades, and repeated attempts by individuals to crawl forward and hurl them proved extremely costly. Also, fallen trees interfered with a clean toss.

Nor was Sato idle. Although content to continue to reinforce his line and to beat off American forays while awaiting the reinforcement landing scheduled for daybreak, he continued, as opportunity presented, to send men down the hill to infiltrate the American line. This was a time-tested Japanese tactic which many times previously had induced the enemy to retreat. Just as did his superiors, Sato relied on the "spiritual strength" of his men to provide what was hoped would be decisively effective, though suicidal, bravery. In one bizarre incident a Japanese, who quite possibly had been a student at an American university a year or two before, came tearing down the hill "screaming like a panther" and yelling in perfect English, "the Japs are right behind me." Quartermaster Clerk Ferguson, who witnessed the incident, was momentarily so taken aback that he did not fire, even though he realized the man was an enemy. Several other marines laughed aloud.

As dawn broke, Ferguson and five of his men decided to try to outflank the Japanese by following the South Shore Road along the south side of the hill. They discovered to their cost that the foe had anticipated this move; automatic weapons rattled and four of the six Americans fell. Accompanied only by Corporal Alvin E. Stewart of Company A of the 803rd Engineers, a soldier who had joined him during the night, Ferguson slipped past the machine-gun coverage and into a roadcut that afforded some protection. Climbing up on the south side the two kept some scarred trees between themselves and the Japanese in Denver's positions above.

Much jabbering among their enemies revealed to the crouching Americans that their advance had been seen. While trying to figure out a way to hurl a grenade, Ferguson was astonished to see the foe begin to climb one by one from their "beautiful and well-nigh impregnable positions" and start for the rear. Silhouetted against the sky, they made perfect targets for Stewart and Ferguson, who shot down some twenty "like ducks in a shooting gallery." Evidently the officer in charge had concluded that he was about to be outflanked and chose the textbook solution, withdrawal. He stubbornly carried through his plan even though his men were toppling over as quickly as they clambered from the splinterproof.

Finally the luck of the audacious pair ran out. Two rifle bullets suddenly hit Ferguson in the face, ripping open the lower end of his nose and cheek. Stewart, whom Ferguson describes as "always cool and collected," bandaged him and then the two men crawled back to their own lines. Ferguson, who had thrilled to the excitement of battle ("I had enjoyed this sensation many times before in Nicaragua"), reported to Major Schaeffer and then walked to Malinta Tunnel for treatment. After eating a handful of sulfa tablets and sleeping pills, this great fighter fell asleep as soon as he left the operating table and did not awake until the afternoon of the next day. Perhaps had all the defenders been like Ferguson and Stewart, or Perkins and Cisneros, Colonel Sato and his "human bullets" would have been annihilated that early morning. But as the sun rose, the enemy still was there. The battle had yet to reach its climax.

14 ☆ The Battle of Water Tank Hill

At about 4:40 A.M., shortly before the first rays of dawn, lookouts on Topside spotted more Japanese landing craft in the North Channel bringing in the scheduled reinforcements. Fort Drum's big rifles, which had been firing on the Cabcaben dock area, shifted to them. Battery Way fired its one remaining mortar, as did Battery Stockade its one 155 mm., and the roving battery, Wright. Some of the men of Lieutenant Harris' 1st Platoon of A Company, still on the beaches anchoring the northern flank of the line, riddled several barges with their two machine guns. The Japanese record their losses in this reinforcement landing as much lower than in the first two, probably because the craft traveled a course that masked them from Lieutenant Lawrence's Scouts and their deadly 75's. Nevertheless, this reinforcement attempt reduced to only twenty-one the number of serviceable landing craft General Homma had left. When word of this as well as of the counterattack of Companies O and P reached him, the Japanese commander, as he said at his postwar trial in Manila, was thrown into "an agony of mind." At this point he believed that the landing had failed.

Shortly after, as soon as it became light, the Japanese Air Force began an all-out bombing effort. The artillery intensified its firing but could not hammer the soldiers and marines below Water Tank Hill because the lines were too closely drawn. It concentrated therefore on repeatedly sweeping the area between Malinta Hill and the firing line. When daylight came Lieutenant Jenkins' marines stationed on the

Bataan side of the hill found the appearance of the terrain about them radically altered as a result of the terrific fire.

The Japanese flyers did not go unscathed—the gunners of the 60th still had some punch left. Boston and Globe somehow had struggled back into action and scattered several flights with their fire. Although confirmation is impossible, Captain Abston's men of Globe were convinced that at least two planes were downed by close bursts. Later in the morning six biplanes on floats attacked Globe from vertical dives, only to miss when the attached .50's of Indiana Battery fired on them so fiercely their bombs fell wild. At about 10:30 that morning Fort Drum was to get its only enemy plane. Its two .50 caliber guns manned by marines splashed a dive bomber which had been trying to silence Battery Wilson's still roaring 14-inch rifles. To the end Drum remained Homma's most formidable foe. As Colonel Motohiko Yoshida, the Chief of Staff of the 4th Division, put it, "Fraile was a constant headache to us."

Another headache was a 155 commanded by Captain Jack Gulick, the son of the former Chief of Coast Artillery. With a crew of Scouts from Battery Cebu, who had manned antiaircraft guns on Bataan, Gulick had emplaced his "roving" battery on Topside between two warehouses which effectively masked the flash from the gun muzzle. The Japanese did not spot him from the air, and wrongly assumed that he was firing from the vicinity of the golf course, located to his rear. Consequently, they gave Abston's Globe a miserable time, but failed to get the energetic Gulick, who kept up a steady fire at the landing barges as they loaded and unloaded at the Cabcaben area throughout the morning of the sixth.

The great ordeal, however, fell on Major William Massello's crew from Battery Erie, which had taken over Battery Way. With no concealment and little protection from Japanese counterbattery, by now registered with extreme accuracy, his men began firing their one remaining 12-inch mortar as soon as the Japanese landing was reported. Their other two serviceable pieces had earlier received direct hits on the gun tubes which had dented one and split the other. Heretofore, Massello's strategy had been to fire for a time and then to lay low and "sweat out" the Japanese reply. Now the chips were down, so Erie's gunners simply kept on firing even with Jap shells pelting about and into the pit. Massello stayed in the open with his men.

At about 3:00 A.M., on orders from Lieutenant Colonel Norman Simmonds, the fire commander, Way shifted its fire directly onto the Japanese beachhead at North Point. However, some of the 670-pound projectiles, which had a lethal radius of over five hundred yards, fell very close to Lieutenant Lawrence, while others endangered the marines and soldiers containing Sato at Water Tank Hill. Reluctantly, Colonel Bunker had to order Simmonds to cease fire.

After this, for the remainder of the morning of May 6, Way fired almost continuously at Bataan and on the landing barges, getting away a round approximately every five minutes. The Japanese replied with counterbattery which Massello describes as "terrific," causing steadily mounting casualties among the gunners. Yet as soon as one crew was knocked out by a direct hit in the pit, another would dash from the safety of the bombproof magazine to take its place. Corporal William A. Graham's gunners fired for an hour before a Japanese salvo wounded four of his men and put a piece of shrapnel through his lung. Graham said, "Well, boys, that's my ticket but you guys keep on firing." He died shortly after. The next crew immediately took over. One of the noncoms, Sergeant Walter A. Kulinski, recalls with wonderment the bravery of the men. "I have never in my life seen men like that crew . . . they were wounded, but they wanted to fire those guns." One man continued servicing the piece although his stomach had been torn open. "You couldn't keep them down. That's the funny thing—I can't understand it. They were fighting fools."

At 5:00 A.M., the last officially designated "gun crew" was shot out. From then on cooks, motor sergeants, communications men, clerks, and other "noncombatants" kept the old mortar firing to the accompaniment of a constant stream of wisecracks from Private Arthur Davis, cook, rammer, and morale-sustainer extraordinary. By this time the emplacement was literally coming to pieces; part of the front wall had collapsed, and concrete fragments lay piled two to three feet high on each side of the runway from the magazine to the mortar. A thick blanket of powder slivers covered the floor of the pit, catching fire with each Japanese salvo. The crews were forced to beat out each blaze with wet burlap. Recoil oil was running short, causing the trunnions to slam "with an awful wallop" against the rubber recoil buffer of the mortar with each round. It was, as Colonel Massello has written, the "last performance of the old concrete artillery," but it was "an honorable end."

In midmorning Massello, who had remained in the mortar pit the whole time and whom Kulinski terms ". . . a fighting man, a real Coast Artillery officer," is reported to have ordered the telephones ripped from the wall of the battery. He did not, he said, want anyone to send him an order to surrender. At about 11:00 A.M. he was badly wounded, with a major leg wound and an arm almost severed. Captain Fred Miller of Jerseyville, Illinois, then assumed command in the pit, although Massello remained on hand in a stretcher. By this time casualties had risen to well over 70 percent, with men hit by shrapnel or knocked unconscious by concussion and flying concrete. Kulinski was out, a victim of shrapnel and backwash concussion suffered while standing near the wall of the pit. The bravery of Private First Class James H. Farmer, Jr., saved many of the wounded. He helped load the casualties onto a truck and then made repeated trips through shell fire and bombing to the battalion aid station at Battery Wheeler.

Massello's wound brought a temporary cease fire, and when the crew tried to resume, it found that the mortar had cooled sufficiently to freeze the breechblock. "The old mortar had finally quit on us," Massello recalls, "but it had lasted long enough to be the last big gun on Corregidor to fire on the enemy."

Dawn brought no comfort to the four anxious commanders,

Beecher, Howard, Moore, and Wainwright, who had spent the night trying without success to learn the details of the fighting. The Japanese had been stopped at Water Tank Hill, they knew, but unless the enemy could be driven from Denver's positions and into the sea, General Homma could reinforce his troops there at will. The reinforcement landing just before dawn had proved that the Rock's batteries could not stop all boat movement in the North Channel. Most significantly, Homma's shortage of landing craft was unknown to them. All Colonel Howard could do was to commit to action the four reserve companies of ill-trained veteran sailors, 275 officers and men under Major "Joe" Williams, the so-called 4th Battalion, 4th Marines, and hope that, somehow, they could drive Sato into the sea.

For some time the 4th Battalion had been in the Malinta Tunnel awaiting orders, having moved out of Government ravine and traversed safely the shell-swept Bottomside area. About 4:30 A.M. it left the tunnel with Q Company, commanded by Captain Paul C. Moore, U.S.A., in the lead, followed by R, S, and T. Sixty artillerymen of Battery B of the 59th CA under the aggressive Captain Herman H. Hauck followed them as a reserve. The men moved willingly like veteran troops, even though the stream of badly wounded men being brought into the tunnel for hospitalization had given them a fairly clear idea of what they were in for. About five hundred yards from the east portal the periodic Japanese artillery barrage dispersed them and inflicted casualities, but the men escaped the heavy losses Companies O and P of the Regimental Reserve had suffered. About two hundred yards from the fighting line they formed as skirmishers and advanced until the line was reached. Q and R reinforced the left flank, while S and T bolstered the center and right. The men took cover while Williams conferred with Schaeffer, and the two marine majors planned their attack strategy.

In the absence of mortars or other supporting weapons all they could do was repeat the tactic of O and P: launch a frontal assault with every available man, and hope for the best. Beginning at 6:15 A.M. the line began to inch forward up the slope toward the two water

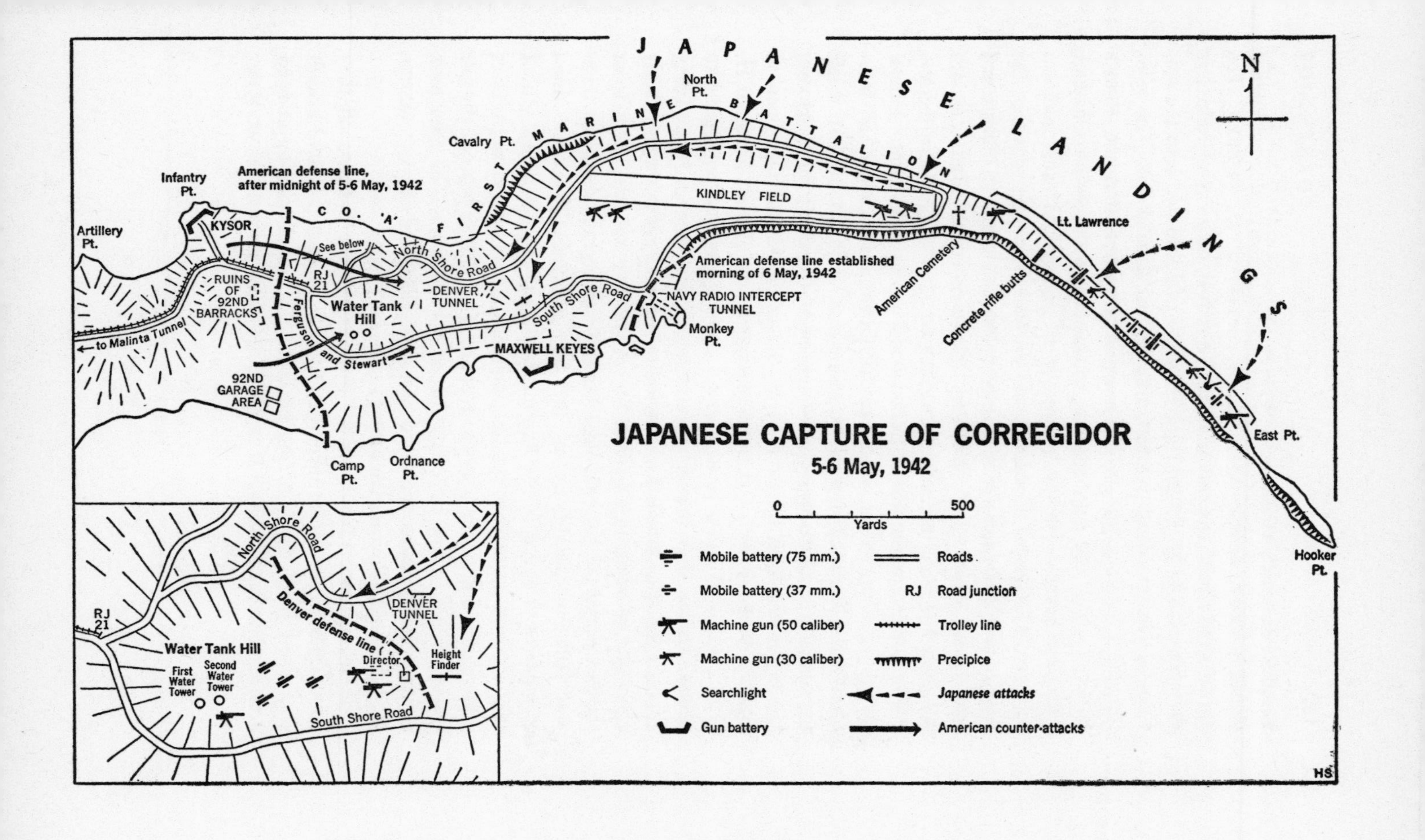

JAPANESE CAPTURE OF CORREGIDOR
5-6 May, 1942
JAPANESE LANDINGS
FIRST MARINE BATTALION
CO. 'A'
North Pt.
Cavalry Pt.
Infantry Pt.
Artillery Pt.
American defense line, after midnight of 5-6 May, 1942
KYSOR
RUINS OF 92ND BARRACKS
to Malinta Tunnel
See below
RJ 21
North Shore Road
Water Tank Hill
DENVER TUNNEL
Ferguson and Stewart
92ND GARAGE AREA
Camp Pt.
Ordnance Pt.
South Shore Road
MAXWELL KEYES
KINDLEY FIELD
American defense line established morning of 6 May, 1942
NAVY RADIO INTERCEPT TUNNEL
Monkey Pt.
American Cemetery
Concrete rifle butts
Lt. Lawrence
East Pt.
Hooker Pt.
N
0
500
Yards
Mobile battery (75 mm.)
Mobile battery (37 mm.)
Machine gun (50 caliber)
Machine gun (30 caliber)
Searchlight
Gun battery
Roads
RJ Road junction
Trolley line
Precipice
Japanese attacks
American counter-attacks
RJ 21
North Shore Road
DENVER TUNNEL
Denver defense line
Water Tank Hill
First Water Tower
Second Water Tower
Director
Height Finder
South Shore Road
HS

towers that gave the hill its name. The men advanced courageously, firing as they went, flushing the Japanese who had tried to infiltrate, scoring a gain of two hundred to three hundred yards on the left flank. Since boyhood Lieutenant Charles B. Brook, U.S.N., S-2 of the extempore battalion, had wondered what it would be like to charge an enemy. Now he found himself doing it, yelling and cursing the foe like the others about him. Near the water towers he and the rest found the fire so intense they had to take cover before reaching the machine guns in Denver's sandbagged positions just beyond. Sheer guts could not substitute for well-served howitzers or mortars. Moreover, by this time Sato's 1st Battalion had been reinforced by the survivors of the 2nd, who had finally crawled up from the beaches, and by others who had come ashore in the reinforcement landing at dawn.

As in the case of the attacks of O and P, only grenades were available to aid the battalion's counterattack. Party after party of eight to ten men crawled forward to silence the enemy guns in Denver's pits only to be cut down with heavy losses and virtually no gain. Lieutenant Bethel B. Otter, U.S.N., commanding Company T, accompanied by Ensign Lloyd and four Navy enlisted men, launched one of the most heroic attacks. At about 7:30 A.M. they crawled forward, and when close enough, Otter and Lloyd jumped up, dashed ahead and threw their grenades. They destroyed an enemy nest, but both men were killed by enemy fire. Not long after, Otter's "exec," Captain Calvin E. Chunn, U.S.A., who had taken over the company, was severely wounded in the chest while attempting to lead a rush against a 75 mm. mountain gun the Japanese were trying to emplace near the water towers. In another attack Lieutenant Brook had a leg mangled by a grenade. Carried back to Malinta Tunnel on a piece of sheet metal, he was taken directly to the operating room where his lower leg was removed under a spinal anesthetic. Reminded of the exclamation of Lord Nelson's, "How cold the steel is!" when the arm of the British naval hero was cut off without anesthesia, Brook thought how cold the knife felt—and calculated his retirement pay.

In a similar action fortune was more kind. Captain Harold Dalness, U.S.A., commanding Company R, together with Lieutenant Otis E. Saalman, U.S.A., led several men up a draw toward a Japanese machine gun sited in a commanding position at the top. From behind cover the party poured in a heavy fire with their Enfields to keep the Japanese low while another man crawled up close with a grenade. The man pitched it into the gun pit, and—just as in the movies—a Japanese soldier snatched it up and rose to throw it back—only to have the deadly missile explode in his hand. The grenade knocked out this Japanese nest, but it did not breech the interlocking chain of automatic weapons Sato's men had skillfully woven across the top of the hill and along its lateral slopes. It would have taken a heavy and extremely accurate artillery barrage to break that web. Apparently nobody had thought of digging in a battery of 75's near the east portal and sending forward a fire control party with a "walkie-talkie" to direct pinpoint fire. Once again a lack of prevision cost the Rock dear.

A pair of rugged marine old-timers, Battalion Sergeant Major John H. Sweeney and Quartermaster Sergeant John Haskin of Companies O and P, undertook the most successful attempt to break the deadlock. Close friends in life, they decided to crawl to one of the water towers, climb up, and from this vantage point hurl grenades squarely into the sandbagged Jap nests. Sweeney threw the grenades with deadly aim, blasting several gun pits, while Haskin apparently climbed and reclimbed the tower several times to bring him more. Their bravery enabled the others to advance a short way along the south flank of the hill, but Haskin finally was killed while reclimbing the tower, and Sweeney, too, died atop the tank, the one on which First Sergeant Brady of Battery Denver had earlier lost his life.

Their gallantry impressed their foes. In a propaganda movie allegedly depicting the fall of Corregidor—a film which some of the Americans saw later in prison camp—the Japanese restaged this episode, but with a Japanese captain in the leading role, hurling down grenades from the water tower and killing hundreds of Americans below.

Major Williams did his best to keep his men moving forward. He was here, there, everywhere along the line, conferring with his company and platoon commanders, organizing parties for grenade attacks, moving forward himself to lay down supporting fire with the rifle he carried. He constantly exposed himself to fire. Though finally wounded, Williams survived the battle, only to succumb in a prison camp in Japan in 1945.

By about 9.00 A.M. Major Williams realized the attack had bogged down. Despite the loss of fifteen officers and at least 150 enlisted men in repeated forays, the 4th Battalion had failed to dislodge Sato. Williams already had committed the last of his reserves, the sixty coast artillerymen under Captain Hauck, against some Japanese trying to sneak around the American line along the south shore.

At about 10:00 A.M. or a little before, some of the men—including Lieutenant Saalman—who had worked their way into a shoulder of the hill on the Bataan side, from where they could look down on Kindley Field, sighted two Japanese tanks. One was still in its landing barge, but the other was crawling up a slide onto the airstrip. The sight of these steel monsters, combined with a Japanese artillery barrage laid just to the rear, panicked the left side of the line briefly, and some men fled their positions. Major Williams stabilized it with effort and sent four men and two officers to the rear to report to Colonel Beecher and try to find a weapon to deal with the tanks. They found nothing.

On learning about the tanks, and also of the severe casualties Williams had suffered, Colonel Howard ordered the defenders to fall back to the old concrete infantry trench near the east portal of the tunnel. Many of the men were indignant at the order; others never received it and remained in their positions. Those who retired were pummeled by the Japanese artillery as they retreated. Only a hundred men or so, joining the gunners of Mobile Battery, occupied the trench to try to make some kind of stand.

Although Colonel Howard did not realize it, matters were not quite so grim as he believed, and his order may have been ill-advised. His only communication was by marine runner, and he had no knowledge of what Herman Hauck was doing with his coast artillerymen or what had been happening in the Monkey Point area. Had he known this, or had he been aware of the Japanese losses of landing barges, he might not have issued the order.

After the break of day, at about seven or eight o'clock in the morning, Captain James R. Bromeyer, U.S.M.C., Lieutenant Mason F. Chronister, U.S.M.C., commander of a platoon of Company B, and attached Air Corps Lieutenants Dayton L. Drachenberg and Edgar D. Whitcomb, together with several other officers, began to organize into a perimeter defense the soldiers and sailors clustered in and around the Radio Intercept Tunnel on Monkey Point. They established a triangular line extending along the high ground for a quarter mile on either side of the tunnel. The men did not advance, but banged away with their rifles at the Japanese on the far side of the airstrip and on the other side of the ridge at the west end of the airfield. For their part, the Japanese replied with a machine gun and small-arms fire and with their nasty little "knee" mortars. Doubtless Colonel Sato was alarmed at this threat suddenly emerging to his left and rear. The line continued to hold and a fire fight still was in progress at the time of surrender.

In the meantime, after the failure of the counterattack of the 4th Battalion, Hauck, aided by some Scouts and a few men from Mobile's 3rd Platoon under Lieutenant Hackett, had attacked Sato's left flank from the vicinity of Battery Maxwell Keyes. Shortly before noon, they actually swept north over the ridge above the west end of the airstrip and down onto the airfield proper, driving the Japanese into the open. Hauck's men were advancing, firing on the Japanese tanks, when word came to give up. Whether they could have driven the Japanese from the field, as Hauck and some of the men believed afterward (and still believe), seems dubious. As it turned out, their counterattack was but a desperate, hopeless attempt to stave off what was in any event inevitable.

The decisive struggle had now resolved itself into a battle for one small hill, fought between units of no more than battalion size, a battle that Colonel Sato's infantrymen had won. Moreover, although the hill was but a few hundred yards from his underground headquarters, few commanders have had less information than "Skinny" Wainwright. That blanket of steel the Japanese artillery on Bataan had been maintaining between Malinta Tunnel and Water Tank Hill had effectively severed his communications and all but isolated the battlefield. "The artillery conquers, the infantry occupies."

Throughout the night the anxious Wainwright had been alternating between Colonel Beecher's command post at the east portal of the Malinta Tunnel and George Moore's H Station lateral. He did not learn of the Japanese tanks until about 10:20 A.M. and then assumed mistakenly that a considerable number had landed. He knew also that the 4th Battalion's counterattack had failed, that Joe Williams and his men had withdrawn to the final defense line, but he was entirely unaware of what Herman Hauck was doing or, apparently, of the presence of three additional coast artillery batteries in the tunnel available as reinforcements. He could not know of Homma's shortage of landing craft; rather, he expected a new landing momentarily on Topside.

In the next ten minutes what apparently loomed largest in Wainwright's thought was the havoc a Japanese tank would cause if it rumbled through Malinta Tunnel, shooting into each lateral as it passed. As he wrote in his memoirs, ". . . it was the terror that is vested in a tank that was the deciding factor." It would be better, he concluded, to surrender rather than to court mass slaughter. Conferring with General Moore and his Chief of Staff, Brigadier General Lewis C. Beebe, he said, "We can't hold out very much longer. Maybe we could last throughout the day, but the end certainly must come tonight. It would be better to clear the situation up now, in daylight." He knew what had happened at Singapore when the British had attempted a night surrender, and of the terror and rapine that had followed when the Japanese troops had gotten out of hand. To Moore he added, "George, I hope I'm doing the right thing. . . . That radiogram of congratulations we got this morning [from President Roosevelt] may mean that we've done about all that's expected of us, anyway."

"The American people," the Commander-in-Chief had radioed Wainwright, "ask no finer example of tenacity, resourcefulness, and steadfast courage. The calm determination of your personal leadership in a desperate situation sets a standard of duty for our soldiers throughout the world. . . . You and your devoted followers have become the living symbols of our war aims and the guarantee of victory."

His decision taken, Wainwright ordered General Beebe to broadcast an already prepared surrender message to General Homma at 10:30 and another in code to Major General William Sharp, the commander of the Filipino and American forces still holding out on Mindanao, releasing him and ordering him to take further commands from General MacArthur in Australia. Finally, he ordered Moore to execute "Pontiac," the code name for a prearranged plan to destroy all weapons above .45 caliber, and also to arrange for the display of a white flag over each of the harbor forts promptly at noon.

In the light of what Wainwright knew and what more we now know, this decision was necessary. The Rock was finished. Colonel Sato was planning to hurl his regiment at Malinta Hill that evening in a night attack, and the 4th Division staff was preparing to abandon the planned Topside landing because of landing craft losses and to send the second attack force of four thousand men onto the already secured beachhead. Beecher's men could not have stopped Sato; it is improbable that Captain Hauck could have pushed his desperate attack much further; and the likely result of continued resistance would have been exactly what Wainwright feared—mass slaughter by frenzied Japanese troops in the tunnel.

As word of the impending surrender at noon spread, the reaction among the men ranged all the way from numbed and resigned acceptance—probably the feeling of the majority—to bitter humiliation and rage. When Lieutenant G. T. Ferguson, a young Navy doctor stationed in Malinta Tunnel, heard it, he went outside despite the shelling and sat down and cried. His chief, Commander Thomas Hayes, the regimental surgeon of the 4th Marines, gave him a shot of precious bourbon to brace him. Colonel Howard put his head in his hands and wept. "My God," he exclaimed, "and I had to be the first marine officer ever to surrender a regiment."

Bunker heard the news by telephone at his C-1 Station. "No," he exclaimed, "I can't believe it." Then slowly, "Well, I guess it had to come." He then ordered his batteries to destroy equipment.

At M Prime West (a fire control post), Lieutenant Frank G. Jonelis, the range officer, picked up a sledge hammer and began smashing the phones and ripping the wiring from the switchboards of his range-finding station. Then he broke up the range-finding equipment and burned the range table books. Opening a can of C rations he ate the clammy food all at once. Then he sat down and listened. "I could hear the wind rustling through the leaves and the insects buzzing in flight. Far off I could hear a few voices. Occasionally a Japanese plane flew over and dropped a lone bomb; here and there an occasional shell screamed through the air. No longer did I pay attention." Unable to stand the solitude he rose and walked to a group of men standing near a blazing fire. "Someone stuck a bottle of whiskey in my hand, but I couldn't drink. I removed my pistol, took out the ammo, and threw the pistol into the flames. . . . I wanted to cry but couldn't."

The marines of the 2nd Battalion stationed in Ramsay ravine, who had been pounded for so long without an opportunity to dish it out, vented their rage on their weapons. Wrote Private William Coghlan, "We tore them apart, stomped on them, cracked them across the wall, and all the time giving vent to our anger with lusty curses for the Japs." Aaron Abston's men of Battery Globe did the same. With vicious yet systematic thoroughness they pierced the recoil cylinders of their 3-inch guns and then fired them, chopped up the fuze cutters with axes, and wrecked the height finder and director with pistol and rifle fire. Then, their commander wrote, "we ate a disconsolate lunch of our emergency rations, and prepared our field bags and rolls to take with us into the unknown future."

At Battery Flint near Cheney ravine, a strafing plane kept interrupting Sergeant John W. Lay's efforts to destroy a .50 caliber machine gun. Angered, Lay fired it at the plane, hitting it and driving it away; then he destroyed the gun.

Rolly Ames's men of Chicago were bewildered and despondent. They had wanted a crack at the enemy. They had manned their defense line and suffered through a heavy barrage on their foxholes at midnight, which had cost them several men. Now they had heard only sporadic and distant firing. Although the situation scarcely seemed desperate enough to warrant surrender, they destroyed their equipment and weapons with a will characteristic of them. When they finally received their orders late in the afternoon to march down to Middleside and turn themselves in, they looked hastily away from their Filipino barber, Elias Monsalund, for fourteen years an employee of the battery. He was sitting by the side of the road, holding his knees, rocking back and forth, sobbing uncontrollably, tears streaming down his face.

The saddest duty fell to Paul Bunker. Promptly at noon, accompanied by his deputy, Lieutenant Colonel Dwight Edison, and a bugler, Bunker marched from his post at C-1 to the flagpole on the parade ground. Ignoring the continuing enemy shelling, he and Edison stood stiffly at attention while the bugler played taps. Then he lowered his nation's colors and later burned them, keeping only a piece of the red cloth, which he later sewed into the sleeve of his own uniform underneath a patch. Half of it has survived to go into the museum at Bunker's alma mater at West Point. With Edison's aid he ran up a white bedsheet on the tall pole. Sergeant Don Hart watched from the parapet of Battery Wheeler: "This was my only time to cry, and this I did, like a baby."

Getting the Japanese to recognize the white flag and to accept the Rock's surrender proved surprisingly difficult. First, Captain Golland L. Clark, Beecher's adjutant, accompanied by Lieutenant Alan S.

Manning, B Company's commander, went forward to Water Tank Hill under a flag of truce with a musician playing until they encountered a Japanese officer. That worthy, strictly obeying orders, sent them back to Malinta Tunnel with word that Wainwright himself would have to come if he desired to discuss terms.

At 2:00 P.M., while heavy Japanese bombing and shelling continued to knock down white flags on all of the Fortified Islands as rapidly as they were raised, Wainwright went forward, accompanied by General Moore and their respective aides. They drove in Moore's car with a white flag fluttering from its fender to Water Tank Hill and then climbed on foot to the Japanese positions, noting with gratification that the dead and dying seemed to be in the proportion of three Japanese to every American. This time a Japanese lieutenant colonel was present, together with an insolent, English-speaking lieutenant named Uramura. After some parleying, Moore and his aide went back to Malinta Tunnel, while Wainwright and his aide, Major Tom Dooley, were escorted to North Point and from there by launch to Cabcaben to meet General Homma.

Minor fighting was continuing between Japanese troops in the tail area and a few cutoff remnants who had not received the surrender order. Sergeant Lloyd A. Catlow, a tough gyrene who had barricaded himself amid some rocks on the south shore, continued to defy the enemy until he finally spotted the white flags and surrendered. Two other marines held out until midafternoon holed up in a cave in a cliff on the north shore. Mute evidence of the valor of an unknown American came to light days later when prisoners on a burial detail found his body in a foxhole with seven Japanese sprawled before him. Unmolested, Lieutenant Ray Lawrence and his men stayed in their positions below the airfield until 5:00 P.M. Then they marched to the airfield and surrendered to the nearest Japanese they found.

Realizing after General Wainwright had appeared that he would meet no further resistance, Colonel Sato sent his two tanks forward on a probing mission and then ordered his 1st and 2nd Battalions to advance to Malinta Tunnel at about 4:00 P.M. They occupied it and the surrounding Bottomside area without incident. Although informed of this, General Homma preferred to consider the battle as still on, and his artillery continued to shell Topside and the other islands, killing and wounding several Americans. The Japanese resumed shelling the next forenoon, May 7, and when their troops landed in midmorning on Topside, and that night on Forts Hughes, Frank, and Drum to take over, they continued the fiction that these operations were combat landings despite the fluttering white flags and complete lack of opposition.

Continuation of an official state of hostilities was part of a brilliantly performed piece of showmanship and psychological warfare that produced exactly the desired effect. When General Wainwright reached Homma's headquarters at Cabcaben on the evening of the sixth, he received most unpleasant news. Homma brutally refused to accept the surrender of the Fortified Islands unless Wainwright also agreed to surrender all other forces in the Philippines. Brushing aside Wainwright's lame attempt to claim that he no longer controlled General Sharp on Mindanao, Homma informed him bluntly that unless these men surrendered with their arms intact neither Wainwright nor his men would be regarded as prisoners of war; instead, they could consider themselves hostages. While avoiding saying so in as many words, this burly, six-foot Japanese commander unquestionably intended to implant forcefully in his antagonist's mind the thought that he must yield or see his men face mistreatment or worse. Whether Homma would have carried out his implied threat had Wainwright refused seems unlikely; but to Wainwright, who recalled the conduct of the Japanese Army at Nanking in China, the threat was real and immediate.

The American commander now found himself in a hopeless impasse. He had no reasonable alternative other than to meet his captor's demand and surrender all of the Philippines. To increase his mental anguish, Homma refused to discuss the subject further, telling the exhausted Wainwright that he would be returned to Corregidor to "think the matter over." If he still wanted to surrender he would have to talk to the local Japanese commander on the scene.

On his arrival late that night Wainwright at once sought out Colonel Sato and drew up a surrender document that conceded every point Homma wanted. At midnight, May 6, his final duty done, he returned to his little whitewashed quarters in Malinta Tunnel, there to hurl himself on his cot and review again and again this bitterest and most humiliating day of his life.

A lack of "prevision," as Colonel Bunker was wont to term it, once more had cost the American cause dearly. By successfully threatening Wainwright, General Homma had unquestionably spared himself the rigors of guerrilla warfare, especially in the central Philippines where Brigadier General Bradford Chynoweth had made thorough preparations for extended resistance. In retrospect it is now apparent that Wainwright should have been publicly withdrawn from his command and the Philippines after the fall of Bataan. Then General Moore, as Harbor Defense commander only, might have been able to claim with success that General Sharp was not his subordinate. Nor would Sharp have felt obligated to obey Moore's orders; Homma's game probably would not have worked.

In return for perhaps as many as 350 killed on the last day of action, the defenders of Corregidor inflicted at least that many deaths on their foe, most of whom perished trying to get ashore. In addition the Japanese lost some five hundred men from malaria before and after the invasion, bringing the total number of Japanese dead to a figure greater than the American, even when 310 additional American dead from the earlier bombing and shelling are added.

Corregidor's last twenty-seven days of resistance knocked the malaria-racked 4th Division from the war. Tokyo had earmarked it, once Corregidor had been conquered, for dispatch to Rabaul to aid in the conquest of New Guinea and the Solomons. Instead, because of the enfeebled condition of the men, General Homma had to return it to Japan for demobilization. This alone made Corregidor's last stand worth the cost in strategic terms.

Although insufficient statistical data are available to warrant a precise judgment, the logistical problem for the Japanese resulting from the Corregidor operation probably was of greater importance than the loss of the 4th Division. Occupation of so many western Pacific islands, each of which required a sizable garrison, imposed a tremendous burden on Japanese shipping. Little remained to support additional offensive operations. Consequently, the tie-up of thousands of tons of shipping for approximately an additional month reduced sharply the tempo of Japanese operations in the Southwest Pacific.

It probably would be saying too much to maintain that Corregidor's continuing resistance in April and the first week of May saved northern Australia from invasion. But the Rock's stand unquestionably slowed the pace of Japanese operations in New Guinea and the Solomons and may have saved one or two steppingstone islands lying between Australia and Hawaii from enemy occupation. Almost certainly, had the Japanese been able to build up faster, General MacArthur's stand in New Guinea would have been gravely endangered. Also, had the Japanese been able to adequately garrison and supply Guadalcanal in the Solomons, the landing there of the American First Marine Division in August, 1942, might not have been possible—a landing that began the great Allied counteroffensive of the Pacific War.

Already noted, but worth repeating, was the role of the Corregidor radio intercept facility, which picked up and relayed the Japanese messages indispensable to the American victories in the crucial aircraft carrier engagements in the Coral Sea and at Midway, battles which saved Port Moresby and Midway Island from invasion and restored the balance of naval air power in the Pacific by sinking five Japanese carriers. Had Admiral Chester Nimitz not known of the Japanese plans in advance, he could not have positioned his carriers to meet the threat.

At the time, Corregidor's holdout had little impact on American morale, military or civilian, because the details were not known. But now that the full account is available, Americans—and Filipinos as well—can take great pride in the tenacity and devotion displayed by the Corregidor garrison. The soldiers, sailors, marines, and Philippine Army men offered their respective nations an inspiring example of bravery and tenacity. The Philippine Scouts deserve special praise for a skillful, polished, and distinguished performance. The final, hopeless counterattack of the ill-trained men of the 4th Battalion, 4th Marines, was in keeping with the highest traditions of a proud corps and fittingly concluded a last stand classic in its proportions.

15 ☆ The Long Wait

COUNTING an additional thousand captives brought over from Fort Hughes on May 8, the Japanese held as hostages about sixteen thousand prisoners on Corregidor to guarantee General Wainwright's compliance with the surrender terms. They kept the captives in this status for two weeks, until satisfied that Wainwright and his staff officers were doing all they reasonably could to induce the commanders of the lesser islands to give up. Wainwright was forced to broadcast personally to General Sharp on Mindanao on May 8 appealing to him to lay down his arms, and one of his officers, Colonel Nicoll F. Galbraith, walked for days through the tangled jungles of northern Luzon in a vain search for Colonel John P. Horan, the commander of Camp John Hay, who still was holding out with a small party. Only on June 9 did the Japanese finally tell Wainwright that he and his men were regular prisoners of war.

For the first two days after the surrender, the captives were allowed to wander almost at will. Some men had a chance to drift back to their positions on Topside and rescue clothing, pictures, Bibles, and other precious items. Then, after shipping in the Fort Hughes garrison on May 8, the Japanese cracked down, and except for eight hundred wounded and sick in the hospital and the hospital staff, plus a few senior officers being held for interrogation, confined all of the men in the so-called 92nd Garage area, a two-block-sized basin on the south shore just east of Malinta Hill. At one time the area had been the island's seaplane station; later it was converted into the motor pool for the 92nd Coast Artillery. For the sixteen thousand miserable Americans and Filipinos it was hellish.

Except for the shrapnel-riddled shells of two large hangars, there was no shade at all. Thousands of vicious, biting, blue-black flies swarmed everywhere. The Filipinos, whom the Japanese had segregated from the Americans, arrived first and appropriated one of the two hangars. The other was reserved for five hundred of the officers. The remaining thousands of men found what comfort they could in the open, on concrete and earth. To escape the painful "Guam blisters" raised by the relentless tropical sun, they erected little shelters from canvas, blankets, and corrugated sheet iron.

For the first several days anarchy reigned. Some of the men seemed to believe—and so said—that their officers no longer had any control over them. Others, joined by some officers, stole, quarreled, bickered, and fought. A few were indiscreet with Japanese 14th Army propagandist "Buddy" Uno, a University of Utah graduate, and blamed their country for their plight. But others, possibly 10 to 15 percent, never gave in, never lost their self-discipline, and worked from the first day to restore order.

The most disagreeable task the men had to perform for their captors was disposing of the Japanese and Filipino and American dead. Following their custom, the Japanese forced details of Americans to gather Japanese cadavers into piles on Kindley Field to burn them. From each they struck off a hand as a sacred memento for later ceremonial cremation, for the deceased warrior would be honored henceforth in the family shrine. About the American bodies they cared nothing beyond getting them underground as rapidly as possible to prevent disease. The chaplains who directed much of the work were not permitted even to compile a casualty roster, and the work details were continually prodded by their captors to hurry their sad task, which was performed for the most part in the rock-hard soil with inadequate hand tools. About all they could do was quickly to scoop a shallow grave wherever they found the casualty, drop in the body, give last rites or a brief prayer, cover it, and hastily search for the next. In two days the job was completed.

Aside from the usual cuffing and beating which the prisoners would soon learn to expect as a matter of course, the Japanese guards committed few of the atrocities which had marked the "Death March" from Bataan. A few wounded prisoners were bayoneted, and Captain Burton C. Thomson, the youthful and highly regarded mess officer of the Malinta hospital, was executed for being "anti-Japanese"; there may have been one or two other executions.

In the tunnel the American and Filipino nurses were not molested, although in anticipation of the worst, they stationed one of their huskier sisters at the entrance to their quarters armed with a large iron skillet. Life for them was anything but pleasant. With nearly a thousand patients to care for, limited to but two slender meals a day, not permitted even to step outside the tunnel for a breath of fresh air, they settled into a numbing, monotonous routine existence. Nearly twenty years later, recalling those days, Dorothy Ludlow McCann could only sigh, "We were *so* hungry, and we worked *so* hard." Together with the doctors and enlisted medical personnel, the nurses finally left Corregidor in early July to spend the rest of the war practicing their profession under slightly better conditions at the Santo Tomas civilian internment camp in Manila.

Colonel Theodore T. ("Tiger") Teague, General Moore's signal officer, showed exemplary courage. He had locked in his mind the sort of information the Japanese wanted most, the details of the workings of America's codes and cryptographic machinery. Even though his captors pressed him hard, Teague's reply was, "To hell with that stuff," and he refused to talk.

A few men escaped capture, most of them only briefly. The most fortunate were a group from the minesweeper *Quail,* headed by the ship's commander, Lieutenant Commander John H. Morrill. On the evening of May 6 they slipped away from Fort Hughes in a thirty-six-foot diesel motor launch. After a narrow escape from a patrolling Japanese destroyer on the night of the seventh, they sailed at an average speed of five knots all the way to Port Darwin, Australia—a tremendous feat of seamanship and mechanical skill. Another escapee was Air Corps Captain Damon J. Gause, who on the day of the surrender made his way by banca and swimming to Bataan, and from thence into the hills where friendly Filipinos took him in. He later joined Colonel William L. Osbourne, a 57th Infantry officer who had escaped on Bataan, and the two finally succeeded in sailing a small boat to Australia to bring MacArthur his first personal account from the Philippines since the surrender. Captain Herman Hauck, the commander of Battery B of the 59th, managed to reach the Cavite shore, where he successfully hid out for a month, only to be turned over to the Japanese, trussed up like a pig, by some Filipinos who were anxious to curry favor with the conqueror.

As the days dragged on in the crowded oven at the 92nd Garage, many of the captives grew more desperate. Two such were Lieutenants Edgar Whitcomb, a Bataan escapee and survivor of the action at Monkey Point, and the valiant commander of the 1st platoon of Company A of Colonel Beecher's 1st Battalion, William (Bill) Harris. Concluding that if they stayed they were as good as dead anyway, the pair slipped away from a wood-gathering detail one afternoon, hid in a hole until dark, and then swam the North Channel to Bataan, a harrowing eight-hour ordeal. In five days, using bananas, cashew nuts, and ants for food, they hiked the length of the peninsula, evaded a Japanese patrol, and took refuge in a Filipino village. The villagers had no banca large enough to sail to China, the pair's intended goal, and so Whitcomb and Harris accepted a smaller one with an outrigger and sailed south for Australia, passing Corregidor well out to sea and moving down the coast of Luzon until a squall wrecked their frail craft.

Again, friendly Filipinos helped them, and they even encountered two enlisted marines, Chamberlain and Armstrong, who had also escaped, hoping to reach Australia. They waited impatiently several weeks until their hosts not only fitted out a larger outrigger, but also provided a precious compass. Setting out once more, the little party soon disagreed over the wisdom of sailing by day, and when the others insisted on risking it to speed their progress, Whitcomb left them and took to foot. Although he presently found companions, a pair of civilian mining engineers, his luck ran out when he and his new friends were turned in by a pro-Japanese mayor.

With the aid of the miners Whitcomb posed successfully as a civilian, secured confinement in Santo Tomas and got to Shanghai, ultimately reaching the United States aboard the Swedish liner *Gripsholm* which exchanged Japanese and American diplomatic and civilian personnel in December, 1943. So far as is known Whitcomb and Captain Gause were the only successful escapees from the Rock. His marine companions, as he had feared, were caught and incarcerated as military prisoners.

On Saturday, May 23, after fifteen days at the 92nd Garage, the prisoners who remained were marched by hundreds to the old stone quarry on the west side of Malinta Hill. After standing for hours in the broiling sun, they moved in the late afternoon to the South Mine Wharf, and from thence in lighters to three ships anchored in San Jose Bay. Aboard the ships it was infernally hot. The men were packed in so tightly they had to stand. There was no food, no water, no medical facilities, not even a latrine. There they spent the night.

The next morning the ships weighed anchor and sailed to Manila. The ship carrying the Filipinos went to a dock, but the two with the Americans anchored off Parañaque Beach. The men scrambled into launches, which carried them part way to shore, and then were ordered into the water, which was in some places armpit deep. On broad Dewey Boulevard near the beach, they reformed into their groups of hundreds, and in columns of fours, flanked by guards, began a roundabout march to Old Bilibid Prison, their initial destination.

With the Sunday crowds on the streets, the Japanese intent soon became vividly clear even to men almost beyond caring: to humiliate the Americans before the Filipino citizenry. But the Japanese no more understood the Filipinos than they had their prisoners. Mur-

murs of sympathy arose at once; men and women ran to get food and water which they offered to the hapless victims, so that the guards who had been urging the crowds forward now beat them back with blows to the stomach from their rifle butts. When the prisoners began lagging from fatigue and hunger, the now jittery guards jabbed them with their bayonets, which the prisoners already had learned to call "vitamin sticks" (with their aid one could do the impossible). Correspondent Royal Arch Gunnison watched one thrust his bayonet completely through the arm of a prisoner.

But perhaps the most pitiful incident of all occurred when a young American mother standing next to Gunnison gasped as she saw her husband. A child of four or five she was holding cried, "Daddy," but she hastily hushed it, saying, "The Japanese will hurt him if you do." The soldier-father saw them, tried to smile, but choked up and had to look away as he went on.

Nevertheless, even a "gloat march" has its compensations. In making it the Corregidor prisoners escaped the infinitely more horrible ordeal of their fellow captives taken on Bataan. The only known death en route was that of Lieutenant Colonel William B. Short, General Moore's artillery engineer, who collapsed before the gate of the column's goal, Old Bilibid Prison. Colonel Paul Bunker went out of his head en route and passed out, as did some others, but was carried by truck to safety.

Old Bilibid marked only a pause. Within a week most of the men shipped out once more, going initially to Cabanatuan Camp No. 3 in the central Luzon plain. From this hellhole, as demands for prisoner labor came in from Japanese occupation authorities, most went to work camps all over the Philippine archipelago. Others went to Formosa, where Paul Bunker died of diseases induced by starvation after losing sixty-nine pounds; to Japan, where even General Wainwright suffered beatings from brutal guards; and to Manchuria and North China.

On May 7, the day after Corregidor's surrender, some of the Bataan POW's in Bilibid Prison in Manila watched their captors raise a huge banner over Rizal Avenue which read, "THE WAR IS OVER—CORREGIDOR FALLS." In one sense it was, for Japan had thereby gained the last of her initial objectives. But her long vain fight to hold them—and the long wait of the prisoners for liberation—had just begun.

Japan's war plan, prepared in the fall of 1941, acknowledged the tremendous war potential of the United States but did not anticipate that American troops would regain the Philippines and Corregidor. Instead, the Japanese assumed, the Americans would bog down battling in the rim of lesser islands surrounding the "Southern Resources Area." In this decisive struggle the High Command in Tokyo was not counting primarily on the strength of Japanese matériel; Japanese army weapons were conventional and by no means superior to the modern arms already beginning to pour in quantity from American arsenals. What the High Command was counting on (in addition to a Hitler victory in Europe) was, again, the suicidally fanatical "spiritual strength" of the individual Japanese soldier, which would offset American mechanical superiority and presumably dismay the "soft" Yankee troops.

To this point in its modern history, Japan had never known defeat. Her troops had defeated China in 1894–1895, Russia in 1904–1905, had conquered Manchuria in 1931–1932, and since 1937 had brought China to the brink of total collapse. The sweeping conquests of 1941–1942 seemed but to confirm an historic pattern and to justify Japanese confidence in their strategy.

What the Army-dominated Japanese planners had not taken into sufficient consideration was the role of sea and air power. Knowing the tremendous scale of President Roosevelt's two-ocean navy program, Admiral Isoroku Yamamoto, the Navy commander, had estimated before the war that for the first year his service would give a good account of itself. After that, he could not guarantee success. Yamamoto proved to be a good prophet. The loss of his aircraft carriers in the Coral Sea and at Midway in May and June of 1942 permanently threw the Japanese Navy onto the defensive. Yamamoto had intended that the Midway battle would give him a lease on life by destroying the American aircraft carrier–heavy cruiser striking forces and remaining battleships that constituted, as he saw it, the backbone of United States naval strength. Instead, by losing four of his six big fleet carriers, Yamamoto had suffered an irreplaceable loss.

Defeat at Midway led swiftly into another at Guadalcanal. Here, not only the Japanese Navy but also the Army suffered. The campaign began on August 7, 1942, when the United States First Marine Division in a spoiling attack seized an airfield the Japanese had nearly completed. Afterward, a savage battle by land, sea, and air raged through the remainder of the year as each side sought to expel the other. Both hurled aircraft carriers into action until few were left on either side. Cruisers, destroyers, and even battleships plunged into desperate, point-blank night battles that the great American naval historian, Samuel Eliot Morison, has likened to barroom brawls with the lights out. Each lost twenty-four ships, but superior American naval strength, already being bolstered with new construction, left the United States in command of the waters about Guadalcanal as the year 1943 dawned—a year that would see the world's greatest industrial nation commission no fewer than seventeen new fleet aircraft carriers and more than a score of escort carriers (CVE's).

American valor at sea was matched by equal valor on land. The First Marines proved worthy successors of the Philippine Scouts of the 57th Infantry and the sailors and leathernecks of the 4th Marines. The Japanese, counting on the willingness of their men to fight without quarter, either had forgotten or did not know that Americans had often battled on the frontier in just this way. In murderous, close-in battles about the perimeter of Henderson Field on Guadalcanal, "spiritual strength" proved inferior to the firepower, discipline, and determination of the marines and Army GIs.

In New Guinea General MacArthur's soldiers fought through the end of 1942 a campaign of equal bitterness to drive the enemy from Papua in New Guinea. At a cost of more than 8,500 battle casualties and many more sick, his Australians and Americans wiped out more than 12,000 Japanese, of whom only 350 permitted themselves to be taken prisoner.

With Guadalcanal and Buna in New Guinea in their hands, and with superiority growing daily at sea and in the air, the Allies now could begin to consider the long road back across the Pacific. Committed to recapture of the Philippines, General MacArthur preferred to strike westward along the New Guinea coast. In the Solomons, a strike to isolate Rabaul seemed logical, if not essential. And in the Central Pacific, as the old Orange Plan had envisaged, Admiral Nimitz proposed striking directly into the Japanese mandated islands.

Had MacArthur and Nimitz been content merely to assault each garrison along the Japanese defense line, the Japanese strategy might have worked. The heavy casualties of a slow, miserable, war of attrition might have induced the American public to demand negotiations. But the commanders soon concluded that capture of every Japanese-held island was not essential. MacArthur could successfully bypass Rabaul, the major Japanese base in the South Pacific, and allow its hundred thousand defenders to "wither on the vine." In the eastern Pacific, Nimitz could bypass completely the heavily defended forward Marshall Islands and land to their southward and rear at Tarawa, Makin, and Kwajalein.

Tarawa was tough. There the Japanese employed the same basic strategy they were to use on other islands, including Corregidor, for the rest of the war. Knowing that the enemy would have to come to them to secure the island, they honeycombed Tarawa with dugouts, pillboxes, and steel and reinforced concrete shelters. Artillery and machine guns swept every beach. The pre-invasion naval and air bombardment failed to destroy many of the fortifications, with the result that three thousand marines—a third of them killed—fell in a short but terrible battle that jolted American attitudes about the war.

Tarawa demonstrated, as nothing else could, how necessary it would be for the Americans to precede their landings not only with heavy, but accurate, naval bombardment, and with better beach reconnaissance by teams of "frogmen" to blast away hidden reefs that fouled landing craft. To carry the initial assault waves ashore, armored amphibious tractors ("amtracs") capable of crawling over reefs and resisting machine-gun and light cannon fire from shore, were needed. Once aground, the troops would need flame throwers and tanks to burn out and shatter the enemy pillboxes.

By mid-September, 1944, as a result of these and other refinements in the art of amphibious warfare, Nimitz held the Mariana Islands, already in the process of conversion into B-29 bases for a concentrated bombing offensive against the Japanese home islands. Leapfrogging along the New Guinea coast and adjacent islands, MacArthur's troops had taken Hollandia in New Guinea and Morotai in the Moluccas, leaving Rabaul cut off far to the rear.

Japanese strategy and tactics thus had failed disastrously. By adopting the leapfrog technique, made possible by sea and air superiority, the Allies had effectively put out of action thousands upon thousands of sorely needed Japanese troops. By lavish use of aircraft, tanks, precision naval bombardment, artillery, and bulldozers, the Americans had kept their losses relatively light—or at least acceptable. As one Japanese prisoner complained, the Americans were "not good" jungle fighters. But after they had been around for a few days, "there was no more jungle." In some cases the GIs found that the easiest way to deal with a cleverly constructed and camouflaged pillbox was simply to attach a dozer blade to a tank, charge it, and bury it under tons of earth.

In fact, "spiritual strength" had become a liability. When all else had failed, the Japanese island garrisons customarily had fortified themselves with sake and loyalty to the Emperor and had launched banzai charges, suicidal blind attacks with whatever weapons they had left: rifles, grenades, samurai swords, and—reminiscent of Japan's early history—even sharpened bamboo sticks. The greatest such assault came on Saipan when some three thousand screaming Japanese rushed to their deaths in trying to annihilate two battalions of the 27th Infantry Division.

By this time the Americans had come to welcome the banzai; it was an easier way of eliminating the enemy than to root him from tunnels and fortifications. The Japanese High Command, however, had begun to frown on the tactic. In nearly every case, it had discovered, the outcome was the reverse of what had been intended, with the Japanese suffering very high losses as against light to moderate American.

Already the "long wait" had consumed more than two years. But MacArthur's long-promised return to the Philippines was next on the agenda. For political and strategic reasons the islands could not be bypassed. Corregidor must become a battleground again.

It was not until the late summer of 1944 that it dawned on the Japanese 14th Army command in Manila that it might have to fight again in the Philippines. Certainly, the average Japanese soldier had no inkling of the danger awaiting him. His own Army's communiqués and newspapers printed only stories of Japanese success.

Until August, 1944, the 14th Army had allocated to garrison Corregidor just three companies of troops, one of infantry and two of artillery, totaling about three hundred men. Since Tokyo would send nothing to assist in rebuilding the Rock's armaments, in June, 1942, the 14th Army began levying drafts of American prisoners to tidy up the sadly shattered installations, to collect scrap and munitions, and to build barracks and quarters. Thus it was that about five hundred men, most of whom had served throughout the siege, found themselves again on Corregidor.

Doubtless reflecting Manila's lack of concern, the garrison did not strain either itself or its POW charges. "The Japanese were apparently satisfied," writes Lieutenant Colonel George A. Sense, a former POW on the Rock, "to have a presentable area where the prisoners could manually retract a disappearing gun, to be tripped into firing position, while visiting V.I.P.'s could 'ooh!' 'ah!' and take pictures." When Captain Ronald O. Pigg, an engineer, asked a Japanese ordnance officer whether his government intended to rebuild the fortifications, the latter replied, "Why?" And he added, "In ten years

Corregidor will be a beautiful Japanese park to which visitors from Manila may come on Sundays."

In their version of "graceful living" the Corregidor Japanese forced their captives to convert the old Philippine Government treasury vault, where the gold and silver had been stored, into an eight-room brothel, in which they confined seven prostitutes from Manila. They lured the girls into coming with the promise of high pay, and then refused them permission to leave. Such an installation on a military post caused wonderment among the American prisoners and much comment in their diaries.

The Japanese even fed the prisoners relatively well. The much better diet on Corregidor saved many men who arrived critically emaciated from Cabanatuan. On the whole the prisoners were treated well. One favorite story recalled by Colonel Sense involved a lone U.S. Army mule and a Japanese guard known by the Americans as "Rat Face." The mule had survived the tremendous shelling and bombing attacks, and for reasons best known to themselves the Japanese thought highly of the stubborn animal. One day "Rat Face" was "plinking" with an American .22 caliber rifle he had found, and to bait him, one of the prisoners belittled his marksmanship, claiming that he couldn't even hit the broadside of the mule, which was conveniently tethered nearby. Thus challenged, "Rat Face" fired—and showed that he could hit the broadside of a mule. To the delight of the prisoners, the next day there was no "Rat Face"; he had disappeared, presumably into the stockade. "But the best part of it," concludes Colonel Sense, "was that the POW's got half the mule. What a feast!"

Had they really made a determined effort, the Japanese probably could have restored at least half of the Rock's big guns. Most of the American crews had attempted to destroy their weapons by firing them with the recoil cylinders drained and the barrels plugged, in accord with standard Coast Artillery doctrine. In a few instances this measure worked well; Battery Smith's gun tube, for example, snapped off when the weapon burst after being fired with a 12-inch projectile rammed nose first into the muzzle. But many pieces were but slightly damaged and would have remained serviceable had not their crews smashed the sights, dented the recoil cylinders and rods with axes and hammers, and tossed gears and handles into the bay. Several rifles of the large batteries were repairable, five of the 155's were entirely unharmed and another was repairable. No guns at Fort Hughes were destroyed because communications with Corregidor had broken down completely on the morning of the surrender, and Colonel Valentine Foster, the fortress commander, did not receive the order to demolish weapons.

Despite this and two years of work by the prisoners on the armament—with at least one POW being co-operative enough to operate willingly a machine shop to replace vital parts—the Japanese accomplished little in the way of restoration. Fort Drum had only its little 3-inch piece, Battery Hoyle, repaired and then removed. The Japanese never did get the turret machinery or casemates to function. On Fort Frank Battery Crofton (one 14-inch) was repaired, as was Hearn (one 12-inch long range) and one gun each of Batteries Wheeler (12-inch), Crockett (12-inch), and Grubbs (10-inch) on Corregidor. Two of Ramsay's 6-inch pieces and one of James's 3-inch guns also were made serviceable. None, however, fired so much as a single test round, none had fire control equipment, and so far as is known the Japanese never provided gun crews.

Sabotage and deliberate go-slow tactics by the prisoners may have been part of the answer. The redoubtable Captain Herman Hauck, still a tiger despite his unsuccessful counterattack on May 6 and his escape attempt, led the "opposition." On one occasion he slipped a link of chain into a recoil cylinder of one of Crockett's supposedly operational 12-inch guns, a measure which would have raised hob with the piece had the Japanese ever tried to fire it. Others slyly sabotaged weapons, powder, and ammunition as opportunity afforded.

After mid-1943 the Japanese progressively reduced the number of Americans until by May 12, 1944, according to an escapee, they had only twenty-one left headed by Major Robert Lothrop, the former post engineer. Four more were on Fort Drum, including Master

Sergeants Dennis Burns and Cy Perkins, both of the 59th CA. Several, including Lothrop, were shipped away in the next few months, but fifteen are believed to have been on the island at the time of its recapture in February, 1945. No trace ever was found of them, and to this day their fate remains a mystery.

16 ☆ Back to Manila

THE DEFENSE of the Philippines constituted the iron test for the Japanese Army. There, for the first time, combat would be on an army instead of a divisional or corps scale, with hundreds of thousands of men involved. If its warriors could not stop the Americans there, they could not stop them anywhere, not even in the Japanese home islands. The Philippine campaign would also be decisive for the Japanese Navy. If it could not check the American fleet in the Philippine Sea, then it could not expect to do so at the entrance to Tokyo Bay. For these massive confrontations the Japanese military leaders mustered everything they had.

For his first landing General MacArthur chose an unexpected place, Leyte Island in the central Philippines, which was garrisoned by only a single Japanese division. MacArthur had sold his Philippine invasion to President Roosevelt with the phrase, "Leyte, Mr. President, then Luzon." This made strategic sense. With Leyte secured, with his land-based air power established and Japanese air power destroyed, MacArthur could repeat the strategy of his enemy in 1941: to land north and south of Manila and entrap the Philippine capital.

For his part General Tomoyuki Yamashita, the conqueror of Singapore who had taken the helm of the 14th Army from General Homma, had no intention of letting MacArthur get away with it. Yamashita had expected his antagonist to strike first at the big southern island, Mindanao, and had disposed his forces accordingly. But wherever MacArthur would land, Yamashita intended to fight him to the finish.

On October 20, 1944, two months ahead of their original schedule, MacArthur's Sixth Army veterans stormed ashore at Tacloban, Leyte, behind a naval bombardment. At first, they drove the Japanese 16th Division northward with ease, but within a few days Yamashita initiated Operation *Ta,* pouring in reinforcing troops from Luzon and adjacent islands by barge and small craft through the western port of Orion. A situation reminiscent of Guadalcanal had developed; MacArthur found himself battling an enemy continually increasing in numbers, forcing him to send in more troops of his own.

Also, as in the case of Guadalcanal, the Japanese Navy reacted to the attack. Admiral Soemu Toyoda, who had followed Yamamoto as commander-in-chief, activated SHO-1, a grandiose plan to destroy the massed invasion fleet off Leyte and its covering force. His plan was clever. Accepting his weakness in air power, Toyoda decided to use his four remaining aircraft carriers, minus most of their planes, as bait to lure Admiral William F. Halsey and his battleships and fast carriers of Task Force 38 northward away from Leyte. Then two powerful surface groups, each operating independently, containing all but two of Japan's battleships, would strike at Leyte Gulf, the site of the landing, by way of San Bernardino and Surigao Straits. If Vice Admiral Takeo Kurita, commanding the Center Force, could get the 18.1-inch guns of his monster 64,000 ton battleships *Yamato* and *Musashi* within range of MacArthur's transports, then the long series of bitter defeats beginning at the Coral Sea and Midway might be avenged.

As it turned out, just one part of Toyoda's scheme worked. His bait force, as expected, did draw Halsey away from Leyte. But in every other respect SHO-1 was a dismal failure. A classic night action virtually annihilated the Southern Force advancing through Surigao Strait as two rebuilt Pearl Harbor victims, the *California* and *West*

Virginia, joined four old U.S. battlewagons to "cross the tee" of the enemy formation. Kurita's Center Force managed to break through San Bernardino Strait by night, after losing battleship *Musashi* to carrier attack, to blunder at daybreak upon a vulnerable task force of six U.S. escort aircraft carriers, which should have been easy pickings. The Japanese Admiral became so disoriented, however, and so harassed by the carriers' planes, that he could sink but two destroyers, a destroyer escort, and only one of the "baby flattops." In return he lost three heavy cruisers—hardly an equal exchange.

Altogether, the Leyte Gulf battle, fought on October 24–25, 1944, in four separate engagements, was the Japanese Navy's worst defeat. Four Japanese carriers and three battleships went down, in addition to numerous cruisers and destroyers. Never again would the Imperial Navy seriously threaten its rival. According to Admiral Morison, more American sailors fought in this one engagement than had been in the entire Navy and Marine Corps in 1938. The two-ocean navy program, supplemented by war emergency programs, had crushed Japanese naval power.

But the Japanese Army remained on Leyte and grew stronger. Yamashita filtered into the fight five additional divisions, four from the Philippines and one from Shanghai, forcing MacArthur to commit seven of his own. Although the issue never was in doubt, tropical rainfall greatly hampered the attackers, stalling airfield construction and preventing the Americans from establishing quickly their customary air supremacy.

On Leyte as elsewhere, superior American firepower provided the margin of superiority. The infantry drove forward until the fall of Ormoc on December 10 virtually severed the Japanese water life line. By January 1, 1945, General MacArthur finally could consider the Leyte campaign concluded except for always difficult mop-up operations. In large-scale combat the Japanese had done no better than in earlier smaller-scale engagements in New Guinea. Their losses totaled about 70,000 nearly all dead, against 15,584 American combat losses, of whom 3,508 were killed.

American success on Leyte buoyed the spirits of the Corregidor prisoners in their Philippine camps. Those near Manila and Clark Field could see American planes sweep overhead and hear the bombings that hinted that liberation was approaching. The trouble was that the Japanese concluded the same thing and decided to remove as many of the prisoners to Japan as possible, aboard troop and supply ships that were going home empty.

This was tragic. In the summer and fall of 1942 prisoners had died like flies in their stinking, malaria-and dysentery-infected camps, only to have the death rate stabilize and sink almost to zero when Red Cross food and medical parcels began arriving after December, 1942. But now, aboard prison ships headed for Japan, they again died by hundreds and even thousands.

A good percentage of the losses, especially among Corregidor officers of the rank of major downward, came when American submarines and planes sank three ships.

Torpedoes blasted the *Shinyo Maru* on September 7, 1944, off Mindanao. Of its 750 POW's only eighty-two survived to be rescued by Filipino guerrillas. The *Arisan Maru,* with 1,790 prisoners embarked, foundered from submarine attack two hundred miles off the coast of China on October 24, 1944, the first day of the battle of Leyte Gulf. The Japanese picked up only four men and fended others away from the escorting destroyers with bamboo poles. By some miracle five swimming prisoners found an empty lifeboat during the night, fished a keg of fresh water from the twenty-foot waves, and rigged a sail which carried them in two days and nights to the only area on the China coast not occupied by a Japanese garrison. Treated royally by the Chinese, entertained with a banquet at every town they entered, the adventurers finally reached Kunming and safety after several weeks of travel.

The greatest horror story of captivity, however, is without question the saga of the prisoners aboard the *Oryoku Maru.* The forty-nine-day ordeal of the 1,619 men of this group, a number of them junior officers from Corregidor, began on December 13, 1944, when they sailed from a Manila dock. The *Oryoku Maru* was a new, graceful, and fast ship, but the men were packed in so tightly that some died because of the panic and filth, even before the ship left Manila Bay.

In Subic Bay the *Oryoku Maru* fell victim to American dive bombers and about 300 of the captives were killed. Somehow, 1,300 survivors, many with wounds, managed to swim or float themselves ashore at Olongapo, where they were concentrated on the grounds of the former U.S. naval station. Taken to San Fernando after five days, "really hurting for water," as Colonel Emil Ulanowicz recalls, they went north by rail to Lingayen Gulf, and thence to Formosa on two ships which were bombed by American planes on arrival in Takao Harbor. One of the ships was hit squarely in a hold containing Corregidor officers; at least 279 men were lost.

From Takao the men went to Japan, this time, fortunately, with no losses to the ships despite a submarine scare. But the starvation continued, and the men were issued so little water that they dehydrated to the point where, if cut, they could not bleed. Hundreds died on this horrible leg of the journey before they arrived—mere walking shadows—in Moji on Kyushu, the southernmost Japanese island. Major G. L. Anloff, Jr., found a scale on the docks and weighed himself. Before the war he had tipped the scales at 187 pounds; now he totaled just 84 pounds with clothes and canteen. Of 1,619 men who had started from Manila, Anloff estimates that 493 reached Moji alive, and that at least 109 of these—including Captain Roland Ames of Battery Chicago—died later from the effects of this most terrible voyage in modern human history.

By the time the typical prisoner in Japan was liberated, he had lost so much weight that he had become quite literally a living skeleton, often unrecognizable to a friend as the man he had known before except by his voice. The subject of food had consumed the prisoners' thoughts, conversations, and nightmares through three and a half long years of captivity. To supplement their slender ration of rice, they had eaten dogs, cats, frogs, snakes—even earthworms and rats ("fine, grain-eating animals"). Altogether, it seems surprising that somehow about two-thirds of the Corregidor prisoners survived captivity.

At about the same time the decision was taken to load the prisoners aboard the "hell ships," the Japanese finally had started to augment Corregidor's defenses. In August, 1944, at the Navy's request, the Japanese Army was forced to bolster the island's modest garrison with two additional infantry companies, bringing personnel strength to five hundred men. In the next month, September, when American carriers began attacking Luzon, the Navy decided to dispatch from Manila a unit of the 31st Naval Special Base Force. These men, Imperial Marines so-called, took with them eight 25 mm. antiaircraft guns and ten "captured" defense guns, presumably American 3-inch or .50 caliber. Corregidor now mustered about eight hundred men.

Toward the end of September the first elements of yet another naval force arrived, this one composed of "Shinyo" units. There were seven of these under the over-all command of Lieutenant Commander Shoichi Koyameda, a regular fleet officer. Each had about two hundred officers and men and a score or so suicide motorboats, for a total of well over a hundred boats. As a weapon the "Shinyo" boat represented the ultimate in desperation tactics. It was only twenty feet long, had a twelve-inch freeboard, carried a one-man volunteer crew, mounted no guns, and with a small (and apparently unreliable) four-cylinder gasoline engine could make about twenty knots. In its bow it carried a five-hundred-pound TNT charge rigged for detonation on impact or by electric key. With a rowboat class of seaworthiness, the "Shinyo" boat was worthless in the open ocean and of questionable value even in the relatively sheltered waters about Corregidor. Nevertheless, the Japanese evidently hoped that by expending them in surprise night attacks they could achieve worthwhile results.

After the Leyte landing in October, the Japanese Navy accelerated its belated efforts to strengthen Corregidor. It sent two batteries of heavy antiaircraft guns and four fortress batteries with ten 150 mm. naval guns manned by 318 men under the command of Navy Lieutenant Endo. Three Imperial Marine construction units also arrived with the specific mission of repairing and putting into service the American fortress guns, which one Japanese source alleges—mistakenly but probably honestly— ". . . had been untouched since the initial Japanese occupation." Since each of these so-called "construction units" actually consisted of about 1,500 trained combat troops, Corregidor again approached the status of a respectable bastion. By about the end of January, 1945, the Japanese had 5,062 men on Corregidor, with an additional 160 at Mariveles, 373 on Fort Hughes, about 400 on Fort Frank, and 65 sailors, survivors from the sunken giant battleship *Musashi,* on Fort Drum. All, including the Army garrison of 827 soldiers under the command of Captain Shinozawa, were designated the Manila Bay Entrance Defense Force and placed under the command of Captain Akira Itagaki, a naval officer. Although the Japanese Army by this time had little interest in either Manila or Corregidor, the Navy was determined to hold the Philippine capital and Corregidor as long as possible, denying Manila Bay to MacArthur and forcing him to redeem in blood his pledge given to General Moore to return to the Rock.

While the Japanese had been reinforcing the Rock, General MacArthur had been planning his Luzon campaign. Wisely, he decided to make his jump to the main island in two stages, keeping well clear of Corregidor in the process. First, he would seize lightly-held Mindoro Island and establish more airfields. Then, he would land at Lingayen Gulf—as General Yamashita expected—but not on the good northern beaches where Homma had landed in 1941 and where the defenses were stronger.

A stimulus to MacArthur's caution had come from a group of Luzon-based Japanese Navy aviators. Acting on their own, they had initiated during the Leyte operation the Kamikaze, or "divine wind" tactic, which was to give the American Navy a very bad time for the rest of the war. Kamikaze pilots, plunging in their bomb-laden aircraft onto enemy ships, did not sink many, but quickly filled the overtaxed forward repair bases with badly damaged warships of all classes. Had Kamikazes been used earlier—say in 1942 or 1943—they might have lengthened the war by years. But now, in the closing weeks of 1944 and in 1945, the American Navy boasted so many ships carrying so many antiaircraft guns that the suicide attacks became only a major nuisance.

Plagued by Kamikazes all of the way, an assault team landed at Mindoro on December 15, quickly routing the five hundred Japanese present and establishing operational airfields. Then, on January 2, a support force of old battleships, cruisers, and escort carriers sailed into the teeth of the "devil birds" to sweep free of mines and bombard the Lingayen Gulf beachhead. "Take it" they had to. Approaching low from over the land so that radar had difficulty picking them up, the Kamikazes struck with fury and skill, killing more than a thousand sailors for the loss of perhaps four hundred or more of their own number. But in expending themselves on the warships the Japanese pilots allowed the safe arrival of the transports packed with troops.

What the Kamikazes had accomplished was bad enough. In a period of a month, between December 13 and January 13, they had sunk twenty-four Allied ships—nearly all destroyer-size and smaller but including an escort carrier. They had damaged thirty badly, including three battleships, five cruisers and four more escort carriers. For some reason they had seemed particularly attracted to H.M.A.S. *Australia,* a heavy cruiser. Five had hit her, but her plucky sailors had gamely kept her in action.

While doubtless pleased with the work of the Kamikazes, General Yamashita had not counted on their checking the invasion. Nor did he believe that he could bar MacArthur from Luzon and Manila. His job, he believed, was to tie up his opponent for as long as possible.

Therefore, he planned to defend only Luzon's mountainous areas. He shunned Bataan, where MacArthur had retired under similar circumstances in 1941–1942, for he regarded the fever-infested peninsula as a cul-de-sac, incapable of sustaining his army of 262,000.

Yamashita divided his 14th Army into three groups. The largest force of 152,000 he held under his personal command in the northern mountains, with headquarters at Baguio. The next largest, 80,000 strong under Lieutenant General Shizuo Yokoyama, he stationed in the mountains to the east and northeast of Manila. The last, of 30,000, he retained in the Clark Field area with orders to dig into the hills just to the west, there to keep the airfield complex within artillery range and unusable for as long as possible.

Initially, he had intended to abandon Manila. But Rear Admiral Sanji Iwabuchi, commanding the 31st Naval Special Base Force of 16,000 men, who already had reinforced Corregidor on his own initiative and who was under separate Navy command, would have none of this. Standing orders enjoined this stubborn sailor to hold the city, and he intended to do so.

Scarcely half of Iwabuchi's men were adequately trained for combat, but for the type of warfare he was preparing to fight this hardly mattered. Rounding up the many antiaircraft guns about the city, especially the light automatic weapons, stripping wrecked aircraft and light warships of their automatic arms, Iwabuchi's sailors amassed formidable firepower. In the modern steel and concrete buildings south of the Intramuros, the old Spanish walled city, they created a series of miniature fortresses, each of which would have to be besieged and taken separately. To the Intramuros itself, designated as a last-ditch defense zone, Iwabuchi and his men planned to retire and to fight to annihilation. In short, Iwabuchi intended to present his opponent with a problem not unlike that encountered by German Field Marshal Friedrich von Paulus at Stalingrad, the city that had marked the high-water point of Hitler's offensive in Russia.

Luzon, then, really contained five separate defense areas, each intended to hold independently of the others. These were: the northern mountains, so heavily garrisoned and vast that Yamashita and 70,000 of his troops would continue in action until Japan's surrender; the mountainous area west of Clark Field; the rugged highlands north and east of Manila; the Philippine capital itself; and finally, Corregidor, commanding the entrance to Manila Bay, garrisoned by about 5,000 men, with another thousand on the lesser islets. In part because of General Yamashita's sound strategy, in part because of the stubbornness of a Navy admiral, the Japanese had stumbled into precisely the combination best suited to their purposes. From these five strongholds they could delay the Yankee enemy for the maximum length of time and inflict upon him maximum casualties.

As a consequence of Yamashita's strategy, General Walter Krueger's Sixth Army veterans had little difficulty in landing at Lingayen on January 9, 1945, and in expanding their beachhead. Heavy surf conditions, slow movement of supplies inland, and—possibly—an excessive concern on the part of Krueger and his commanders for the security of their flanks, slowed the advance toward Manila, but by the last week of January the only center of severe resistance, the Clark Field complex and the adjacent hills to the west, had been overcome.

Prodded by an impatient MacArthur, who was extremely anxious to liberate the capital and to free the Allied POW's and civilian internees he knew were there, Krueger cut loose combat teams of his 1st Cavalry and 37th Infantry Divisions on January 27. Three days later, on the last day of the month, he landed the 8th Army's 11th Airborne Division at Nasugbu, fifty-five miles south of Manila, to spring a trap on the defenders. Advancing at times at speeds up to fifty miles an hour, a troop of the 1st Cavalry entered Manila from the north on the afternoon of February 3 to seize Santo Tomas University and free the civilian internees, the Corregidor nurses included, after thirty-three months of captivity. Not to be outdone, the competing 37th Infantry Division pushed a combat team to Old Bilibid Prison the next day, liberating eight hundred POW's, including Charles Brook and Dayton Drachenberg, cripples from the final battle for Corregidor.

Greatly cheered by these events, a jubilant MacArthur announced to the press that Manila had fallen, while his staff planned a victory parade to be led by the Supreme Commander himself, following what everyone hoped would be mopping-up operations. The paratroopers of the 11th Airborne, locked in a bitter struggle at Nichols Field at the southern edge of the city, could have told them otherwise. The swiftness of the final rush had caught the Japanese by surprise and unready in the half of the city north of the Pasig River. But in the southern half, which included the modern buildings and the Intramuros, they were much better prepared.

Only fifty Americans and about fifteen hundred Japanese had been killed north of the Pasig. But the struggle for the southern half rapidly turned into one of the most savage—and certainly the most tragic—of all of the great battles of the Pacific War. Between February 7 and March 3 the Americans lost another 950 killed as against about 14,500 Japanese, but what was far worse, an estimated hundred thousand Filipinos, innocents "caught in the middle" or held hostage by the Japanese, also perished. Long before the struggle had ended, the plan for the victory parade had been quietly dropped.

In a vain effort to spare civilian lives, MacArthur had prohibited bombing in Manila. Nevertheless, the *only* way that the embattled infantry and troopers of the 37th and 1st Cavalry Divisions could overcome the enemy's fanatical resistance was to use direct fire from tanks, M-7 S.P.M.'s (105 mm. self-propelled gun carriages), and field artillery to blast enemy automatic weapons positions. Sometimes, whole buildings had to be leveled before the men could approach. In taking a building the troops, most of whom had had street-fighting indoctrination in basic training, discovered that the best method was to seize the roof and top story first. Then holes could be chopped in each lower floor and grenades dropped through to clear the remainder of the building. On reaching the basement, however, the men often found that the Japanese had escaped through a tunnel to the next building, forcing them to begin all over again.

Perhaps the nastiest fighting took place in the Commonwealth Government structures bordering the Intramuros to the south, and in the apartments, clubs, and hotels along Dewey Boulevard. In the General Post Office, for example, tank and S.P.M. fire did little damage, for each room had strong, thick walls that confined the blast and fragments from the shell. Finally, troops of the 37th Division managed to break through a second-story window, and the Japanese retired to a large, dark basement, to be finished off in a particularly dirty fight.

Troop B of the 5th Cavalry had a difficult task trying to take Rizal Hall of the University of the Philippines. On February 20 one of its platoons burst into the building and fought its way with slight loss to the top floor. Then the Japanese touched off a suicide blast, killing a trooper and wounding four more, forcing the platoon to retire. The next day the fight had to begin all over again. The 250 Japanese defenders battled on until the night of February 23–24, when the remaining seventy-five committed suicide.

Rather than battle at close quarters in the medieval walled city, the Intramuros, the GIs decided to subdue the foe with massive artillery support. They liberally employed 240 mm. and 8-inch howitzers, with the result that the ancient landmark dating from Spanish times was virtually leveled. Doubtless civilian loss of life was regrettably high, but under the circumstances it hardly could have been avoided no matter what the troops did. Losses to the attacking 37th Division were relatively low, only 25 killed and 265 wounded.

The fall of the Finance Building on the night of March 3 ended a full month of fighting. The last Japanese strongpoint having been reduced, the Battle of Manila was over. Again in American hands was the shattered remains of what had been one of the most beautiful cities of the Orient.

17 ☆ Confronting the Rock

WITH THE BATTLE STILL RAGING IN MANILA, Americans once again after nearly fifty years confronted Corregidor as an obstacle to victory in the Philippines. The Rock had to fall before Clark Field and Manila would be of any use. Otherwise, the Japanese could deny entrance to Manila Bay. Storming the island would not be easy; Japanese experience in 1942 and the bitter fighting under way in Manila had demonstrated that.

On February 3, 1945, in a radiogram to General Krueger, Douglas MacArthur briefly outlined his idea of how the job should be done. First, Bataan had to be overrun quickly to prevent the Japanese in the Manila area from escaping into it. Second, Corregidor and its sister islands had to be captured. Third, the Ternate area had to be cleared to eliminate all Japanese forces from the bay shore. MacArthur did not presume to tell Krueger precisely how to recapture the Rock, but he suggested the assault might be made either by a shore-to-shore amphibious landing, or by an airborne drop, or both, depending on the tactical situation.

MacArthur's message did not catch Krueger's skilled planners by surprise; two days later they had a plan ready for MacArthur's approval. Accepting his chief's suggestion, Krueger proposed to overrun Bataan by rushing a regimental combat team from the Luzon plain down the east coast of the peninsula. Simultaneously, on the morning of February 15, the 38th Division's 151st Regimental Combat Team would board landing craft in Subic Bay—already in American hands—to land inside Mariveles Harbor, rout the Japanese there, and move out to link up with the regiment moving down the east coast of Bataan. This would seal off the Bataan Peninsula.

The next day, February 16, would be Corregidor's turn. In the wake of a heavy air and sea bombardment, a battalion of paratroopers of the 503rd Parachute Infantry Regiment, an experienced outfit that had jumped before in the Markham Valley in New Guinea, would fly up in the early morning hours from their Mindoro base to drop squarely on Topside at 8:30 A.M. Two hours later infantry of the 3rd Battalion of the 24th Division's 34th Regiment would board landing craft in newly captured Mariveles Harbor and land on Bottomside to seize Malinta Hill and the adjacent area. With key positions on the high ground at Topside and Malinta Hill in American hands, reinforcement drops of the remaining two battalions of the 503rd would put enough troops on Corregidor to deal easily with the estimated eight hundred to a thousand Japanese defenders.

In placing the Japanese numbers so low, instead of at the more than five thousand actually present, both the Sixth Army's and MacArthur's intelligence had erred. Evidently, the low estimate was based on information received from four men of the 59th and 60th Coast Artillery who had escaped from Fort Frank in May, 1944, and had then joined guerrillas in Cavite Province. Aerial photography taken as late as the end of January, 1945, had shown no evidence of reinforcement because the Japanese were living mostly underground. Guerrilla reports in November and December had noted increased ship travel back and forth from Manila—ships which could have been hauling away supplies from a depot the Japanese were known to have on the Rock—but little else. To be on the safe side, the Sixth Army's "Estimate of the Enemy Situation" had taken the report of three hundred Japanese from the prisoners, noted "this is considered low," and guessed, "Present strength may approximate 1,000 troops."

So it had come about that despite reasonably good sources of information, and all of the advantages that the highly developed art of photo interpretation could bring, MacArthur's planners had been grievously misled. Through nobody's fault the last-minute shipment of Imperial Marines had gone undetected, and the plans and preparations for recapture were predicated on the assumption that the enemy was but one-fifth his actual numbers. Fortunately, it was not the habit of MacArthur—or of Krueger—to send a boy to do a man's job.

General Krueger personally selected the drop zones for the airborne landing. He rejected a proposal by one of his staff officers to parachute the troopers onto Kindley Field, the only really suitable drop site on the island. A paradrop there, Krueger pointed out, would accomplish nothing that could not be done better by a seaborne landing. Moreover, it would leave untouched Malinta Hill and Topside, which if taken by surprise would provide an excellent base to attack from the rear the Japanese cave positions around the rim of the island.

The catch was that Topside was a terrible place for a paradrop. Only two areas were in the least suitable: the old parade ground in front of Topside Barracks, designated for planning purposes area "A"; and the sloping nine-hole golf course where Aaron Abston and his men of Globe had manned their guns three years before, designated area "B." Both were diminutive—less than a thousand feet long by 450 feet wide—pinpoint targets for an airdrop. In addition, the area was littered by clods, rocks, scrap iron, and tin roofing, and surrounded by splintered trees, wrecked buildings, and tangled undergrowth. If the wind blew during the operation it could push many of the troopers over the cliffs. To counteract the effect of the wind, the transports were ordered to fly into it. Thus the wind would act as a brake on each jumper and enable him to control his drop. Both the Sixth Army and 503rd Regiment planners agreed that 20 percent—every fifth man—would suffer serious injury, and the youthful Colonel George M. Jones, the commander of the 503rd, after inspecting the Rock from a bomber, feared that his jump casualties might run as high as 50 percent and certainly not less than 10 percent.

Nevertheless, the risk was accepted. The planners hoped that the jump injuries would comprise the majority of casualties in the operation, leading to an otherwise relatively easy and bloodless victory. Better to have broken legs than mass butchery from shell hits in packed landing craft. But the jump had to go *exactly* right, for "the margin of safety was nil."

With the invasion plan established, the job of preparing the way for the men who would land on the Rock got under way.

Roaring over the island in November, 1944, two P-47's of General George Kenney's Fifth Air Force had taken the first crack at the Japanese on Corregidor and had begun a procession of air attacks that already had vastly exceeded anything General Moore's garrison had endured three years earlier. The aviators' principal mission was to destroy the batteries so that when the cruisers and destroyers of Task Group 77.3 arrived to bombard the island and protect the mine sweepers clearing the bay, they would not be pummeled by shells from American-made 12-inch guns.

In late January lumbering B-24 Liberators of the 307th Bomb Group systematically had begun to pattern the island with heavy demolition bombs, concentrating on Topside and Malinta Hill. On January 28 they dropped nearly one hundred tons and maintained this intensity of attack until February 7, when they doubled the tonnage. In the days following, A-20 attack bombers, the "Grim Reapers" of the 3rd Attack Group, joined the heavyweights, taking on the neutralization of Battery Woodruff on Fort Hughes. Captain Itagaki's battered defenders were granted a respite on February 12 and 13 while the bombers softened up Mariveles for the landing scheduled for the 15th, but the A-20's and Liberators returned during the next two days to give the Rock its most terrific blasting to date. Altogether, Corregidor was hammered by 3,128 tons of bombs during the pre-invasion air offensive, the most concentrated pasting any target would receive in the entire Pacific War.

In the absence of Japanese records or survivors the effect of these attacks can only be guessed. Personnel casualties probably were light, since most of the defenders undoubtedly stayed deep in their tunnels.

But the bombers knocked out all the repaired coast defense guns as well as the two batteries of 5-inch dual-purpose guns the Japanese had installed the previous fall. When American troops reached the site of Battery Ramsay (three 6-inchers) they found its gun mounts destroyed and a crater twenty-five feet deep where a magazine had been. Evidently this installation had suffered the same fate that befell Battery Geary in the 1942 siege.

Most important, the bombings drove the Japanese away from the exposed high ground on Topside, including the barracks area, the golf course, and the parade ground, into the safety of tunnels around the rim of the island and under Malinta Hill. In seeking refuge Itagaki's men avoided losses but forfeited their ability to deal with a paradrop, exactly as Krueger's planners had hoped.

To support the mine sweepers clearing the bay and the landing operations against both Mariveles and Corregidor, Rear Admiral R. S. Berkey moved in a force of light cruisers and destroyers. The cruisers included the veterans *Phoenix* and *Boise* and the new *Denver, Montpelier,* and *Cleveland,* the latter three commissioned after Corregidor's surrender in 1942. Itagaki's marines were about to experience "the terrible firepower of a light cruiser," a lethal deluge of shells from 6-inch guns.

On Tuesday morning, February 13, under a clear sky, with a fresh breeze strong enough to sweep away the haze and provide excellent visibility—conditions that prevailed throughout—the complex operation to recover Corregidor began. With the mine sweepers in the van and the cruisers and destroyers in the rear, Berkey patiently began the exacting and time-consuming task of sweeping up the mines—no Dewey-like dash could be made with these menaces lurking below—and adding his share to the tons of high explosive heaped onto the Rock by the B-24's and "Grim Reapers."

Following Berkey's carefully worked-out plan, the cruisers and destroyers split into two groups, with Berkey's flagship, *Phoenix,* accompanied by the *Boise* and four of the "cans," escorting the first group of mine sweepers into the North Channel; the *Denver, Cleve-*

land, and three other destroyers followed a second group into the South Channel. They remained most of the day, firing methodically at all the Fortified Islands, while the mine sweepers' paravanes cut loose hundreds of horned mines for the destroyers to explode or sink with gunfire. In the North Channel they discovered that the U.S. Navy had indeed solved the problem of laying mines in deep tropical waters; those cut loose there were live Mark 6A's from the former Navy contact field between La Monja and Bataan which the Japanese had left unswept and had incorporated into their own mine defense system for Manila Bay.

Not once did an American ship detect a retaliatory shot from Lieutenant Endo's Navy gunners. But instead of taking this as a favorable omen, Admiral Berkey was perturbed. From intelligence reports he knew the Japanese had sent 150 mm. guns to Corregidor and on the basis of previous experience at Saipan he believed that they had tunneled them into Topside's vertical cliffs, allowing hanging vines and dense jungle growth to furnish natural camouflage. Berkey was right; this is exactly what Endo's men had done. But they had been too cagey to accept the "bait" Berkey had dangled in the form of cruisers, destroyers and mine sweepers operating at point-blank range.

After spending the night in Subic Bay, Berkey returned at sunrise the next morning, the 14th, to cover the last phase of the mine-sweeping operation, which included clearing Mariveles Harbor. This time Captain Itagaki allowed Lieutenant Endo to shoot, and at 9:33 A.M. several of the mine sweepers radioed they were under fire from batteries located in caves on both Corregidor and Fort Hughes. They and their covering destroyers briskly replied in kind and the batteries fell silent.

At about noon *YMS-48* and a small group of wooden sweepers began the dangerous job of clearing Mariveles Harbor. The destroyers *Hopewell* and *Fletcher* idled at the harbor mouth, their guns trained inshore to silence any enemy battery that might try to interfere and also to sink or blow up mines bobbing to the surface in the wake of the sweeping gear. When at 1:30 P.M. the *Fletcher* stopped dead in the water to lower a boat to scuttle a small buoy its machine gunners could not seem to hit, Endo seized his opportunity. His first salvo straddled her and his second, moments later, smashed a 150 mm. shell into the destroyer's forecastle, killing five sailors and wounding six.

Retaliation was swift. The blast of one of the pieces had raised enough dust and smoke for the *Phoenix*'s observers to spot its approximate position in the cliffside a little to the west of Morrison Point. Joined by two destroyers the cruiser promptly forced Endo to silence. *Fletcher* was not holed badly and continued in action, but the heroism of Water Tender 2nd Class Elmer C. Bigelow prevented her blowing up. Discovering a fire blazing in the forward powder magazine, Bigelow rushed inside with two CO_2 fire extinguishers and saved his ship. In the process he breathed so much of the acrid powder fumes that he caught pneumonia and died ten days later. His grateful skipper, Commander J. L. Foster, recommended him for the posthumous award of the nation's highest honor, the Congressional Medal of Honor.

The *Phoenix* had neither cowed nor permanently silenced Endo. A half hour later, at 2:00 P.M., his guns fired once more, this time starting a mortal blaze aboard the wooden *YMS-48,* and a few minutes later, as the *Hopewell* was closing the sweeper to rescue her crew, he scored three hits on the destroyer. Two shells struck the funnel and a third the base of the destroyer's quintuple torpedo tubes, killing six men, wounding eleven, blasting holes in the stack, wrecking the torpedo mount, and knocking out the ship's sonar, telephone, and forward lighting system.

This was too much for an angry Berkey. Along with her destroyers the *Phoenix* at once began rapid fire, and in the next eight minutes they lashed a thousand 5- and 6-inch shells at Endo's positions, silencing him once more. They continued a slow fire the rest of the day to keep him quiet. Progressive blasting away of the jungle growth finally pinpointed three of the gun positions, including the masonry-lined tunnel containing the most troublesome, *Hopewell*'s nemesis. The destroyers spotted three more low along the shore line, but could not get an exact plot. The other four went undetected. Endo held his peace, but in sinking a mine sweeper and damaging two destroyers he and his men had done their share for the Emperor that day. Their shooting had been deadly accurate; Paul Bunker would have given his grudging admiration.

When Berkey and his captains reviewed the day's operations that evening, they agreed that plenty of fire support would be needed to protect the landing craft ferrying the infantry into Mariveles the next morning. More mine sweeping seemed necessary, also, since two of the destroyers had been badly damaged in striking mines in waters already swept twice. An air strike on Endo's cave positions seemed advisable, so Berkey passed their co-ordinates to the Fifth Air Force with a request for glide and dive-bomber attacks by P-47's.

At 4:38 A.M. on the fifteenth the cruisers got under way from Subic escorting the landing ships bearing the infantry to Mariveles Harbor. On nearing Corregidor at first light, they began a slow, steady fire at the Rock's cliffs. Endo replied once, at 7:30, only to have everyone plaster him and force him to silence. At 9:00 A.M. the P-47's warmed up Endo's caves with both high-explosive and the terrible napalm (jellied gasoline) incendiary bombs. Patient, careful aiming of single shots by the *Phoenix* finally paid big dividends when one of its 6-inch shells went "right down the throat" of the masonry-lined tunnel. After that Endo fired just once more, at 10:40 A.M., and with his usual phenomenally good aim, he succeeded in holing one of the LSM's at the water line, disabling it. Otherwise, the landing was completely successful; the troops met no fire from the Mariveles beaches as they waded ashore.

Even though Endo was virtually out of business, all danger to the American invaders had not yet passed. Captain Itagaki still had Lieutenant Commander Koyameda's "Shinyo" boats, the suicide craft, and that night he dispatched about thirty of them after some landing craft anchored for the night in Mariveles Harbor. Most either lost their way, stalled, or swamped en route, but about a dozen reached the harbor to hurl themselves in pairs at the four landing-craft gunboats patrolling the entrance. Six exploded against three of the small gunboats, which apparently were unaware of their presence until they struck, sinking them immediately. The others were spotted by an alert lookout on *LCS (L) 27,* whose crew opened fire and destroyed at least five, blowing up the last one at a range so close that she herself suffered severe damage. The Japanese tactic had worked in that three vessels were sunk and another damaged at relatively little cost to themselves, but because none of the LST's and other landing craft inside the bay were attacked, it had not materially affected the forthcoming landing operation. Why Itagaki did not expend all his "Shinyo" boats, and perhaps work a few into the harbor among the landing craft, remains a mystery. He still had a number in serviceable condition in Corregidor's caves and may have had it in mind to save them for use against the amphibious landing he correctly expected would be launched the next day against the Rock.

On their return to Manila Bay the next morning, February 16, D day for Corregidor, Berkey's task force sighted and sank three stalled "Shinyo" boats, and thanked their lucky stars no ship had hit any of the hundred previously cut mines found drifting aimlessly about.

At 7:15 A.M. Berkey began shooting, this time concentrating on Topside as well as on Endo's tunnels. He fired until 7:50, when the first flight of B-24's arrived for the pre-invasion bombing. The big planes dropped forty 240-pound fragmentation bombs apiece on Topside, a tactic intended to encourage the Japanese to scurry for their caves. Close behind came eleven B-25's and thirty-one A-20's, sweeping in low, firing .50 caliber machine guns and dropping deadly 260-pound "parademo" bombs, demolition bombs with parachutes attached to give the planes time to get clear. The intent was to stun any Japanese who had ducked into foxholes in the exposed areas. The "Grim Reapers" then swung back to strafe the Topside cliffs again and again for the next hour to keep the Japanese away from the tunnel mouths and blind them to what was happening on Topside.

Just before 8:30, as the *Montpelier*'s youthful crew was watching with awe the tremendous ferocity of the air attack, the cruiser's lookouts spotted still another wave of fifty-one planes approaching in two long columns, flying so low and slow they seemed to be floating. The distant specks gradually assumed the distinctive shape of that work horse of the Air Force, the C-47 transport. As the first plane of this fleet, piloted by Colonel John Lackey, commander of the 317th Troop Carrier Group, passed over Topside at about 8:32 or 8:33 A.M. with its flaps extended, eight little specks spilled quickly from it, and eight white parachutes blossomed in the air. Borne swiftly on the brisk wind, they drifted down rapidly into the smoke over Topside and disappeared from sight. By the world's most modern and exotic means of warfare the first Americans had returned to the Rock.

18 ☆ The Perilous Jump

THE MEN who floated down over Corregidor on that sparkling morning of February 16, 1945, represented not only a new era of warfare, but also a new breed of American soldier, the paratrooper. This was the sort of soldier who had brought a new dimension to attack. At Normandy in France, in Sicily, in New Guinea, and in other actions, they had been tough and aggressive and had suffered grave losses. In this action the boss of the entire invasion was Colonel George M. Jones, a slim, intense, thirty-three-year-old West Pointer from the class of 1936, the very class that had produced several of Corregidor's best battery commanders of 1942.

Appropriately labeled "Rock Force," Jones's command included his own 503rd Parachute Infantry Regiment, the 3rd Battalion (Reinforced) of the 34th Infantry Regiment, the 462nd Parachute Field Artillery Battalion, a platoon of tanks and self-propelled guns, an airborne engineer company, and a few lesser units. It mustered 4,560 men, somewhat less than Captain Itagaki's defenders.

The first man to jump was Lietuenant Colonel John L. Erickson, the commander of the 503rd's 3rd Battalion, closely followed by T/5 Arthur O. Smithback and Private First Class Stanley J. Grochala. Leaping from the lead plane at about five hundred feet, Erickson was carried rapidly by the twenty-five-mile-per-hour wind, which was ten miles an hour too strong for normal jumping, to the cliffside about a hundred yards below Battery Wheeler, far from his intended landing point on the parade ground. "Considering the location of my landing," he writes, "the terrain, and the fact that the area was covered with the jagged stumps of bomb-blasted trees, I was lucky. I had only minor bruises and scratches and was able to get on with the job." Hiking back up over the top of Battery Wheeler, unaware that its bombproofs teemed with hiding Japanese, he joined his men to begin clearing the enemy from the immediate area around both drop zones, the parade ground and golf course.

For the next hour men continued to hit with bruising jolts wherever the wind decreed. Those who could, quickly slipped from their chute harnesses and hobbled over the broken and littered ground to their assigned assembly areas. They watched for enemy fire and also kept an eye on the sky, for to have a heavy supply bundle or another paratrooper crash onto one's head could be fatal. Some unfortunates drifted over the cliffs onto enemy positions, but even then the Japanese did not have it all their own way. Initially there was little enemy fire to worry about. Meanwhile, Private First Class Donald E. Rich of Company I shot two snipers while dangling from a tree, and Private Earl J. Williams hit two more with a pistol even while he was entangled in his chute.

In the drop zones and about Topside Barracks the defenders were scattered in twos and threes without a semblance of an organized defense. The airdrop had taken Itagaki completely by surprise. A prisoner later revealed that Tokyo had warned the captain to guard against an airborne landing, but that he had completely discounted this possibility and instead had disposed over half of his men to cover James, Cheney, and Ramsay ravines and the north slopes of Malinta Hill on the assumption that attack would come by sea. Itagaki's own survey of Topside had convinced him that paratroopers could not land there.

This proved fatal to him. Itagaki had noticed the infantrymen of the 34th Infantry's 3rd Battalion boarding landing barges in Mariveles Harbor at about 8:00 A.M. and, anticipating their early departure for Corregidor, had rushed to an observation point near Breakwater Point. So intently did he watch the barges that he failed to notice the C-47's approaching and did not alert his command to the impending airdrop. A few minutes later some twenty-five to thirty of the troopers, blown three hundred yards from the golf course, plummeted about his position. The Japanese began firing, but the aggressive chutists formed up, laid down covering fire, and attacked the O.P., killing Itagaki and eight of his men with grenades. Thus, at the outset of the battle, the Japanese had lost their commander, their communications "central" in the old bombproof telephone exchange on Topside, and their ability to organize an immediate counterattack.

Had they known of Itagaki's estimate of the unsuitability of Topside for an airdrop, the men of the 3rd Battalion would have agreed. But they also faced pain and losses. Unanimously, they felt that Topside was ". . . the worst jump field ever used for an airborne operation." Most of the men landed outside the drop zones, crashing onto jagged chunks of concrete, into trees, into gun emplacements, onto buildings, and into bomb craters. One man had a "streamer"—an incompletely opened chute—and plummeted into the now empty Fort Mills swimming pool; his chute rapidly became saturated with blood. Yet even on this first drop, made initially too high and too soon, casualties had approximated only the expected 20 percent. Of the thousand who jumped in the first lift about 750 were in action immediately, with others joining after receiving first aid. ". . . It should be remembered," reminds Colonel Erickson, "that we did not consider a man a casualty unless he was immobile as a result of a broken bone or was suffering shock as the result of wounds or injuries. Otherwise he was treated, bandaged, and continued to fight."

Bizarre adventures during the parachute landings were many. Lieutenant Edward T. Flash of Company F recalls hitting "like a brick" on the golf course after leaping from the dangerously low altitude of only 450 feet, so low his chute made but one oscillation after the opening shock. Good conditioning and fall training, he believes, saved him and many others from severe injury. Captain Henry W. Gibson, the commander of Battery B of the 462nd Field Artillery, landed on the edge of a bomb crater, rolled in, and became so ensnarled in his shroud lines that two of his men had to untangle him. Captain Donald D. Burke of Headquarters, 462nd, sat stunned in a bomb crater. When the cobwebs finally began to clear, he realized that his chute harness was off and that a map was being thrust under one of his arms. The cheery voice of one of the outfit "yardbirds," who had been in the stockade both in the States and Australia, said, "Here, Captain, you lookin' for one of these."

Perhaps the ultimate of bizarre experiences happened to the 503rd's Catholic chaplain, Father John J. Powers. Powers was holed through the leg by a Japanese sharpshooter on the way down, and in his own words, "I was foolishly examining the wound instead of watching where I was going to land and thereby directing my parachute accordingly." He glanced off an artillery piece on the cliff's edge, breaking several ribs and causing a concussion ". . . which did not make me unconscious, but only forgetful." His clerk, Jimmy Fraser, had jumped with him and after landing found him sitting on the ground in front of a Japanese-occupied cave ". . . with a foolish grin on my face." "All that I can tell you now, and for some time, is hearsay," Father Powers continues his account, "because I do not remember. But for the next three hours or so I kept repeating the same questions over and over. . . ."

> I said: "Jimmy, where are we?" and Jimmy would tell me that we were on Corregidor Island. I would then ask the location of Corregidor and I would inquire as to our purpose for being here; and when Jimmy told me we were here to fight Japs I would regularly reply: "Get me a knife and let us get going." I am braver out of my head than in it. When I was pulling out of my unconsciousness (?) some hours later I caught myself asking these questions and this is when Jimmy told me I had been asking these same questions for several hours, almost driving him out of his mind.

With his groggy charge still asking questions, Fraser had managed to find refuge for the pair behind a small hummock of earth tossed up by a bomb explosion. There were several other troopers there, including a doctor with a broken leg. Unfortunately, there were also some inconsiderate Japanese on the other side who kept tossing over hand grenades. Powers remembers kicking one away which did not explode. Coming somewhat to his senses, Powers finally directed two men to either side of the hillock and another toward the top ". . . so that our Japanese friends would not make a surprise rush against us." A little later the enemy stopped grenading and the Americans crawled away and sent back a litter team to pick up the injured doctor.

Wounded, hurt, unarmed, and out of his head, Father Powers had proved a formidable adversary. At his landing place, he had kept twenty-one Japanese pinned in a cave ". . . who must have been scared to death of me, a defenseless chaplain." A patrol later killed them all. At his second site he and the others pinned down more Japanese who might otherwise have been firing into the drop zones.

One of Rock Force's doctors, Captain Emmet R. Spicer of the 462nd, successfully landed with the first lift, but at 9:15 A.M., a few minutes before the last parachutists landed, he made the decision that cost him his life. Captain Albert L. Tait spotted him moving toward a gully controlled by the Japanese. "He said there were wounded soldiers in there and he was going in. That was the last time I saw Doc alive." Later a poignant slip of paper revealed what had happened to this "fine Southern gentleman." Spicer was hit by a sniper, and realizing the wound was fatal, sat down and wrote out his death certificate, correctly diagnosed. Giving himself a shot of morphine, he lay down to wait. The only incomplete item on the certificate was the actual time of death.

The airborne landing was one of the most—if not *the* most—daring, unusual, and successful in the history of airborne operations. A careful analysis of wind and other conditions by Colonel Jones's S-3 had indicated that each stick of six to eight paratroopers would have approximately a one-hundred-foot margin of error. Since a C-47 flying at a drop speed of 110 miles per hour travels 160 feet per second, and the men required three to four seconds to leave the plane, a second's error in jumping would land at least one paratrooper in each stick outside either extremity of the drop zone. A sudden gust of wind could produce the same result for the whole stick, as could a wind diminution or a slight error by the pilot in switching on the "Go" light in the cabin as he flew over his predetermined landmark on his pass.

On their first run, the C-47's came over at 550 feet, much too high. Consequently, the men drifted past the drop zones, and since the wind was somewhat more northeasterly than expected, some went over the cliffs south of the golf course. None fell into the water, but nine landed so near the water they had to be rescued by PT boats positioned off the coast to pick up strays. Witnessing the error from his command plane, Colonel Jones quickly radioed the pilots to come in as low as 400 feet, and directed the jumpmasters to count from five to ten seconds longer after the "Go" lights flicked on in the cabin. The result was that in the second and third passes more paratroopers landed in the drop zones with correspondingly fewer injuries. When the second lift carrying the 2nd Battalion jumped in the early afternoon, the procedure had been refined so well that most of the troopers landed in the D.Z.'s.

Of the 2,065 men of both lifts, about 280, or approximately 13.5 percent, were killed or severely injured. Of these, 210 were injured on landing, and another 50 wounded either in the air or on grounding. Some 180 had to be evacuated and hospitalized. Three men who suffered chute malfunctions and two who swung into the sides of buildings were killed, and an unfortunate eight—mostly men who blew over the cliffs and landed in front of Japanese caves—were slain in the air or before they could get free of their chutes. Six remained missing after the final count was in.

Only one man refused to jump and that because his best judgment dictated otherwise. "I wanted to be in on the fight, not on the rocks." He came later, by water. A C-47 carrying the 503rd's demolition team suffered an engine failure just before swinging into its drop pattern and ejected its troopers over Bataan. No planes crashed, although several were hit by enemy fire and had aircrew and paratroopers wounded.

The Corregidor recapture was one of the best photographed of the

Pacific War. A complete team with still and motion-picture cameras jumped with Lieutenant Dick Williams of New York City in command. A naval liaison gunfire control party (JASCO) and a Nisei intelligence interrogation team also jumped, six for the first time. Finally, in their version of "gracious living," the paratroopers brought along Mr. Harold Templeman, a Red Cross civilian and trained parachutist. By the afternoon of the first day Mr. Templeman had set up his canteen in the relatively undamaged bombproof lower floor of Topside Barracks and was brewing hot coffee for the wounded and injured.

By about 9:40 A.M., while Colonel Erickson's 3rd Battalion was clearing Topside Barracks and surrounding buildings, the C-47's were dropping their last sticks. The A-20's of the "Grim Reapers" also stopped their strafing runs along the sides of the cliffs and swung away. Out on the parade ground, with enemy sniper bullets zipping about, Private First Class Clyde I. Bates and T/5 Frank Arrigo, both of Headquarters Company, 503rd, were laboriously climbing the tallest remaining pole. A few minutes later Old Glory fluttered once more from Topside; Colonel Paul Bunker's humiliation of May 6, 1942, had at last been avenged.

Next the 3rd Battalion's combat companies, G, H, and I, shoved out vigorously from Topside to seize the high ground covering the routes leading up from Bottomside, while the headquarters men, the airborne engineers, and the field artillerymen flushed snipers from the nearby post exchange and the hospital buildings at Middleside. Finding little opposition, H Company killed three sentries in overrunning the 60th's Middleside Barracks and aggressively thrust a platoon onto Morrison Hill, taking from the rear the Japanese positions in Chicago's gun pits of three years before. G Company, also advancing against very light opposition, secured the area overlooking Ramsay ravine and emplaced a pair of .50 caliber machine guns just in time to support the amphibious landing of the 3rd Battalion GIs across the beaches below.

When the second lift, consisting of Major Lawson B. Caskey's 2nd

Battalion and attached units, began jumping at 12:40 P.M., it found the situation well in hand. Erickson's 3rd Battalion already had established a snug perimeter on Topside's highest ground, had seized the dominating terrain above Bottomside, and had gained all of the day's initial objectives. Some harassing fire from snipers and machine gunners located in pillboxes around the rim of Topside was bouncing off the chipped and battered concrete of Topside Barracks, mostly from the direction of Batteries Crockett, Cheney, and Wheeler, which the Japanese held firmly. It gradually grew heavier as the Japanese recovered from the shock of the bombardment, until in midafternoon the 503rd's supply section was forced to abandon attempts to recover supply bundles on the exposed parade ground.

To stop the fire Captain Henry W. Gibson, commander of Battery B of the 462nd, had a 75 mm. pack howitzer disassembled and carried to the second floor of a ruined officers' quarters. This gave sufficient clearance to allow fire on the most dangerous enemy position, a tunnel under the high ground north of Battery Wheeler. Once in position on the balcony with their piece assembled, the gunners discovered a parachute canopy dangling in their line of fire. To free it a cannoneer, Private First Class John P. Prettyman, crawled forward and jerked at the canopy, but it would not pull free. At this the Japanese began splattering the concrete building with machine-gun fire, evidently aware that something was brewing. During a lull Prettyman sprang up on the railing, grabbed the chute, and yanked it free, only to catch a full burst of machine-gun fire in the chest at the same instant. "All caution went out of that gun crew," Captain Gibson recalls. "They poured shell after shell into that hill for about fifteen minutes when I ordered them to cease fire." That silenced the machine gun, but the medics could not help Prettyman. All that could be done was to award him the Silver Star posthumously.

Aside from providing one of the hundreds of acts of individual heroism, this episode demonstrated S-3's wisdom in having Major Arlis E. Kline's 462nd Field Artillery (Parachute) come along. Someone's "prevision" had led to a last-minute decision to include it.

Again and again during the remainder of the operation the pack howitzers proved their worth. The gunners often manhandled them into difficult positions and blasted with direct fire Japanese caves and other strong points that could not otherwise be approached. They also kept Japanese-held ravines and gullies under harassment fire during the night while the 503rd slept inside its perimeter.

While the first lift of paratroopers was winging toward its destination, the ground-bound GIs of the 3rd Battalion (Reinforced) of the 34th Infantry Regiment, 24th Division, were boarding the twenty-five LSM's (Landing Ships, Medium) that were to ferry them to Bottomside. While doing so they filched so much extra gear from piles heaped on the beach that they called themselves "Postlethwait's thousand thieves," in honor of their C.O., Lieutenant Colonel Edward M. Postlethwait, a tall West Pointer. Sweating in the already uncomfortable heat, his men stowed their weapons, slipped their packs from rounded shoulders, and scrunched uncomfortably on the decks of the beaching craft for the jarring ride across the North Channel. Their destination was Black Beach, a narrow two-hundred-yard strand of south shore squarely in front of the empty gap that once had been San Jose barrio.

Anticipating that the Japanese would expect a landing on the more obvious north side or at the 92nd Garage area on the tail, the planners had chosen Black Beach despite its narrowness in the hope that its defenses would be a little weaker. They also hoped that the intense bombardment by the ships and planes, combined with the confusion induced by the paradrop, would so dislocate the Japanese defenses that the 3rd Battalion could overrun the first objectives, Bottomside and Malinta Hill, at reasonable cost. Heavy naval shelling already had brought down a rock slide over the three entrances to the Navy tunnels overlooking the beach. A Japanese 75 firing from these tunnels could have raised hob with the landing. Following the seizure of Malinta Hill and Bottomside, the plan merely called for the GIs to clear out the caves in the immediate vicinity, and then sit tight and hold a barrier across the island. This would cut the Japanese defense in two, preventing those on the eastern half of the island from joining their fellows on Topside.

Colonel Postlethwait's greatest worry was mines on Black Beach. An air strike supposed to detonate them had not come off, and his ordnance lieutenant had insisted he needed a truck to carry his mine-disposal equipment. Since there was no room for the truck, no mine-disposal equipment accompanied the first wave.

Shortly after 8:00 A.M. the LSM's got under way. Forming into five assault waves of five ships each, and accompanied by two armed LCM's, a picket boat, a maintenance boat, and the regimental crash boat, they headed across the North Channel and around the bulbous head of the Tadpole. There they met Navy rocket boats that would drive ahead to stun the defenders with a shower of missiles.

Off Black Beach destroyers *Picking, Young,* and *Wilkes* inched nearer until their 5-inch guns were smashing shells into the Rock's cliffs from as close as five hundred yards. They did a systematic job of it, carefully getting the range on the caves with single shots, and then letting go with murderous salvos. Even so, when the rocket boats went in, enemy shells began casting up waterspouts. *LCI (R) 338* was unlucky, taking four hits from a gun of about 3-inch caliber. Nevertheless she continued on, applying damage control as she went, firing with her own 40 mm. and machine guns, and discharging at the release line her deadly rockets. Then she retired under her own power to succor her wounded.

Close behind came the first five LSM's, and they too began to receive fire, mostly from machine guns, from foes holed up in the cliffs just east of Ramsay ravine, where nineteen suicide boats still lay hidden in their caves. Three of the five LSM's were hit, but none of the troops, who were all flat on their bellies, were touched. Grounding two minutes early, at 10:28 A.M., the GIs scrambled out and raced ashore without loss.

The four succeeding boat waves encountered more resistance as the Japanese began to recover from the rocket bombardment. Wave three came under heavy fire as it grounded six minutes late. A mortar shell exploded aboard one of the LSM's; forty bullets riddled another. Waves four and five in the rear took a worse beating. Nevertheless, all of the LSM's succeeded in retracting under their own power, including one that had one of its two engines shot out of action. Losses were astonishingly light among the troops; only two were killed and another six wounded. The GIs had escaped the kind of slaughter Colonel Sato's "human bullets" had suffered in 1942.

Accompanied by seven nervous war correspondents, Colonel Postlethwait was in a boat of the third wave, the one riddled by the forty bullets. A Japanese 20 mm. had opened with an "over" on the first burst, but was "on" with the second, with one round ("It sounded like a sledge hammer hitting the boat") passing through the conning tower and the coxswain, killing him. The wave leader had grabbed the wheel and directed the boat toward the beach as the gunner raked the boat with his third burst. Postlethwait inched behind a truck, only to discover he was next to its fuel tank. The Japanese gunner did not loose a fourth burst, probably because he had expended his belt of ammunition and had to reload. In addition to the coxswain, one other man had been killed.

As Postlethwait had feared, Black Beach was mined. Rows of 130 anti-vehicle mines were spaced seven to fifteen feet apart along 125 yards of beach. All were of the kind that poked their firing mechanisms out of the sand, and the infantrymen had skipped over them, keeping a sharp eye out for trip wires as they ran inland. But against the vehicles which followed they proved extremely effective. One of the first out, an M-7 self-propelled gun, hit a mine after leaving the ramp of its LSM. So did an M-4 Sherman tank of the 603rd Tank Company, and a jeep towing a 37 mm. antitank gun. Machine-gun fire pelting about indiscriminately accentuated the confusion, slowing the off-loading of additional vehicles. A mortar shell hit a truck. An engineer noncom acted first, organizing a party to mark an exit lane through the mines to get vehicles moving inland and out of the fire. Another climbed aboard a bulldozer and began pushing stalled equipment clear of the beach. By 10:53 A.M. all of the landing craft had unloaded and retracted. The mines had cost Postlethwait twenty-nine men and about half of his vehicles.

K and L Companies, the first two ashore, had as their mission the seizure of Malinta Hill, while the following three, I, M, and the attached A, were to seize Bottomside, help unload equipment, and block the west entrance of Malinta Tunnel, the Navy tunnels, and the North and South Shore roads running around either side of Malinta Hill. Expecting the worst, K and L Company's GIs raced two hundred yards inland on the double and then swerved off to scramble up Malinta Hill on hands and knees like men possessed. "We climbed like hell-bent apes," the novelist-historian of the 24th Division, Jan Valtin, quotes one of them as saying. "There's no place to go, once you're there, but forward," Colonel Postlethwait had admonished them. On top they dropped, panting in exhaustion, amazed at their good fortune. Not a man had been hit; what everyone had fully expected to be a carnage had been a piece of cake. Captain Frank Centenni, commanding K Company, expressed everyone's sentiments by exclaiming, "I'll be damned!" The only enemies present were nasty, biting flies such as had helped make life such a hell at the 92nd Garage three years before.

There was no time to waste. Centenni and his men well knew they were sitting atop plenty of foes hidden directly beneath their feet in the recesses of Malinta Tunnel. As soon as they had caught their breath, they moved out by squads and platoons, L Company to the south, K Company to the north, toward Malinta Point, to seize the dominating ground over the tunnel entrances and throw a barrier across Malinta Hill. That was their job: to grab the high ground, dig in, and hang on for dear life. We simply hold the hill, Colonel Postlethwait had summarized, ". . . until we kill all the Japs or the Japs have killed all of us. . . ."

As K Company moved out, a soldier cautiously poking into the tunnel where Lieutenant Friedline had lost his life discovered four enemy soldiers crouching behind the remains of No. 8 searchlight. A quick tommygun blast dispatched them. The 3rd Platoon, heading across Bottomside toward Malinta Point, came under fire briefly from the hospital portal of the tunnel but sprinted past and kept going until it reached its goal, leaving the enemy between it and the remainder of the company. Though cut off by enemy fire, its men had a good position with excellent cover blocking the road behind the beach in front. Two other squads slid down Malinta Hill to occupy two promontories lying between the crest and Malinta Point, one dubbed "Goal Post Ridge," because it had a cable hoist on it resembling a football goal post, the other "Little Knob." Wire was strung linking all elements, after which quiet descended for the remainder of a long afternoon, ruptured only by shooting from Bottomside where the other three companies of the 34th gingerly probed caves, tunnels, and rubble. L Company had the prize lookout point, the East Defense Officer's Station located at the very top of the hill. Below it all Bottomside and the entire tail of the island spread out like a map.

Far below, the men of M Company, the weapons company, armed with machine guns and mortars, and A Company, the attached reserve, were constructing defenses to keep the Japanese in their tunnels while I Company secured the Bottomside area. The west portal to Malinta Tunnel in the old rock quarry was partially closed by a rock slide caused by the pre-invasion bombardment, but machine guns were positioned to cover it if the Japanese tried to dig out. For the same reason the blocked entrances to the Navy tunnels also were guarded. Even the trackless disabled tank was towed up from the beach and used as a stationary pillbox. The Japanese had egress from the eastern end of the tunnel and from the hospital entrance, but the North and South Shore roads around each side of the hill were blocked. From the hilltop, L Company could spot Japanese escaping in daylight from the east entrance, but lacked the firepower and manpower to do much more than harass them. Nevertheless, the GIs had been as successful in seizing their initial objectives as the paratroopers; the enemy serpent was cut in two.

Colonel Jones, who had jumped on the third pass of the lead plane, was so encouraged by the progress on Topside and about Malinta

Hill by late afternoon that he asked XI Corps Headquarters to cancel the airdrop of Major Robert H. Woods's 1st Battalion, 503rd. Plans had called for it to parachute in at 8:30 the next morning, the seventeenth. Instead, Jones recommended flying it to San Marcelino Airfield above Subic Bay and having it come by water to Black Beach to avoid the inevitable drop injuries. He saw no point in landing by parachute if there was an easier way. He was convinced that his 2nd and 3rd Battalions would have no difficulty in holding their perimeter that night, even though he already knew that the Rock was infested with more Japanese than intelligence had estimated. Aside from the drop injuries, his losses had been light: only nine additional men killed and thirty-four wounded against a total of fifty counted Japanese dead.

Jones's supply situation also was good, although his Regimental S-4, Captain Robert M. Atkins, has since confessed that his status of supply report issued that evening was "somewhat meaningless." The only real shortage was of water; too many men had emptied both of their canteens and would have to suck their tongues until the C-47's could get around to dropping more.

The first twelve hours of the American return to the Rock were nearing their close. A brilliant lodgment against an enemy superior in numbers had been made with faultess timing and moderate losses. Together, the paratroopers and GIs had seized positions of advantage much superior to those held by Colonel Sato three years earlier and with far fewer casualties. In this situation Wainwright, unwilling to sacrifice his men and women, had surrendered. But even with their commander dead, their forces fragmented, their communications severed, and sure death awaiting them, the Japanese would not give up. To them, Corregidor still could be a victory if they could inflict equal or greater loss on their foe. A merciless fight lay ahead. Quarter would not be asked; neither would it—nor could it—be given.

19 ☆ "Let 'Em Come"

A SOFT TROPICAL NIGHT had come to Corregidor on this first day of the recapture operation, bringing out millions of stars. Thirsty GIs and paratroopers appreciated its coolness and the sudden departure of the annoying flies, but they paid little heed to the stellar display, for night was when the Japanese preferred to fight. Atop Malinta Hill stomachs tightened and nerves strained wire-taut as the GIs of Company K waited, packed uneasily together in a perimeter little larger than a couple of good-sized rooms, unable to burrow into the rock beneath. Soon, they feared, the darkness would ring to the fanatical screams of the foe. But they had to stay. "We were on top," recalls medic Ed Stachlek, "and that was it."

Just before midnight a burst of rifle fire and the staccato sputter of tommy guns erupted from the two squads isolated below on Goal Post Ridge and Little Knob. The telephone line went dead. Then shells from the nasty little Japanese knee mortars began bursting atop the hill.

A panting and groaning revealed someone laboring up the slope. It was Private Rivers P. Bourque carrying on his back a man with a mangled leg and dragging another whose hands dripped blood. He gasped his story to Captain Centenni; the Japanese had attacked the squad on Little Knob, killing or wounding everyone except himself and Private Cassie, who had volunteered to stay behind with two wounded men. Moments later two unwounded but angry survivors arrived from Goal Post Ridge to report that the enemy had killed nine of their eleven men. The Japanese had severed K Company's lightly held link between Malinta Hill and Malinta Point, freeing the hospital portal from fire, threatening the rest of the company atop the hill, the 3rd Platoon isolated on Malinta Point, and the companies below manning the barrier across Bottomside.

Bourque had scarcely finished his story when—in the words of Jan Valtin—"the night exploded in fury and death." Scrambling with the determination of the damned up the near-vertical northeast slope of Malinta Hill came the Japanese Imperial Marines, armed with rifles or captured stockade double-barrel shotguns and grenades. K Company held its fire, then blazed away with everything it had, following with a shower of grenades. Private Adolf Neament emptied his rifle into the face of a howling foe, while Private Ray Crenshaw kicked aside a grenade and knocked its thrower sprawling with a slug from his Garand. For an hour and a half they came, hurling furious small-scale rushes, but Company K stayed, checking its foe ten feet from its perimeter. When hit, the Imperial Marines tumbled all the way to the bottom.

On L Company's south end of the hill all was quiet as its GIs listened with concern and fear to the din of battle on the other side. On Topside, where the 503rd's paratroopers were spending a fairly quiet night except for scattered sniper fire, men awoke and sat up. The screams of the Imperial Marines told them that someone was on the receiving end of a banzai charge. Looking down from its hill-top at dawn's first light, K Company counted thirty-five enemy shapes sprawled grotesquely far below.

The next morning Colonel Postlethwait ordered Captain Centenni to find out what had happened on Goal Post Ridge and Little Knob and to rescue the wounded survivors. An eight-man patrol found one still alive on Goal Post Ridge, but lost half its number trying to push on further to Little Knob. Centenni mustered another patrol, leading it himself because he was short of manpower. With Centenni walking upright in the lead, the men crawled and slithered past the point where the other patrol had halted. Suddenly rifles cracked and grenades popped; the men hugged the earth. Centenni's riddled body toppled over a hummock of earth beyond their reach.

The 3rd Platoon on Malinta Point, which also had beaten off an attack the night before, remained cut off all that day, the seventeenth, as did three men manning an advanced outpost above the North Shore Road. These three, Sergeant Lewis Vershun, Private Emil Ehrenhold, and Private Ronald Paeth, remained isolated from February 16 through the twenty-third, beating off nightly attacks and killing twenty-three Japanese in the last and most ferocious charge. At Bottomside A Company killed twenty-three enemy swimmers in the water and H Company another fifty on the beach who had attempted to slip around their positions.

The morning of the seventeenth brought relative quiet, which prevailed until the late afternoon when the 503rd's 1st Battalion arrived by water and drew fire. Until then the chief excitement had been provided by a suicide-minded Japanese who had strapped a block of TNT about his waist and crawled underneath to blow up the motor—but not the cargo—of a truck loaded with explosives. During the day M and A Companies slowly worked over the caves along the beaches while I Company cleared the North Dock area with the aid of the serviceable tank.

That night, between midnight and 3:00 A.M. of the eighteenth, the Japanese tried for the second time to dislodge K Company, which had been resupplied—but not reinforced—during the daylight hours. They came cat-footed at first, until a lieutenant heard them and fired a flare. Then they charged in a frenzied scramble up the precipitous slope. Driven back by grenades and rifle fire, they inflicted twenty more casualties on Company K and left the GIs desperately short of grenades and ammunition. A worried L Company, again spending a quiet night, lent them more. By morning only thirty-three unwounded men and three officers remained to hold the entire northern half of the hill and contain the enemy in possession of Little Knob and Goal Post Ridge below.

Daylight of the eighteenth brought relief in the form of three platoons from I Company. Mortars blasted the Japanese, driving them from Goal Post Ridge. Covered by fire from its 3rd Platoon, I Company attacked, recoiled, attacked again, and won the ridge, plugging the hard-won hole the enemy had bored in Colonel Postlethwait's block across Malinta Hill. K Company's ordeal was over; of the 161 men who had climbed the hill two days before, 93, including the walking wounded, came down to flop exhausted in the sand, oblivious to the swarming flies and the stench of the 150 unburied Japanese cadavers on the slopes above.

With his weakened K Company replaced atop Malinta Hill and his block across Bottomside firmly established, Postlethwait's main problem now centered about finding some means to harass the several hundred Japanese still inside the tunnel. Opportunity soon came. On the night of the nineteenth an amazed L Company observer in the East Defense Officer's Station rubbed his eyes as he watched about two hundred of his adversaries march out of the east portal in a column of fours as if on parade. No one "clutched," no one started shooting prematurely; instead the observer rang up the naval fire control liaison team, and the night stand-by destroyer hurried over, its skipper hollering frantically over voice radio, "Wait for me!" Joined by the GIs' mortars and machine guns, it opened up with its 5-inchers, first with star shell, then with high explosives as the enemy scattered. At least thirty were killed, but the Japanese still continued to use the east portal, albeit more cautiously.

In the meantime, while the GIs had been maintaining their barricade, the paratroopers of the 503rd, with murderous expertise, had been slowly working their way around the rim of Topside, cave by cave, ably supported by the 462nd's pack howitzers, by air strikes, and by naval gunfire.

At 8:30 A.M. on the second day, the seventeenth, engines had drummed as Colonel Lackey's C-47's swung over the parade ground once more to drop the 1st Battalion's equipment bundles before flying on to San Marcelino Airfield to off-load the men. Surprisingly, this drop met the heaviest antiaircraft fire, which holed sixteen of forty-four planes and wounded five aircrew members, confirming Colonel Jones's wisdom in having the 1st Battalion come by sea. Had they come by paradrop, many men would have been hit in their chutes.

Subsequent effective harassment by the pack howitzers of the 462nd drove the enemy machine-gunners back into their caves, enabling thirty-three of the C-47's to fly that afternoon a resupply mission requiring 191 separate low passes without suffering a single hit.

In the meantime, Colonel Erickson's 3rd Battalion, 503rd, had again seized Morrison Hill, which the persistent enemy had reoccupied after the paratroopers had pulled back into perimeter for the night. As before, the Japanese made little effort to hold, although stubborn resistance would have delayed clearing the only usable road leading from Bottomside to Topside. By noon the hill was again in American hands.

The other side of the island was much tougher, Major Lawson B. Caskey's 2nd Battalion having gotten into a terrific fight for Battery Wheeler, which the Japanese had converted into a miniature fortress. Company F lost three of six officers trying to root the foe from the magazines, and Company D had to assist. Between them the two companies secured the battery by late afternoon, killing about sixty at a cost of several killed and more than a dozen wounded. While Company D was occupying the gun pits that night, the entrenched foe in one of the interlocking tunnels tried the first of many similar suicidal tactics. The Japanese blew up some ammunition inside, killing a paratrooper and forcing the other Americans to pull out. The Japanese lost sixty of their own number. The next morning D Company had to take the battery all over again.

The most important operations of the 17th, blasting out a link between the GIs and paratroopers, took place along the main road running from Bottomside to Topside. Erickson's G Company attacked from the west while elements of Postlethwait's I Company worked the other direction from Bottomside. Here the one undamaged Sherman tank and the two M-7 self-propelled howitzers (SPM's) proved their worth. Clattering up the road with small-arms fire glancing from their armor, they would wheel about with a roar, aim their cannon squarely into the mouths of the caves dug into the upper side of the road, and fire.

At the 503rd's end a demolition team under Lieutenant Bill Blake helped Erickson's Company G clear a stretch containing six cave openings. Blake and two of his team edged cautiously to within five yards of the caves, to be welcomed with a pair of grenades that wounded one of the men in his lower legs. Blake countered with a white phosphorous grenade, driving the enemy deeper inside and enabling his flamethrower man to spring out and spray three of the openings. Immediately nine screaming, flaming Japanese emerged, nearly trampling Blake and setting Corporal Delbert L. Parsons' clothing afire as they passed. They were shot down and released from their agony by I Company riflemen covering the team. The remaining Japanese stayed quietly in the other three caves while Blake propped heavy charges inside the entrances and buried them alive.

In the early afternoon before the cave clearance was finished, two self-propelled-howitzer men, Sergeant Bill Hartman and Corporal Mike Nolan, learned that the 503rd's medics on Topside were short of blood plasma. They volunteered to run the gauntlet up the road and try to get some through. Gunning their chunky monster, named the "Sad Sack," they started up past uncleared caves with small-arms fire sprinkling from their mount's none-too-thickly armored sides. A damaged bridge gave them a bad moment but held, and they delivered the plasma at the 503rd's aid station, only to learn there that the medics direly needed water. Taking aboard two seriously wounded men they returned and made the perilous run a second time with the precious water cans. Afterward Nolan decided to count the bullet scars on the sides of his M-7, but gave up after reaching two hundred.

When Major Woods's 1st Battalion arrived via LCVP's at Black Beach in the late afternoon of the seventeenth it discovered the hard way that the enemy was far from licked. Heavy machine-gun fire from caves near Ramsay ravine pinned the second wave to the beach, fortunately without losses. The troopers rose from their bellies only after the destroyer *Claxton* cowed the enemy gunners with 5-inch broadsides. Then they climbed quickly to Topside to take their assigned place in the perimeter.

Despite this contretemps Colonel Jones could take as much satisfaction at the end of his second day on Corregidor as from his first. Company K had held for another night on Malinta Hill, his 1st Battalion was ashore without loss, he had conferred personally with Colonel Postlethwait and now had some inkling of the location of the main Japanese concentrations, and against three hundred counted enemy dead he had lost but eight killed during the day. By dusk the road to Topside was virtually free of live Japanese, although not from annoying machine-gun and sniper fire from the direction of the old cold-storage and power plant, which was still in enemy hands. Personnel but not vehicles could move freely from Topside to Bottomside on trails. Jones knew he would have to abandon some ground so as to tighten his perimeter, for he realized that the Japanese were present in vastly greater numbers than G-2 had estimated. Yet if he could hold a nighttime perimeter, his superior firepower by land, sea, and air would insure a systematic mop-up at a reasonable price.

February 18, the third day of the operation, was largely a repeat of the day before. The 1st Battalion took over a sector to clear, while the GIs below cleaned out troublesome Power Plant ravine with the aid of the SPM's. To free Black Beach from all enemy fire, Jones's 3rd Battalion began working along the cliffside and shore near Breakwater Point, assisted by destroyer gunfire and occasional air strikes by P-47's. Rock Force losses for the day were slightly higher, at nineteen dead, but the count of Japanese dead rose steeply to over seven hundred for the day. That his men had to recapture some positions taken the day before and abandoned at nightfall did not worry Jones. He could not secure the island without killing the enemy, and doing this in positions attacked before was easier than assailing new ones.

For their part the Japanese were growing desperate. Deprived of wire communications by the paratroopers holding their "central," and with their forces severed by Postlethwait's block across Malinta Hill, their doom was certain unless they could break Jones's stranglehold on Topside. Like Wainwright's defenders three years before they needed water. In a week or two more, even if their tormentors left them alone, many would perish from thirst. Instead of reviving the extensive well system of Fort Mills and reconditioning all the local pumps for use in an emergency, the Japanese had established only four water points. Isolated, forced into a molelike existence in hundreds of caves and dugouts, they were dependent on such reserves as individual prevision had led them to store. In Malinta Tunnel, a prisoner later reported, they were living entirely on canned juices and seepage from the walls. On Malinta Hill L Company's GIs spent the long afternoons by picking off Japanese attempting to fill their water jugs at a well on the Rock's tail. The Japanese in Cheney and James ravines were luckier, enjoying bubbling springs, until the paratroopers finally found them and pre-empted their cool (and badly needed) refreshment for themselves.

By nightfall on the eighteenth, the third day of action, Lieutenant Endo, now the senior Japanese officer on Topside, believed the time had come for an all-out banzai charge. By runner Endo passed the word around topside's cliffs: charge at 6:00 A.M., the dark hour before the dawn of the nineteenth.

An example of the sort of self-sacrificing fanaticism Endo was counting on came at 1:05 A.M. well in advance of the main attack. A group of about forty Japanese exploded a heavy charge in a tunnel beneath a building Company A of the 1st Battalion was using as its command post, killing or injuring twenty of the troopers in a blast felt all around the Topside perimeter. Half the Japanese were killed, achieving their goal of perishing and taking an equal number of the enemy with them; but the others emerged from their tunnel, squatted in a circle chanting slogans, pulled the pins from grenades which they pressed into their stomachs, and ceremoniously blew themselves up.

After a series of feints Endo's main assault got under way at 6:00 A.M. when six hundred or more screaming Japanese marines carrying grenades, rifles, and even bayonets on sticks poured out of Cheney ravine and from positions near Batteries Crockett and Wheeler in a frenzied stampede. Through sheer weight of numbers they broke through the perimeter held by D and F Companies in the 2nd Battalion sector between Wheeler and Cheney and hammered away at A Company's positions near Breakwater Point.

D Company was hardest hit. Stationed around the rim of the parapet of Battery Wheeler, it found itself enveloped on either side. The pitch darkness made it dangerous to move without being fired on by one's own buddies, but Staff Sergeant Nelson H. Howard managed to work a few men and a machine-gun team close to the point of the attack. From there the two young lads on the stuttering gun littered the ground with enemy dead. But not without cost; D Company had thirteen killed, including one of the heroic gunners and its company commander, First Lieutenant Joseph A. Turinsky, who died from a grenade thrown into his command post in the plotting room of Battery Wheeler. A dozen more lay wounded.

Company F might have suffered its sister company's fate had not Endo's marines run into a one-man army. Private Lloyd G. McCarter was lying near his buddies in a foxhole atop a small, bare hill overlooking a draw that led up to Topside. Already he was a hero; on the sixteenth a few minutes after landing by parachute he had dashed thirty yards across open ground to silence a machine gun with grenades. Two days later, on the eighteenth, he had killed six enemy snipers. Now, on the night of the nineteenth and morning of the twentieth, he was virtually to shatter Endo's attack on Company F singlehanded.

At about 10:00 P.M. when the Japanese began their preliminary jockeying, McCarter shifted to a more exposed position down the hill, the better to sense his prey. For the remainder of the night he poured fire into the draw whenever he heard movement there, using in turn, until each jammed, a tommy gun, an automatic rifle, and a Garand, yelling repeatedly to his buddies up behind him, "How are you making out, boys?" When Endo's main attack began just before dawn, McCarter stood erect, completely exposing himself, to determine the base of the Japanese supporting machine-gun and knee-mortar fire. A bullet knocked him down, seriously wounding him, but as he fell he located the enemy, and he refused evacuation until he had told his squad mates where the foe was, enabling the 503rd's mortars to zero in with support that stopped Endo's infantry before they could banzai. The sun rose on thirty dead Imperial Marines in the draw below McCarter's position. Mortars and supporting fire had killed a hundred more massed in a cut below, where McCarter had spotted them. "I believe," wrote Staff Sergeant Chris W. Johnson, "if Private McCarter had not stayed in that dangerous position we would have had many more men killed and possibly lost the hill." For his feat McCarter was awarded the Congressional Medal of Honor, the only man so honored in the recapture of Corregidor.

Three Japanese infiltrated as far as Topside Barracks, where one tossed in a grenade that wounded four men of the regimental supply section. Captain Robert M. Atkins rallied his men, who were clad only in their shorts, and from the shattered third story they poured volley after volley of carbine fire into the darkness. The Japanese supported their attack with mortars, dropping shells as close as ten yards from the barracks.

At some points on the perimeter hand-to-hand fighting developed when the Japanese burst into the American positions. Private James J. Edgar of Battery D of the 462nd found himself in a tug of war with a determined Japanese marine over a .50 caliber machine gun. Since he was holding the butt end, Edgar won the contest by charging the weapon and pulling the trigger.

When daylight came Endo's men retired as abruptly as the tropical night, leaving dead littered everywhere. To tally them the paratroopers "counted arms and divided by two." One Japanese marine, clad in green coveralls that looked dangerously like those worn by the 503rd, lay just ten feet from the Topside Barracks. Apparently he was the one who had thrown the grenade, and evidently he had been shot when about to hurl another, for he had only one arm to count. By anyone's standard, even Endo's, the banzai had failed. Casualties to the troopers had been comparatively light despite the shooting and commotion, principally because of their good fire discipline. As ordered, they had stayed in their foxholes, except in heavily overrun points on the outer perimeter, letting the enemy do the moving, firing when they had a target. The pack howitzers of the 462nd helped tremendously as they fired at almost maximum rates for an hour on the Japanese routes of approach.

Mopping up after daylight was dangerous work. Individual Japanese marines were hiding all over Topside, forcing Colonel Jones to send patrols to inspect every building. Feigning death, others rose to hurl grenades at the rear of patrols as they passed. Three prisoners gave Colonel Jones's S-2, Captain Francis X. Donovan, his first "hard" information on the numbers and dispositions of the enemy. Some three thousand men, the prisoners agreed, had been on Topside, and another two thousand or more were stationed from Malinta Tunnel eastward. One said another banzai charge would be made that night with a thousand men. When this cheerful prospect reached F Company, the anonymous recorder of its daily log noted philosophically, "If it's true, let 'em come. We'll get it over with one big banzai. I'll close this journal down for the night."

In anticipation Colonel Jones tightened his perimeter when dusk fell on the nineteenth but no banzai came. The paratroopers had broken the backbone of Endo's resistance the morning before. From then on, wrote an officer-observer, ". . . the Jap could read the 'OFF LIMITS' sign on Topside and contented himself with life (and death) in the caves and ravines." February 19 had been hectic. The Japanese had lost an estimated five hundred men, mostly in Endo's banzai, against American losses of thirty-three killed and seventy-five wounded. Lopsided as it was, this was the second-best relative score the Japanese would achieve in the campaign.

In the days following, the troopers fought their way down the ravines to the water's edge and started sealing the caves in the cliffs. James ravine, where heavy resistance had been expected, was cleared easily following two days of extremely effective strikes by P-47's armed with both five-hundred pound high-explosive bombs and napalm. Patrols discovered afterward that the searing, suffocating flame of the napalm had penetrated thirty-five feet into the chief center of resistance, the old underground infantry barracks, killing all of the Japanese inside by suffocation. A heavy bomb had transformed the lone enemy tank on Corregidor into an almost unrecognizable pile of junk. An E Company probe of six men commanded by Lieutenant Joe M. Whitson, Jr., encountered but slight opposition in the ravine and took a prisoner but found the stench of rotting flesh difficult to bear.

Elsewhere the Japanese tried a few local rushes when the troopers approached, often trying to toss grenades from ranges fatal to themselves and their enemy. By February 23 little resistance remained on Topside. Both James and Cheney ravines were free of enemies and the largest remaining group was at Wheeler Point, where some hundred to two hundred of Endo's men had dug shafts into the almost vertical cliffs, accessible only by sliding down a rope from above. Others were in caverns along the water line of the point, where approach from the open beach was hazardous. As an F Company diarist put it, "It's a rough go—you have to get into every one and then close it up with demolition or the Nips will go back in."

On the night of February 21–22, while Postlethwait's I and L Companies still were camped patiently above them, the Japanese in Malinta Tunnel decided to try their variant of the suicide explosion and banzai charge. Their point of desperation came on the afternoon of the twentieth when they realized that they would have to break out or die of thirst. Accordingly, they decided to explode some of the huge stores of ammunition in the tunnel to stun the Americans and blast away the landslide at the west entrances. Then troops, massed at all portals, including the hospital and Navy exits, would march out, rush Topside, and annihilate their tormentors.

The possibility that the Japanese might try to blow up Malinta Hill had worried Colonel Postlethwait for some time. He had kept to himself the details of a captured manifest of the ammunition stored in the tunnel. The total tonnage came too close for peace of mind to the figure his battalion engineer, after fiddling with his slide rule, had calculated would suffice to blow the hill and I and L Companies atop it sky-high. Granted it was unlikely the Japanese could touch off all of it at once—but.

Suddenly at 11:30 P.M. Corregidor rolled like a ship at sea and Bataan shook. Flames shot from all the tunnel entrances and from the ventilation shafts above, lighting up the sky. From the side of the hill an avalanche of rock poured down, erasing a segment of the South Shore Road and burying six men of Postlethwait's A Company guarding caves near a roadblock. I and L Companies bounced about in their positions atop the hill but otherwise were unhurt. The nagging question that had lurked in the Colonel's mind was answered; Malinta Hill could take it.

The following banzai charge did not amount to much. Fifty Japanese—probably dazed survivors of a much larger force crowded there—marched in a column of twos from the west entrance and were cut down. Another group of fifty to a hundred ran out of the hospital entrance and started around the North Shore Road only to be driven back by machine-gun, tank, and mortar fire. Six hundred others escaped from the east entrance to the tail of the island, probably after discovering that the slide had frustrated their intent of charging around the south side of the hill. A prisoner revealed later that the explosion had gotten out of hand, generating much more power than intended, and that it had killed or stunned many of the attackers crowded at the tunnel portals.

Two days later, on February 23, Colonel Postlethwait undertook to open the North Shore Road in preparation for the cleanup of the Rock's tail. His 81 mm. mortars fired preparation, and his GIs overran a small knob above the old Enlisted Men's Bathing Beach at Engineer Cove. A platoon led the assault along the road, with a tank leading to blast the hospital portal of the tunnel. Just as the tank arrived some Japanese banzaied out. "A Tennessee boy," Postlethwait recalls, "shot a Jap from the hip and cartwheeled him into the bushes, then spat!" A few rounds from the tank drove the others back. Then the infantrymen piled up stones and brush to seal the tunnel entrance. After eight days K Company's isolated Third Platoon on Malinta Point was no longer cut off.

By 6:00 P.M. of February 23 the Japanese had lost a cumulative total of 2,466 counted dead and six prisoners of war. In addition an unknown number were sealed, dead or alive, in Malinta Tunnel and countless caves. Rock Force, including both the paratroopers and the GIs, had lost 118 killed in action and 314 wounded or injured. It was time for Colonel Jones to begin the last phase of the reconquest, the sweep from Malinta Hill to Hooker Point to exterminate all remaining enemies.

20 ☆ Mop-Up

FOR HIS FINAL ADVANCE down the tail of Corregidor Colonel Jones selected his 1st Battalion as a spearhead with his 3rd bringing up the rear in support. The hard-hit 2nd was given a "rest," the cleanup of Topside. Jones left Postlethwait's 3rd Battalion GIs in place to contain the surviving Japanese in Malinta Tunnel, but beginning at 3:00 A.M. on February 24, the morning of the attack, the chanting enemy conveniently eliminated himself by setting off six more distinct blasts that turned the entire subterranean cavern into a man-made volcano.

The 1st Battalion kicked off at 8:30 A.M., moving out briskly past the tunnel's sullenly smoking east entrance, while shells from the 462nd's nine 75's, now massed at the eastern edge of the parade ground on Topside, whistled over their heads in a rolling barrage. Recalls Captain William Bossert, the commander of Company A, the attack was ". . . an Infantry School textbook ideal for 'small unit on the attack.' " His men moved along the same road and ridge where Joe Williams' sailors of the 4th Battalion, 4th Marines, had marched with Enfields and Lewis guns but three years before. By late afternoon, supported by two Sherman tanks, they had reached Camp Point, just short of Water Tank Hill, while B and C Companies cleaned up Infantry Point on the other side of the ridge. To their rear Erickson's 3rd Battalion followed, eliminating nests of bypassed Japanese.

So far it had been easy. The enemy was mostly in caves along the shore and could be approached safely from the rear. Often point-blank fire from PT boats or landing-craft gunboats sufficed to destroy him. On one occasion Captain Bossert watched a destroyer "walk" its 5-inch projectiles into an enemy nest and blow it to bits. ". . . An exhilarating luxury," he recalls, "to have a destroyer attached to a rifle company." P-47's also helped with strike after strike with five-hundred-pound bombs and tanks of napalm. During their advance Bossert and his company had counted 101 Japanese dead. They scarcely had been able to believe their eyes as they watched ". . . a Japanese officer waving a samurai sword, screaming courage into a group of his grim-faced men, who then dutifully staggered forward over the rubble directly into our aimed fire!"

On nearing Water Tank Hill, where Colonel Sato's infantrymen had held out so successfully in 1942, the 1st Battalion ran into serious trouble. The Second Platoon of A Company tried to take the hill before nightfall but bogged down fifty yards short of the first water tower despite strong mortar support and directed fire from the 75's. With two men wounded it recoiled to join the 1st and 3rd Platoons in establishing a perimeter for the night just below the hill.

With the coming of darkness, the unknown Japanese commander, who had his command post in the former Navy Radio Intercept Tunnel at Monkey Point, was not content merely to hold his ground. In true Bushido spirit he proposed to ignore the odds and counter-attack all the way to Topside. Beginning about 9:00 P.M. he had his men set up their mortars and begin pummeling the 1st Battalion's perimeter with accurate fire. They dropped a round directly into the bomb crater which was serving as Major Robert H. Wood's command post, killing him and two others and wounding several of his 1st Battalion staff.

The survivors promptly rang up the 462nd and asked the artillerymen to fire a "search" for the offending mortar. The resulting deluge of 75 mm. shells caught the Japanese at the worst possible moment, a prisoner reported later, as six hundred were trying to form up for a banzai charge down Water Tank Hill. Despite the barrage the Japanese officers doggedly refused to let their men disperse and take cover, with the result that about half the force was killed or wounded before the attack began. Consequently, if the prisoner was correct, the Japanese were weakened in almost the exact proportion as Companies O and P of the 4th Marines had been three years before in the predawn hours of May 6, 1942.

The survivors attacked at about 3:00 A.M. and for the next hour or two gave the 1st Battalion a very hard time. Company A had three killed and twenty-one wounded before the foes finally slunk back to their positions. Only some 165 Japanese remained. Once again firepower and good discipline had triumphed over "spiritual strength."

Despite their near crippling losses, the survivors made a stiff fight of it the next morning, February 25, when A Company and its sisters again attacked Water Tank Hill at 10:45 A.M. As the troopers cautiously advanced, enemy riflemen fired briskly and killed Private John C. Pace and two companions by rushing from a small tunnel dug into one of the ridge's ravines. Had the paratroopers been forced to rely solely on rifles and grenades, as Williams' sailors had had to do in 1942, the attack might have failed, but strong tank, mortar, and artillery support gradually wore down the Japanese. Major John N. Davis, now the battalion commander, wisely decided to send his forces to the flank of the east end of the hill, where Denver's height finder had been located, rather than to attempt a frontal assault as Williams had done. Consequently, by 6:00 P.M. the 1st Battalion held all of the high ground overlooking Kindley Field.

Against sixteen paratroopers killed, the Japanese had lost over five hundred men, including the casualties of the previous night. More unusual than the disproportionate losses was the capture of ten POW's picked up by an LCM while they were trying to swim from Rock Point on Topside to Bataan. The day's count brought the total of Japanese dead since the first landing to over 3,700, making it evident that not many more could possibly remain in the Radio Intercept Tunnel and on the Tadpole's narrow tail. After darkness fell, the absence of customary sniper and mortar fire confirmed the heavy losses.

The next morning at 8:00 A.M. on the twenty-sixth, the tenth day of the brutal operation, the 1st Battalion relentlessly attacked once more, aided by the two Sherman tanks, to close the tunnel and clear Monkey Point. By 11:05 Company A was atop the little ridge on Monkey Point, squarely above the Japanese in the Radio Intercept Tunnel below. Company "B" was guarding a lower entrance. Major Davis, the battalion commander, was standing on top of the concrete upper entrance on the ridge, watching an artillery and air preparation for an attack down Kindley Field. His men were squatting, resting, while one of the Shermans cleaned out a nest of small caves on the ridge, firing its 75 into each in turn. Suddenly, almost simultaneously with the blast of the tank's gun, a tremendous underground explosion lifted the entire ridge above the tunnel into the air, sending bodies, Japanese and American alike, flying in pieces, shaking the entire Rock like a leaf, even more than did the Malinta Tunnel blast. Debris flew thousands of yards, a sizable chunk landing on a destroyer over a mile away. The Japanese had touched off some tons of explosives they had stored in the intercept tunnel. The thirty-five-ton tank tumbled end over end like a child's toy for nearly fifty feet, killing all but one of its crew. Ironically, it was Bossert's A Company, once before the victim of a Japanese suicide blast, that suffered the heaviest casualties. But C and B Companies also had many men killed and injured from falling boulders and debris.

Major Davis was propelled from his tunnel entrance perch, which remained intact, flew perhaps twenty to thirty feet through the air, and on landing had his wind knocked out. When the smoke and dust cleared and he had recovered enough to see, he was horrified. "I have never seen such a sight in my life—utter carnage—bodies laying everywhere, *everywhere*." A few feet from where he had been the concrete tunnel abruptly opened into a huge, oblong crater 130 feet long, 70 feet wide, and 30 feet deep. The little ridge over Monkey Point was now a hole in the ground.

Captain Bossert was about a hundred yards away talking over a walkie-talkie to one of his platoon commanders, Lieutenant René E.

Stievenart, who was killed in the blast, when the explosion came. ". . . The whole hill shook," he recalls. ". . . I fell to my knees; my helmet was knocked off, but I recovered it and clung to the straps, crouching, as the sky rained down coral, boulders, scrap iron, and bodies. I was hammered flat and partially buried, but some of my men found me quickly and dug me out." Bossert had a rib broken, his chest was partially crushed; "I was coughing blood like a Grade B movie hero!"

Lieutenant Edward J. Callahan, commanding a platoon of Company B guarding the lower entrance to the Radio Intercept Tunnel, was more fortunate. Noticing smoke seeping from the concrete entrance a few moments before the explosion, he had ordered his platoon down the hill into the underbrush, remaining himself with his radio operator. "Suddenly I dove for protection out of reflex action. . . . Everything was pitch black." When he came to his senses, Callahan found himself lying on his back, injured, covered with a thick layer of dust.

Disaster had stopped the 1st Battalion. Fifty-two men had been killed and scores wounded and injured for a total of 196 casualties. By this Kamikaze tactic the Japanese for once had succeeded in inflicting a greater loss than they themselves had suffered, even though about 150 of them were blown to bits.

Colonel Jones at once rushed all possible medical support to his stricken 1st Battalion, but did not let the catastrophe shake his military judgment. He ordered the 3rd Battalion to continue the advance while the Japanese still were numbed from the shock. Colonel Erickson's men moved out immediately, with Company I in the lead, and H and G following on the flanks. Bulldozing aside light resistance, the rugged troopers overran Kindley Field and pushed a platoon all the way to East Point by 4:00 P.M. There they dug in and traded bullets with some die-hard defenders who were holding out to the bitter end on Hooker Point, the narrow islet off the tip of the Tadpole.

After reorganizing in the Monkey Point area, the battered 1st

Battalion limped back to Water Tank Hill to go into a perimeter for the night. Although unwounded, many men were suffering from concussion—"shell shock" in the World War I vernacular—and they badly needed rest. Counting noses, A Company found it had only 2 officers and 42 men left of the 6 officers and 126 men who had landed on Bottomside on February 17. It had suffered the heaviest casualties of any unit engaged in the recapture of Corregidor.

The night of February 26–27 passed quietly. All enemy concentrations of any size now were gone. While the 1st and 3rd Battalions were capturing the Rock's tail, Company D of the 2nd Battalion on Topside had been co-operating with the Navy in the cleanup of the troublesome Japanese caves at Wheeler Point. It had lost three killed and five wounded in this dangerous work; at one point some of its men became so thoroughly pinned to the beach by fire from a large cave, that a landing craft had to close and take them off while another pumped in bullets to keep snipers away from the entrance.

Many Japanese tried to flee from the overrun tail of the island on the twenty-seventh, slipping down from their bypassed caves into the water. The Navy's PT boats, other small craft, Air Force P-47's, and even Lieutenant James R. Thomas, the 462nd's liaison pilot, flying his little Piper Cub with one hand and wielding a tommy gun with the other, ruthlessly hunted them down. A few undoubtedly escaped to Bataan or to Fort Hughes, but several dozen did not. Very few tried to surrender, and the Navy had learned long ago that it was dangerous to seize them forcefully in the water. Most of them carried a grenade, a pistol, or knife and resisted when approached. One prisoner, captured in the 2nd Battalion's mop-up on Topside, attacked his Nisei interpreter, forcing his guards to club and kick him to death. The Japanese on Corregidor had been as fanatical—as determined to fight and die for the Emperor—as Colonel Sato's "human bullets" had been three and one half years earlier.

Against 4,506 counted dead, Jones's men had taken only 21 prisoners by March 2, and 2 of these died later of wounds previously inflicted. An estimated 500 more were sealed in caves and another

200 killed in the water. Jones's Rock Force, paratroopers and GIs combined, had suffered a grand total of 197 dead and 1,022 wounded and injured, a quarter of its strength.

In the midmorning of March 2, 1945, a bright, sparkling day with a fresh breeze, General MacArthur stepped from a PT boat at Bottomside and surveyed his former command. Plenty of brass accompanied him, and all turned to watch a show staged by the Air Force, the bombing of Fort Hughes by twelve P-47's. After viewing the still-smoking east entrance to Malinta Tunnel, the General then jeeped up the dusty road to Topside accompanied by Colonel Jones.

Arriving at about 11:00 A.M., MacArthur first visited Topside Barracks. Then he went to Battery Wheeler and spent ten or fifteen minutes looking it over. Returning to the parade ground, where Jones's grimy paratroopers were drawn up, trying in spite of the dirt to look their best, he reviewed the men and then turned to Jones. Proudly the Colonel saluted, reporting, "Sir, I present you the fortress Corregidor." Then MacArthur made some short, quiet, to-the-point remarks, concluding with, "I see that the old flagpole still stands. . . . Hoist the colors to its peak and let no enemy ever haul them down." Everyone turned, saluted, and Old Glory fluttered once more before the old Post Headquarters. From a hospital cot outside Topside Barracks, from which he had been carried by some of his A Company men, a misty-eyed William Bossert watched it rise.

History had turned full cycle.

The capture of Corregidor had put the hard-fighting paratroopers of the 503rd temporarily out of a job. On March 8 the regiment left the island, backing away from Black Beach in LCI's, headed ultimately for Negros Island and another hard fight. The 151st Infantry's 2nd Battalion remained behind to furnish garrison and prepare for the capture of the Rock's lesser sisters.

Even though none of the lesser islands had a cannon left intact, XI Corps Headquarters decreed that Forts Hughes, Drum, and Frank must be taken. Leaving their enemy garrisons to wither on the vine would not do, because they had the habit of taking pot-shots with their rifles and machine guns at every ship venturing within range. A reconnaissance platoon on March 20 discovered the hard way that the foe on Hughes was still in a belligerent mood. After landing without molestation it was pinned to the beach; the enemy had holed up in Battery Craighill's twin mortar pits and in the prewar tunnel running up through the hill and connecting with the pits.

On March 27, at 9:00 A.M., Companies E and F of the 151st, under the command of Lieutenant Colonel Paul R. La Masters, landed unopposed on Hughes after savage naval and air bombardment. Against fairly light opposition they secured all of the island in just two days except for the two mortar pits, but there they hit a snag. Every time a curious infantryman would peer over into the pits, as one of the GIs put it, ". . . 'ping,' and another casualty was counted." The Japanese inside numbered at least fifty, with many more in the tunnel and magazines, and they were armed with rifles, machine guns, and 20 mm. light cannon. Tossing over grenades, heavy satchel charges, and even rolling down two five-hundred-pound aerial bombs accomplished nothing, and flame-throwing tanks could not get up the hill. Inspired by their Army Day on April 4, the Japanese launched a banzai charge which cost them eighty of their remaining men but also nearly wiped out E Company's command post.

What finally destroyed them was a scheme concocted by the engineers. Rigging a four-inch pipline from a landing barge, they pumped into the pits and tunnel three thousand gallons of an oil and gasoline mixture. Two doses pumped in and set afire on successive days suffocated the 50 survivors of the 280 Japanese originally on the island. Just 3 allowed themselves to accept capture.

Drum, the concrete battleship, still glowering sullen and silent in the South Channel, had looked so tough that some thought was given simply to routing shipping past out of rifle range of the *Musashi* sailors manning it. The success of the oil and gas mixture at Fort Hughes, however, led Lieutenant Colonel Fred C. Dyer, G-4 of the 38th Division, the 151st Regiment's parent organization, to suggest a similar treatment for Drum. He had the deck of Drum exactly duplicated on the Corregidor parade ground, with each air vent, gun turret, and opening marked. Then he rehearsed a platoon of riflemen from Company F of the 151st until each man knew exactly where to squat and point his weapon to keep the enemy below decks.

In the meantime engineers of the 113th Engineer Battalion had been building on an LSM a ramp resembling a gangway or Roman corvus, much the same arrangement the Republic's legionnaires had used in the First Punic War to win their naval victory over Carthage at Mylae. The idea was that the gangway would be dropped from the landing ship's conning tower onto Drum's deck, after which the riflemen—even as had Rome's soldiers—would race across and take their stations. Then a platoon of engineers would rig a pipeline, pump in 2,200 gallons of the terrible oil-gas mixture, and lay and light a six-hundred-pound charge of tetryl in a hatchway on the starboard side of the fort. Then everyone would "run like hell" for the landing ship, the better to be a long way off when she blew.

On the morning of Friday, April 13, the landing ship moved in on Drum and the gangway crashed down. The infantrymen quickly boarded the fort, the engineers rigged the pipe, pumped in the oil and gas, and set and lit the charge. Twenty-five minutes later it went off with a disappointingly small "whump," only to be followed in a few minutes by a tremendous blast as the gasoline and oil suddenly exploded, touching off the fort's filled magazines. A huge flat object, later identified as a twelve-foot-square slab of armor over the magazine, sailed hundreds of feet into the air to cap a mushroom column and fall back on the deck. For two days Drum burned fiercely, and when a patrol finally entered the fort some days later, after it had cooled, it found eight Japanese dead on the second deck and sixty more, burned beyond all recognition, on the third. By way of contrast only three Americans had been slightly wounded as the LSM pulled away. The concrete battleship itself was so gutted and melted even the souvenir hunting was poor. Only the hulking turrets of Batteries Wilson and Marshall remained intact on the deck, their 14-inch guns still in place, to identify what once had been the pride of the Coast Artillery Corps.

In view of the difficulty in taking Hughes, nobody was anxious to rush Fort Frank, with its hundred-foot vertical cliffs. An elaborate program of naval bombardment, bombing, and reconnaissance was laid on, while the 1st Battalion, 151st, under Major Morton K. Sitten, rehearsed with the utmost care for what uneasy divisional planners feared would be a massacre. Yet when the troops attacked, after another tremendous aerial and naval preparation, all they found were two dead Japanese and one live pig. The garrison of 350 marines had fled to the nearby Cavite mainland to become guerrillas in the hills. Now all four of the once-proud Fortified Islands of Manila and Subic Bays were again in American hands, shattered, battered, explosive-ripped wrecks already overtaken by history and rusting into obscurity.

21 ☆ The Monument

Only a lone Quartermaster Graves Registration Company remained on Corregidor after the occupation of Fort Frank in April, 1945. Protected by an infantry company against possible Japanese stragglers, it probed for the next year and a half for the American dead of two campaigns. In September an official survey team headed by Colonel Reinold Melberg inspected the Rock to determine what, if anything, was salvageable of its 150 million dollars' worth of prewar coast defenses. Its conclusion was—nothing. The great rifles and mortars were just so much scrap, providing mute testimony that the day of the fixed fortress had ended.

As the graves registration men continued their sad, gruesome work, they began to realize that they were not alone. Telltale footprints and stealthy rustlings at night beyond the guard perimeter led them to suspect that some of the Japanese sealed in the caves by the 503rd had dug their way out and still were alive.

On New Year's Day of 1946 Sergeant James "Moon" Mullen was astonished to see a formation of twenty Japanese, headed by an Army junior officer, marching toward him and waving surrender flags. Mullen noted that all appeared to be "exceptionally soldierly," indicating that they had not been suffering from short rations during their long sojourn underground. Bowing, the officer presented a document written in excellent English proffering their capitulation. Later interrogation revealed that the party had not learned of Japan's surrender until a few weeks previously, when one of the men had found an old newspaper while venturing forth at night for water. A long debate followed until all were convinced that surrender was the Emperor's will and therefore their duty. After that, they had decided to search for comrades bottled up in other caves before turning themselves in. Their persistence was rewarded; they found two Navy men. This done, they had shaved, cleaned up, put on fresh uniforms, and marched forth from their hiding place as befitting loyal subjects of the Emperor.

During the next twenty-two months the jungle quickly reclaimed Corregidor. Not since Spanish times had the island been so deserted and overgrown. On the parade ground, where the Americans of the 59th and 60th and Philippine Scouts of the 91st and 92nd Regiments had once so proudly marched, waist-high grass and ipil-ipil overran everything, concealing treacherous jagged shrapnel, dented helmets—Japanese and two styles of American—and unexploded bombs and shells. Growing with incredible swiftness after an aerial seeding operation, the jungle trees quickly soared to the rooftops of the shattered officers' quarters; yet on the bulletin board in the ruins of Topside Barracks a few yellowed orders of the day still fluttered to remind occasional parties of visitors of the housekeeping of the 503rd. Smashed footlockers and moldering personal gear served as mementos of the long occupancy of the old 59th Coast Artillery, and of the subsequent looting by the infantrymen of His Imperial Majesty's 4th Division. Rows of rusting shells still lay in fire-gutted Malinta Tunnel, while nearby, a bleached skull grinned hideously from a pole. A small garrison of Philippine Scouts maintained a compound at Bottomside and kept the road open to the renovated lighthouse on Topside; thus Corregidor preserved its early role as a guard and guide to ships entering Manila Bay.

For one day only, on October 12, 1947, the Rock's old luster returned. In a moving and colorful ceremony the Honorable Emmet O'Neal, the United States Ambassador, officiated over the transfer of the sovereignty of Corregidor to the new Philippine Republic. President Manuel A. Roxas accepted the island in the name of the Philippine people, noting that the Rock ". . . is sacred to the memory not only of Filipinos, but of American soldier dead." Among the several hundred assembled was George Moore, a survivor of captivity and now Lieutenant General in command of all United States forces in the Philippines and Ryukyus. ". . . It was on this very spot," the tired veteran spoke sadly, "that I suffered the most bitter experience of my life." And he added, "Certainly I can say that my best years as a soldier have been spent on Corregidor." Then both national anthems were played, the Stars and Stripes fluttered down for the last time, the flag of the Philippine Republic rose, and the small detachment of veteran Scouts turned over their guard duty to an equally small Philippine Army unit. An exchange of notes completed the ceremony.

Following the transfer, Corregidor was left alone, all but forgotten. Burdened with many problems, including a Hukubulap rebellion, the Philippine government could do little to restore the island. Only a small Army detachment remained to escort visitors and to prevent smugglers from spiriting away its mementos, guns and munitions.

Nor for some time did the United States show interest. Only in 1953 did Congress establish the Corregidor-Bataan Memorial Commission to assist in erecting a suitable memorial on the island. Failure to provide funds stalled action, until the Commission's chairman, former Ambassador O'Neal, and its executive director, Captain Samuel G. Kelly, U.S.N. (Ret.), took the cause directly to President John F. Kennedy. Observing that his budget did not permit a large outlay, Mr. Kennedy suggested that for a modest sum a battlefield park on the order of Gettysburg might be built. After clearing the idea with Philippine Vice-President Emmanuel Pelaez, Kennedy sponsored legislation in 1962 to appropriate $1,500,000 for the battlefield park, an amount to be matched by the Philippine government as co-sponsor. Planning then got under way and is continuing as of this writing for an appropriate memorial, while the Philippine government began clearing the Topside and Bottomside areas of duds, debris, and jungle growth.

Today, the visitor to the island may take a hydrofoil boat which makes the excursion from Manila in just forty-five minutes, following at a faster speed the route of the daily trips of the harbor boat *General Miley* in the lazy years of the twenties and thirties. Disembarking at South Dock and riding up the narrow, twisting road to Topside, he may visit Battery Way, where "Wild Bill" Massello and his Erie crew fought long past the point of hopelessness. He may hike the trail to the head of the Tadpole, there to admire Bataan Province's mountains from beside Battery Hearn, still intact on its circular bull's-eye of concrete. Crossing Topside he can visit Battery Crockett, where Dr. Fox suffered his agony, and call at Batteries Wheeler and Cheney, where paratroopers hunted Japanese marines in the ruined galleries. On the parade ground before mangled Topside Barracks, he can stand by the flagpole near the ruins of the old Post Headquarters. Perhaps he might imagine seeing the parachutes of the 503rd's Third Battalion, as the men drifted past level ground to thud onto the rocks and debris where Battery Boston had trained its 3-inchers at high-flying "Sallys" during the siege of 1942.

Leaving Topside's cooling breeze, the visitor can drop down the hill past the ruins of Middleside's utilities to enter Malinta Tunnel, Kilbourne's and Embick's prewar miracle in concrete. Following the old streetcar tracks, he can turn off into the hospital complex to emerge at the north entrance to sit where the desperately tired nurses took their breaks in the defiladed road cut, safe from the menacing Japanese 240's.

If he doesn't mind the steep climb, the visitor can scramble up the precipitous slopes of Malinta Hill, there to stand on the room-sized spot where Company K fought off screaming, dedicated enemies. And, going a little further, he can view the ruins of Number 8 searchlight, where Stan Friedline and his Mobile Battery crew were killed by a freak 240 shot. Turning about, he may look toward the tail, and toward the first water tank, where Dewey Brady bravely stood and died, and where John Sweeney and John Haskin, marines, offered up their lives for the honor of the Corps. Far down the curving tail, the visitor may see where Ray Lawrence and his Scouts took their awesome toll of Japanese landing craft on the night of May 5–6, 1942.

At night, just as in the pleasant years before the war, one can gaze at the lights of Manila winking across the bay. In the stillness before moonrise, the stars shine with piercing brightness, as they did when the GIs and paratroopers on Topside and Malinta Hill sweated out the banzai charges. To the north and south the mountains of Bataan and Cavite loom high. When the moon rises, the contours of Corregidor's hills and ridges are etched weirdly in the pale light, and their shadows edge onto the beaches and into the ravines. Except for the strange sounds of tropic life, all is silent. The relics of war have been covered by trees and vines and grass, the sounds of gunfire have faded with time. But for those survivors—American, Filipino, and Japanese—of the desperate battles to take or to hold the Rock, the memories of this Gibraltar turned Alamo of modern times lives on.

☆ Note on Sources

IN THEIR SEVEN YEARS of research for this book the authors have utilized three sources of information. First, they have gone to the men who participated in the 1942 siege and the 1945 recapture of Corregidor. Second, they have used the documentary sources available at the World War II Records Center of the National Archives in Alexandria, Virginia, at the Army Administration Center in St. Louis, and at the historical divisions of the Army, Navy, and Marine Corps in Washington, D.C. Third, they have read all relevant published articles and monographs.

The authors have found that interviews and correspondence with participants have been indispensable to their research. The memories of the participants have proved to be unexpectedly fresh; the shattering experience of more than three years of captivity as prisoners of war has not eclipsed memories of the siege among the 1942 veterans. Also, some participants have furnished additional documentary material of exceptional value.

Colonel Paul Cornwall loaned to the authors his "War History of Battery 'D,' 60th CA (AA)," written by him in 1942 while in captivity. Colonel William Massello supplied an account he had written in 1946 on the last fight of Battery Way, the details of which did not reach the archives. Brigadier General Curtis T. Beecher supplied an account written in captivity of the action of his First Battalion, 4th Marines, and Colonel Louis Bowler loaned to the authors the text of an unpublished seventy-page narrative written shortly after the war.

Colonel Ray Lawrence's letter covering the action of his command on the Rock's tail on May 5–6, 1942, must stand as a unique historical document, as must Major Richard Ivey's "Narrative of Experiences," written for the authors, relating his work in directing fire in the mountains of Cavite Province in February, 1942. Colonel Napoleon Boudreau's letter describing the siege of Fort Frank is exceedingly detailed and accurate. Mr. William Bossert has related in masterful prose the action of his Company A of the 503rd Parachute Infantry. Many enlisted men have displayed powers of description as able as that of their former officers. To mention only two, more or less at random: Mr. Harold Shrode's account, based on his personal diary, tracing in detail his experiences as a height-finder operator in Battery Denver; Mr. Don Hart's account relating his experiences at Battery Wheeler.

Interviews proved very rewarding. The narration of Colonel Thomas W. Davis, III, of the action at Battery Geary on May 2, 1942, is matched in interest only by Colonel Jesus Villamor's account of his heroic reconnaissance flight over the Japanese batteries in Cavite Province on February 7, 1942. Two lengthy interviews with Colonels Edward M. Postlethwait and John N. Davis revealed many important details not in the official records of the recapture of the Rock in 1945. A lengthy, tape-recorded interview with Mr. Art Bressi produced valuable details on every aspect of the siege of 1942, and particularly of the daily routine of life at Battery Chicago on exposed Morrison Hill.

A number of correspondents went "beyond the call of duty" in locating individuals and obtaining additional information requested by the persistent authors. Perhaps no other correspondent—unless it be Mrs. June Davis, the widow of Captain Frederick Miller of Battery Erie—has worked so hard to help as Colonel Valentine P. Foster, commander of Fort Hughes during the siege of 1942. The authors are especially indebted to Colonel Ray M. O'Day of Seattle, a Bataan "March of Death" survivor, who provided them with hundreds of current addresses of Corregidor veterans, and to Mr. Andrew J. Amaty of Brooklyn, who edits the newsletter of the 503rd Parachute Infantry Regiment Association. Brigadier General George M. Jones, the 503rd's wartime commander, also furnished valuable information and addresses.

The authors would like to thank Major General William B. Bunker, U.S.A., for permission to use the diary of his late father, Colonel Paul D. Bunker; Mrs. Rita Ferguson for permission to use the notebooks of her late father, Staff Sergeant Bernard O. Hopkins; and Mrs. Katherine Gehrkens for permission to use the diary of her late husband, Captain Godfrey R. Ames. All three of these gallant soldiers were as able with their pens as they were in going about their military duties.

Space considerations unfortunately prohibit further mention of individual correspondents and interviewees. A partial list has been appended to this Note.

Three documentary collections comprise the backbone of the written source material. These are: first, the postwar report of the late Major General George F. Moore, Corregidor's commanding officer in 1941–1942; second, the report of operations of the 503rd Parachute Infantry Regiment; and third, "Operation M-7," the report of action on Corregidor of the 3rd Battalion, 34th Infantry Regiment.

Of these reports the first, General Moore's, was prepared by him and a number of his former staff officers after hostilities had ended as part of the larger report on the Philippine campaign prepared by General Wainwright. Moore's former operations officer, Colonel William C. Braly, drafted the day-to-day account of the combat action, utilizing his G-3 operations diary, which he smuggled through captivity, his personal diary, and the memories of the participants. Other officers, largely from memory since most records were lost, prepared annexes relating to their supply, personnel, engineering, and antiaircraft activities. A valuable supplement to the Moore report is one prepared in 1943 by Colonel Stephen M. Mellnik, Moore's assistant supply officer, who escaped from prison camp on Mindanao Island and reached Australia.

The 503rd Parachute Infantry's report includes the report of Colonel George M. Jones, the Rock Force commander in 1945, and the detailed observations of a USAFFE Board inspection team. The report incorporates verbatim the war diaries of Colonel Jones's S-1, S-2, S-3, and S-4, and also of Companies A, D, E, and F. These, plus a mass of appended individual documents, furnish an exceptionally complete record of the 503rd in action. Nevertheless, since the official reports seldom record individual heroism or exploits, the authors have had to rely heavily on correspondence and interviews to secure additional details.

Like the report of General Moore, the action report of the 34th Infantry's 3rd Battalion is in the form of a narrative. Colorfully written, evidently by personnel of the 24th Division's historical section, it is reasonably detailed and accurate. Nevertheless, the authors found their interview with the unit's commander, Colonel E. M. Postlethwait, indispensable to corroborate and expand the report.

The authors have by no means relied entirely on these three abovementioned reports. They sought out as much additional documentary material as they could find. They turned up many hundreds of individual documents in various files, ranging from engineering construction reports to texts of citations for awards granted to individuals. This type of material is almost too abundant for the 1945 recapture and relatively sparse for the 1942 siege. By far the most valuable "find" came in the form of Japanese monographs prepared for the American occupation authorities in Tokyo after the war, relating from enemy records the story of the siege of 1942 and recapture of 1945. Also, records of interviews with former Japanese officers helped to fill out the picture.

The third category of information used by the authors has been the published literature. It is surprisingly abundant; they have located no fewer than 84 relevant monographs and 103 articles. Their search for this material has taken them to both coasts, to the Library of Congress, to the New York Public Library, to the Newberry Library in Chicago, and to the libraries of a half-dozen colleges and universities, including the service academies. By far the most useful volumes, however, have been the official histories of the U.S. Army, Navy, and Marine Corps dealing with the Philipine campaign. The admirable volume of Dr. Louis Morton and the survey of Robert Ross Smith, covering respectively the defeat in the Philippines in 1942 and the recapture in 1945, both were indispensable. The authors invite inquiry from scholars interested in pursuing further detailed research.

We are grateful to the following correspondents and participants who were gracious enough to grant us interviews. They are: M/Sgt. Abie Abraham, Lt. Col. Aaron A. Abston, Carl L. Allen, Andrew J. Amaty, Col. Arnold D. Amoroso, Frederick C. Amos, Capt. Louise M. Anschiks, William H. Arterburn, Col. Robert M. Atkins, Robert F. Augur, Rev. Herman C. Baumann, Dr. James B. Becker, Brig. Gen. Curtis T. Beecher, USMC, Clarence E. Boehrs, Jesse C. Booth, William Bossert, Col. Napoleon Boudreau, Col. Louis J. Bowler, Dr. Charles H. Bradford, Col. William C. Braly, C.W.O. Robert K. Branch, Winfred B. Brannon, Maj. Hattie R. Brantley, Rev. Albert Braun, Arthur A. Bressi, Mark F. Britain, Rear Adm. Charles B. Brook, Lt. Col. Stockton D. Bruns, Chester L. Buchholz, Maj. Gen. William B. Bunker, Lt. Col. Donald D. Burke, Rhynard Byars, Edward J. Callahan, Anson H. Cartwright, Col. Clifton H. Chamberlain, L. B. Chevaillier, Dr. Calvin E. Chunn, Charles A. Cobb, Col. J. H. Cochran, James F. Cook, Col. Wibb E. Cooper, M.D., Albert L. Corn, Col. Paul R. Cornwall, Brig. Gen. James B. Crawford, Brig. Gen. Donald T. Curtis, USMC, Col. Alfred J. D'Arezzo, Col. John N. Davis, June R. Davis, Thomas J. Davis, Col. Thomas W. Davis, III, William E. Davis, Kenneth Day, Col. Octave De Carre, R. A. Densmore, Henry N. Depanian, Col. Thomas Dooley, Capt. Dayton L. Drachenberg, Robert W. Erdwin, Col. John L. Erickson, Calmer A. Ersness, Col. Stephen C. Farris, James O. Faulkner, Brig. Gen. Bonner F. Fellers, Capt. Clara M. Fensch, Lt. Col. F. W. Ferguson, USMC, Lt. Col. Edward T. Flash, Maj. Adele F. Foreman, Col. Valentine P. Foster, Dr. Lester I. Fox, M.D., Alfred Galler, Katherine Gehrkens, Col. Henry W. Gibson, Frank Gomez, Rear Adm. H. W. Goodall, Clarence M. Graham, T/Sgt. Arthur T. Green, W. O. Odas A. Greer, Lt. Col. John McM. Gulick, Benson Guyton, B. Osbury Haller, Lt. Col. William A. Hamilton, Col. Stanley H. Hankins, Donald V. Hart, Lt. Col. Milton D. Hawes, Myron D. Hayes, Bertha D. Henderson, Loyal C. Henrich, S.F.C. Carl P. Hill, First Sergeant John A. Hillmon, Col. Armand Hopkins, Henry R. Hudson, Theodore Ince, Maj. Richard G. Ivey, Paul Jackson, Frankie L. Jarrett, Lt. Col. Frank G. Jonelis, Brig. Gen. George M. Jones, Lucy Wilson Jopling, Darnell W. Kadolph, Edwin Kalbfleish, Jr., Lt. Gen. Charles E. Kilbourne, Garrett G. King, Weldon King, Walter A. Kulinski, Col. John H. Lackey Jr., USAF, Alonzo E. Langworthy, Lt. Col. Ray G. Lawrence, John W. Lay, Wilbur Mason Marrs, Harold D. Martelle, Jr., Col. William Massello, Jr., Charles E. Maurer, Dr. Priscilla Maury, Lt. Col. George G. Maxfield, Dorothy Ludlow McCann, Rear Adm. Melvyn H. McCoy, Col. Riley E. McGarraugh, Estie M. McLouth, Brig. Gen. Stephen M. Mellnik, Ralph W. Middlebrooks, Col. Lloyd E. Mielenz, S. Harrison Mitchell, Major George M. Moore, C. W. Montgomery, Dr. Charles H. Morhouse, M.D., William M. Murrell, Capt. David Nash, USN, V. Randolph Neblett, Fleet Adm. Chester W. Nimitz, Dr. Robert L. Obourn, M.D., Col. Ray M. O'Day, Col. Arthur C. Peterson, Lester L. Petrie, M/Sgt. Ben A. Pierce, Jr., Lloyd A. Ponder, Col. Edward M. Postlethwait, Rev. John J. Powers, Major Gen. John R. Pugh, M/Sgt. Charles C. Reel, Col. Franklin B. Reybold, Ray L. Riddle, Boyd C. Ringo, E. O. Roberts, Jr., Col. Dorsey J. Rutherford, Major Otis E. Saalman, Jean Kennedy Schmidt, Clement P. Schmitt, Lt. Col. George A. Sense, Harold J. Shrode, Col. Harry A. Skerry, Cmdr. Alexander N. Slimmon, Charles F. Snyder, Albert N. Sondergaard, Alfred N. Sorensen, Spec. 5th Cl. Edward Stachlek, Frederick T. Stolley, Minnie Breeze Stubbs, Kenneth Stull, Harlow Tainter, Col. Albert L. Tait, J. C. Tannehill, Edward Templeman, Brig. Gen. Clesen H. Tenney, T/Sgt. Paul W. Tomlinson, Col. Emil M. Ulanowicz, Lt. Col. Madeline M. Ullom, Joseph A. Vater, Col. J. A. Villamor, Beulah M. Walcher, Ben D. Waldron, Col. Frederick A. Ward, Pierce L. Wardlow, Paul W. Wasson, Gen. Albert C. Wedemeyer, Rear Adm. Kenneth R. Wheeler, Edgar D. Whitcomb, Col. (Ch.) Perry O. Wilcox, Lt. Col. Maude D. Williams, Maj. Gen. Charles A. Willoughby, Dr. Warren A. Wilson, M.D., Gene W. Wooten, and Brig. Gen. John M. Wright, Jr.

INDEX

About the Authors

James H. and William M. Belote are professional historians with extensive backgrounds in military and naval history. They are veterans of the North African campaigns of World War II. Born in Bellevue, Washington, the authors, who are twin brothers, are graduates of the University of Washington in Seattle and received their doctorates from the University of California at Berkeley. William Belote is currently Associate Professor of History at the United States Naval Academy at Annapolis. He is a co-author of a book, *The Great Sea War,* edited by Admiral Chester W. Nimitz, and has published several articles. James H. Belote was for six years a military affairs analyst for a United States government agency in Washington, D.C. He is at present Associate Professor of History at Principia College in Elsah, Illinois.

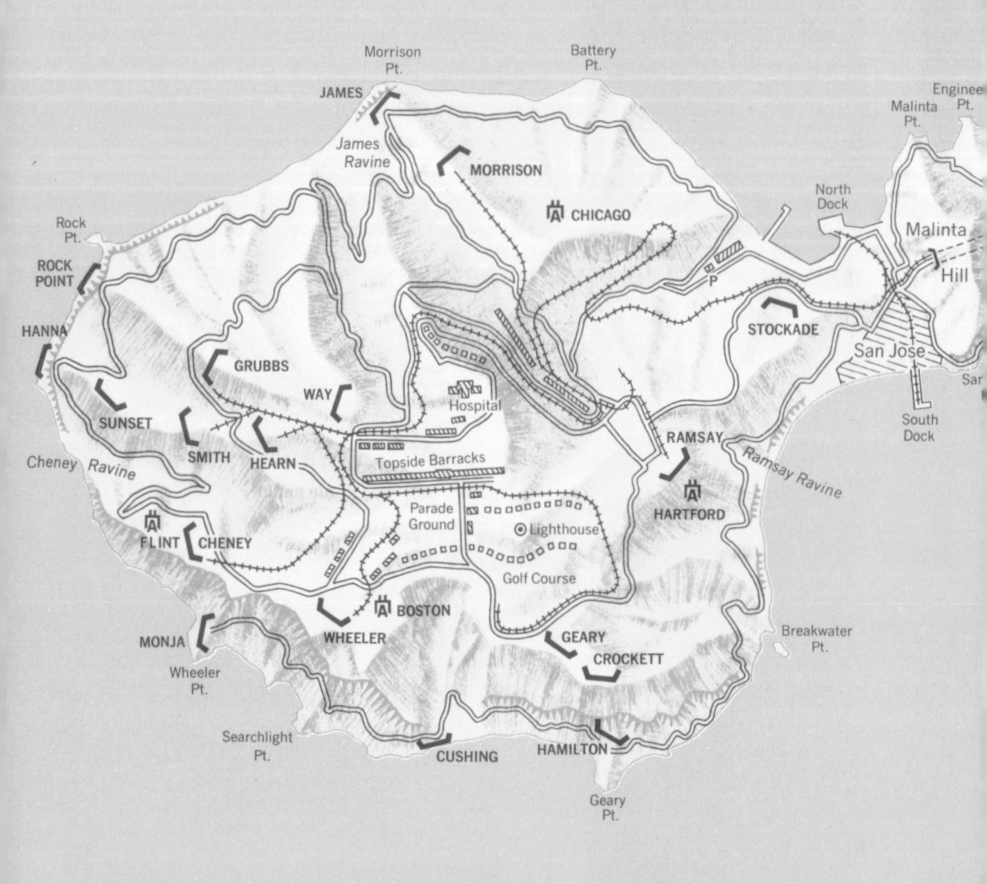

CORREGIDOR ISLAND

December, 1941

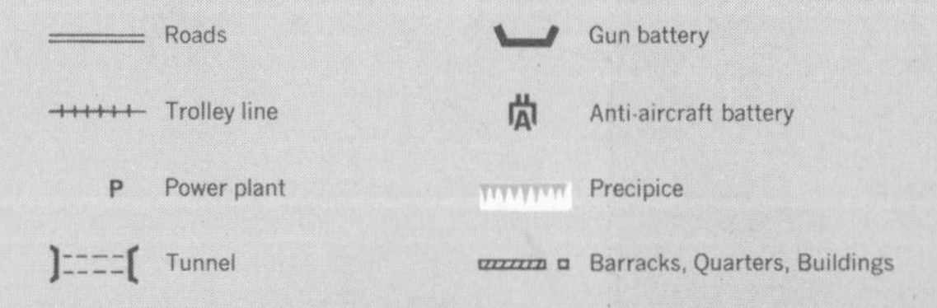

This map not intended to show all structures on the island